Rewilding Earth

Rewilding Earth

Best of 2019

Edited by
John Davis & Susan Morgan

Essex Editions

Rewilding Earth: Best of 2019
Copyright © 2020
Editors John Davis & Susan Morgan
Cover Painting © Steven Kellogg
Photos on Back Cover:
Susan Morgan © John Miles
John Davis © Kim Vacariu

All rights reserved. No part of this book may be reproduced or transmitted in any form or by any means, electronic or mechanical, including photocopying, recording or by any information storage and retrieval system, without written permission from the publisher, except for educational purposes or for the inclusion of brief quotations in a review.

Published in the United States by Essex Editions.

ISBN: 978-1-7335190-3-8

Library of Congress Control Number: 2020905445

Essex Editions
Post Office Box 25
Essex, New York 12936
www.essexeditions.com
contact@essexeditions.com

Table of Contents

Introduction by John Miles and Susan Morgan 1

Eagle Mountain Success by Jon Leibowitz 3

Forever Wild by Sophi Veltrop 8

Adirondack Wildways Update by John Davis 9

Wildlife Crossings in the Adirondacks by Kevin Webb 11

Something Wicked This Way Comes: The Menace of Deep-Sea Mining by Eileen Crist 20

You are the Last Whale by Gary Lawless 26

Wild Carbon by Mark Anderson and Jon Leibowitz 27

Profile of the Northern Forest Atlas Project by the Editors 30

Box Creek Biodiversity by Christopher R. Wilson 32

The Librarians by Robert Michael Pyle 36

Drifting from Rewilding by Mark Fisher 37

Rewilding Scotland by Kenyon Fields 40

European Experiments in Rewilding: Elbe River Biosphere Reserve by David T. Schwartz 43

How to Bring the Bison Home by Susie O'Keeffe 47

Days of Fire by Stuart Pimm 48

Will You Join Us in Defending the Arctic Refuge? by Brad Meiklejohn 51

Tongass National Forest Alert by Andrew Thoms 52

Citizen Scientist: Searching for Heroes and Hope in an Age of Extinction
    by Mary Ellen Hannibal, Reviewed by John Miles 54

White Birds of Winter by Saul Weisberg 58

A Tale of Three Weasels by Paula Mackay 59

The River I and The River II by Tim McNulty 64

Rio Mora Seasons by Brian Miller 65

Embers from the Campfire, When Republicans Loved Endangered Species by Uncle Dave Foreman 69

Cow-Bombing the World's Largest Organism by Andy Kerr 70

Wildlife Versus Livestock in the Upper Green by George Wuerthner 74

New Mexico's Wildlife Corridors Act: A Path Toward Success by Michael Dax 76

Embers from the Campfire, Quitobaquito Springs by Uncle Dave Foreman 80

Tapping the Third-Rail: Wildlife Watching and State Wildlife Funding Reform by Chris Spatz 81

Planting for Bees and Butterflies by Gary Lawless 84

Wilderness in the Anthropocene: What Future for its Untrammeled Wildness? by Roger Kaye 85

Train #7, North Dakota by Susie O'Keeffe 89

Combat Overpopulation Denial by Richard Grossman, M.D. 90

Ecotone by David Crews 92

The Cliff Edge: Generating Political Will for the Required Level of Change by Randy Hayes 94

From No Sense of Wild to a Need to Rewild North America by John Miles 97

Appendix
 About the Cover Artist 105
 About the Contributors 106
 About The Rewilding Institute and Rewilding Earth 115
 Rewilding Earth Website Post Index 117
 About the Rewilding Bookstore 128
 Sponsors 131

Dedication

We dedicate this book to our friends and close colleagues Dave Foreman and Nancy Morton. If the concept of rewilding has parents, they are Dave and Nancy.

Dave Foreman is rightly and widely celebrated for his half-century of leadership on wilderness and wildlife issues (please see the bio we wrote for him in Appendix). Nancy (arguably, the real head of their household—with the only ones who'd challenge that claim being their two cats!) gets less recognition but has been a powerful conservation leader for nearly as long, most recently as president of the New Mexico Wilderness Alliance.

Whole books will be written about the lasting influence of and wild places saved by this daring duo of wilderness champions. For now, just let it be known, these pages honor all who speak out for wild places and creatures, but especially Nancy Morton and her husband Dave Foreman, spiritual leaders of our little band of rewilding advocates. May this work help realize their vision of vast wildways stretching across North America and beyond, teeming with life, including those ultimate wildeors, Pumas and Wolves.

—*Rewilding Earth* editors, spring 2020

Petroglyph © Karen Boeger

Diablo Canyon © Janice St. Marie

Introduction

By John Miles and Susan Morgan of The Rewilding Institute

Despite these anxious times about the fate of the wild and all life on Earth, we believe despair is not an option. It's true, there are too many humans who want too much stuff, cause too much destruction, and believe with too little humility that economic growth and technology will solve all their problems, and they do pose serious existential threats. Now that we are facing a world-wide pandemic with no rational national leadership, we must be even more alert to short- and long-range effects to our natural world. Public lands continue to be targeted while much of the public is isolated and distracted. We will have to change our strategy and tactics to address this toxic combination of threats, and in this collection from *Rewilding Earth* (rewilding.org) you will read about projects to defend wild nature that offer cause for hope and inspiration.

Here we present some of the finest articles we collected during 2019 that feature good thinking and diligent work being done to restore and rewild parts of the natural world.

The Rewilding Institute promotes the idea of rewilding as "giving the land back to wildlife and wildlife back to the land," and is dedicated to defining what rewilding should be at various scales and in many contexts. *Rewilding Earth: Best of 2019* presents promising work in North America and Europe; accounts of courageous actions by adventurers and wilderness advocates in Alaska; persistent advocacy around the country, such as Wyoming's Upper Green River and New Mexico's Rio Mora National Wildlife Refuge; encouraging legislation for New Mexico's wildlife corridors; and scouting locations for wildlife crossings in the Adirondacks. We are featuring an update on Adirondack Wildways, two thoughtful overpopulation articles, a book review about *Citizen Science*, a profile of the impressive *Northern Forest Atlas Project*, and stimulating overviews of rewilding projects in Germany and Scotland. We are calling attention to challenges such as the threats of deep-sea mining, the devastating fires in Brazil, the cow-bombing of aspen clones, and the need for state wildlife funding reform. We are heralding the successes of Eagle Mountain in New York's Adirondack Park and Box Creek Wilderness in the Southern Appalachians. We present wild ideas of wildness in the Anthropocene, an overview of how conservation has evolved to rewilding, and two brief eloquent pleas for wild things from our founder Dave Foreman—all complimented by beautiful poetry and art.

"Cumulative effects" is a phrase often used to describe how small insults to nature add up to big impacts. A positive cumulative effect envisioned by The Rewilding Institute is the recovery produced by hundreds and thousands of rewilding projects adding incrementally to major gains for the natural world in general and its wild denizens in particular. The goal of *Rewilding Earth* and this anthology is to highlight the good work being done and to inspire a growing movement to launch rewilding projects all across North America and around the world, offering examples and ideas from which to draw inspiration.

Eminent scientist E.O. Wilson argues that "only by committing half of the planet's surface to nature can we hope to save the immensity of life forms that compose it." He adds that "it is past time to broaden the discussion of the human future and connect it to the rest of life." His prescription seems large and daunting, but people climb Mount Everest one step at a time. The action Wilson calls for can be similarly achieved, one project at a time, and herein are presented some steps toward that goal. Wilson also alludes to a core truth in his call to connect the human future to the rest of life—the flourishing of human life depends on the flourishing of the rest of life. *Rewilding Earth 2019* offers examples of how to reject denial of this truth and build a future in which all life can flourish.

Petroglyph © Karen Boeger

Eagle Mountain © Brendan Wiltse. Northeast Wilderness Trust's Eagle Mountain Wilderness Preserve protects another vital part of Adirondack Park and bolsters west-east and south-north habitat connections.

Eagle Mountain Success

By Jon Leibowitz, Executive Director, Northeast Wilderness Trust

A century-old tradition continues in New York's Adirondack Park to solve the ecological crises of today and give us hope.

Old Forest

With the slap of her tail, the beaver formally welcomed us to her domain. She dipped back under the tannin-brown water, reemerged, slapped again, and zigzagged around her lodge. This river was her home, not ours; we were interlopers in her wild place.

We were six or so miles into a canoe trip up and down the Oswegatchie River within the Five Ponds Wilderness in the western Adirondacks. The Five Ponds landscape looks and feels different from most places across the northeastern United States, and for good reason. Within this New York State-designated forever-wild landscape remain approximately 50,000 acres of ancient forest. This expanse is recognized as the largest uncut forest in the Northeast. The river itself is lined with countless stately eastern white pines towering above 100 feet. The forests beyond host larger and older trees, everywhere, than I ever find, anywhere, in my home state of Vermont.

A few days into the trip we turned off the Oswegatchie and paddled up an unnamed tributary. We made our way over beaver dams submerged under swollen spring waters, just barely passable without portage. As we meandered further up the watershed, schools of trout darted beneath my canoe through clear water bounded by sandy riverbeds. Eventually, the local engineers proved too successful, and we parked our canoes just below a series of higher dams and headed off into the forest.

We began our walk amongst beautiful, old hardwoods. We passed the largest black cherry I have ever seen. Soon followed the largest yellow birch. What left me in awe was not the superlatives but the regularity and commonality of large trees—everywhere. Old growth, ancient, virgin, primary, primeval, pre-European-- whatever one chooses to call it—looks and feels different from most forests across the Northeast. By some estimates, 99% of the forest across the vast Northern Forest has been logged—the remaining one percent is what's left of the forest that stood before European arrival and the subsequent warfare upon forests.

After a snack, we left the hardwoods behind and crested an esker that stood between ponds. This heap of sediment and boulders, left behind by some ancient glacial event, afforded us a view in all directions. What lay before me was a forest that rivaled the "park-like" appearance of this continent's stately western ponderosa pine forests (my former home) and California's redwood groves. Towering white pines dotted the terrain in every direction, with many over 125' by our estimation. One was too large for three grown men to wrap our arms around. Yes, it felt juvenile to hug the tree. Yes, it also felt thrilling, hopeful, and joyous.

Elder giants strewn across the forest floor by old age or tremendous storms created wide, clear walkways. It brought me right back to a college ramble through the redwoods many years ago, where giant round red bridges punctuated towering trunks reaching for the sky and lush green ferns carpeting the earth.

Walking this forest was the first time in the Northeast that an experience in the woods evoked in me that feeling of wild magnificence, of old, grand, *original forest*; the same way I used to often feel tramping through wilderness areas out West. There is a definition for what constitutes old growth. It's scientific and it likely makes sense to someone. I don't know the precise point at which a secondary forest can be formally defined as old growth, nor do I care to know. What I do know, is that to me, ancient forests are self-apparent; I can feel it in my bones when I'm in one.

I left the Five Ponds with a full soul, a rejuvenated spirit, and an optimistic outlook on my work.

Ecological Amnesia

It wasn't so long ago that most of the Northern Forest resembled the Five Ponds and rivaled western forests in splendor and size. It was not so long ago that witnessing a smooth-barked beech was the rule, not the exception; that flocks of passenger pigeons darkened the skies above the forest canopy; that catamounts stalked prey in a forest that stretched a third of the way across the continent. Nor was it so long ago that rivers were the highways for annual migrations of millions of Atlantic salmon, American eel, and other diadromous species—a phenomenon that thankfully still continues in places like the Great Bear Rainforest of the Pacific Northwest.

Today the passenger pigeon—once accounting for 40% of the entire bird population of North America—is extinct. Catamounts have been extirpated from the Northeast. The cyclical, life-giving transfer of ocean nutrients hundreds of miles inland thanks to the migratory salmon and eels has functionally halted. The only sizeable Atlantic salmon populations today are raised in enormous, industrial offshore nets. Many of the regal white pines like those along the Oswegatchie were cut for the Crown's Navy centuries ago, and a majority of the forest that stood upon European arrival was cut altogether by the late 1800s. Those original natural wonders brought richness to human life and great beauty and diversity to life itself. The absence of those wild denizens and grand eastern forests has become our collective baseline; the great forgetting. We all suffer from this ecological amnesia.

Before European "settlement"—read conquest—of America, there was no such thing as "old-growth," no such thing as "native forest," no such thing as "ancient forest," because all of the forests were mixed old growth, they were all native, they were all diverse, ancient communities. Difficult as all of this may be to imagine, living as we do in this time of extraordinary ecological impoverishment, all of these images of fecundity are from near-contemporary accounts easy enough to find, if only we bother to look.
— Derrick Jenson, *Strangely Like War: The Global Assault on Forests*

The Northern Forest has changed and continues to do so, both of natural and not so natural causes. We are born into an environment lacking apex predators, large trees, and landscapes with multi-generational communities of life. We lack deep understanding of and direct connection with the rhythms and laws of nature. It's easy to accept that what surrounds us is normal. It isn't.

The diminished has become our baseline; the empty, our cognitive reality, and the implications are drastic. With each generation that unwittingly accepts a less diverse planet as natural and normal, we collectively become more detached from the full diversity of life. As our original memory diminishes, it becomes ever harder to reimagine what the wild world should look like and what steps should be taken to rebalance our species with the planet, emotionally, physically, and spiritually.

A coral reef ravaged by climate change, bleached stone-dead as far as the eye can see, is unsurprisingly less inspiring than a reef overflowing with the psychedelic technicolor spectacle of thousands of species. Likewise, a hardwood forest of young spindly trees of the same age and diameter, devoid of stalking big cats and the full diversity of the land community, inspires one less than an old forest full of life. Less inspiration means greater apathy.

This ecological amnesia, or shifting baseline syndrome, may be one of the greatest threats to rebalancing our coexistence with natural systems. It's predictable that fewer *wander in* and *wonder at* the natural world. It's no surprise that more choose to escape into the digital world rather than the natural one. Those living today have been wholesale ripped off by those that preceded us! And, the cycle *could* continue in an endless negative feedback loop of more losses, more amnesia. But it doesn't have to. There is a clear path to a more hopeful future.

Taking Stock of Where We Are

The Adirondacks are perhaps the world's greatest experiment in ecological recovery, a place hard used a century ago and now slowly recovering, slowly proving that where humanity backs off, nature rebounds.
— Bill McKibben

Over the past 100+ years, the Northern Forest has returned. These tenacious woods have proven their resilience. This recovery has followed two parallel tracks: the intentional and the accidental. The intentional track includes watershed moments like the creation of the Adirondack Park and the inclusion of forever-wild language in the New York Constitution in 1892; the creation of the White and Green Mountain National Forests in 1918 and 1932, respectively; the donation of land that became Baxter State Park in 1932; and the passage of the Federal Wilderness Act in 1964 and subsequent Federal actions in 1975, 1984, and 2006 that designated significant portions of the Greens and Whites as Wilderness.

Those intentional efforts are laudable, but as a region that is approximately 90% privately owned, arguably the more widespread occurrence has been the "accidental" rewilding of the region. This most fortuitous recovery resulted from the exodus of the dairy and wool markets in the late 1800s, as farmers fled west to gentler, more fertile ground. This economic shift was furthered by the abandonment of the charcoal industry, which petered out with the diminishing timber supply. With a sheer lack of humans, much of New England and the Adirondacks had a chance to rest and heal. As Bill McKibben so aptly states, when we back off, nature rebounds.

The report from Harvard Forest, *Wildlands and Woodlands*, calls for 70% of New England (30 million acres) to be preserved as forest, and 10% of that (3 million acres) to be preserved as Wildlands. (New York is not included in the report.) We can celebrate the fact that the Northern Forest has largely recovered from its decimated state a hundred years ago. Thanks to the tireless work of the conservation movement, we are lucky that more than 25% of the region's natural terrain has some sort of legal protection, largely from development. However, only about 3-4% of the Northeast is legally protected as forever-wild. Only such places—those with permanent forever-wild legal protections—are guaranteed to continue rewilding, growing old, and becoming more complex. This is not nearly enough, and we have a long way to go before we reach 3 million forever-wild acres across New England.

We are between two forested worlds—the natural forest of pre-settlement North America and the recovered forest of the future...The earlier forested

Bald Eagle © KIT West Designs

> *world is not dead. We are studying and struggling to preserve its living remnants. And we do not believe that the future forest is powerless to be born. These remnants—with our help—will become the seeds from which a renewed forest spreads.*
> — Mary Byrd Davis, *Eastern Old-Growth Forests: Prospects for Rediscovery and Recovery*

Most protected forests in the Northeast have been preserved for people: for natural resource extraction, recreation, or motorized vehicle access. And that's OK! However, it is within our power to change the ratio toward a more nature-centered future. The act of rewilding is to give land back to wildlife and wildlife back to the land. The Five Ponds Wilderness is a blueprint of a more hopeful future, not a relic of a distant past never to return.

Rewilding Forests and Imaginations by Reimagining Wilderness

Henry David Thorough wrote more than 200 years ago that, "In Wildness is the Preservation of the World."

Today, in wildness is the tonic to our many modern ecological dilemmas. Wild places simply have a right to exist, but let's also acknowledge that wilderness conservation in its historic context has been sidelined by the assumption that it is not relevant to vast segments of society. Today, that argument no longer holds water, and a reimagining of what wilderness means provides tangible and measurable hope in an otherwise bleak state of ecological affairs.

Only through more forever-wild conservation can we unleash the full potential of our region's carbon sequestering forests. Only through landscape-scale rewilding efforts can we stave off the biodiversity crisis. And, only through the humble act of setting aside vast and connected places that are left to their own devices will wonder and amazement be accessible to more people. Through rewilding, we can flip the script of ecological amnesia and create a positive feedback loop where more people connect with and care for wild places.

You have to love something before you are moved to save it!
— Sylvia Earle

In the 21st century, conserving the recovered woodlands of the Northern Forest as forever-wild is the most cost effective, scalable, and efficient tool in our arsenal to combat the interconnected crises of climate change and biodiversity loss. Such a *new wilderness* builds on the foundational ideas of the wilderness movement. When Howard Zahniser conjured up the language for the Wilderness Act in 1964, he knew that wilderness could grow as well as shrink, and he consciously used the obscure word 'untrammeled' in the law's definition of wilderness. The Wilderness Act does not contain the words 'pristine' or 'untouched'. Something that is trammeled is bound or caught; something untrammeled is free or unimpeded.

Today, conserving wild places is about far more than setting aside land to remain untrammeled; it's about our *survival*. Life itself hangs in the balance—human and non-human alike. We must celebrate that by recognizing such self-evident value, we are also helping ourselves. These ends are not mutually exclusive.

Backing off, rewilding, and reconnecting landscapes has been the work of Northeast Wilderness Trust since 2002. By applying the model of private land conservation to the ideals of wilderness enshrined in the federal Wilderness Act and New York Constitution, the Wilderness Trust has helped conserve more than 35,000 acres of forever-wild landscapes across the Northern Forest. This has been accomplished through land acquisitions and forever-wild conservation easements. The Wilderness Trust's guiding vision is that of a connected landscape of resilient wildlands shared by a human culture that deeply respects wild places.

The Wilderness Trust most recently purchased the Eagle Mountain Wilderness Preserve. The initiative to protect this place was featured in *Rewilding Earth*, and now that it has been preserved, not only from future development but also from extractive industries like logging; it is growing wilder by the month. The Preserve is situated between two critical ecosystems—the fertile lowlands of the Champlain Valley to the east and the rugged High Peaks to the west. It is the latest in a two-decade long effort to conserve these transition lands. In the Split Rock Wildway to the south, the Wilderness Trust has completed nine transactions to protect the wildlife corridor. Eagle Mountain's successful purchase expanded on this concept and helps secure connectivity in a critical corridor to the north. Acre by acre, parcel by parcel, this sort of slow but steady conservation is bringing wildness and hope back to the Northeast.

Eagle Mountain is not pristine. It's been heavily logged for a century. Old, grown-in timber roads crisscross the property. Yet, a wild character permeates this landscape. At over 2,400 acres and sitting between two large conserved forest blocks, the property is quintessential Adirondack wildland. The strategically located parcel also conserves wilderness in an area underrepresented by conservation lands within the Adirondack Park, wilderness or otherwise. Beautiful ponds provide sustenance for otters, peregrine falcons nest on its cliffs, and mother bears raise their young among dense forests. The terrain teems with wildlife.

Much like the lands that Zahniser considered in drafting the Wilderness Act, Eagle Mountain is not untouched, but from the moment Northeast Wilderness Trust signed the deed, the land became untrammeled and the long process of rewilding began. At the Wilderness Trust, we say that wilderness is not simply a special kind of place, but rather a special commitment we make to a place.

No, Eagle Mountain Wilderness Preserve is not the Five Ponds Wilderness today, but on a small scale, it will be tomorrow.

Wilderness is Relevant; Wilderness is Hope

As we consider the implications of a new wilderness for the 21st century and the hopeful reawakening of our collective connection with *Wild Earth*, places like Eagle Mountain can help lead the way. The property was purchased not for people, but for nature. It was protected so the forest could regain its original foothold and be self-willed, in every sense of the term. And in doing so, the benefits to people will be both measurable and immeasurable. Measurably, it will store carbon and provide safe harbor to wildlife. Immeasurably, it will rekindle imagination and wonder for generations of people to come. That in and of itself fills me with hope.

Flight: Blue Heron © PLMeriam.Art. Celebrating the strength of art to bring attention to nature's beauty and fragility.

Forever Wild

By Sophi Veltrop

Northeast Wilderness Trust's Forever-Wild Circle of monthly donors is a community of the region's most committed wilderness advocates and supporters. The Wilderness Trust is thanking Forever-Wild Circle members with custom bandannas, featuring the artwork of Patricia Leahey Meriam and hand-dyed with local indigo from Honey Hill Studios. Donating monthly is an effective and efficient way to ensure a forever-wild future for the land and wildlife of the Northeast. Your sustaining gift allows Northeast Wilderness Trust to focus its resources on the ground where our work matters most.

Adirondack Wildways Update

By John Davis

Adirondack Old-growth Forest © Rob Leverett

Connectivity work continues in New York's Adirondack Park and beyond. Priority areas and species include Split Rock Wildway, Algonquin to Adirondack axis (A2A), Puma reintroduction, dam removal for native fish, and American Chestnut replanting.

Northeast Wilderness Trust (newildernesstrust.org) is striving to extend Split Rock Wildway protection westward by acquiring a 2,400-acre block of pond- and wetland-enriched forest called Eagle Mountain. [See "Eagle Mountain Success" by Jon Leibowitz in this volume.] Its partner the Eddy Foundation (theeddy.org) is working to raise more money for conservation acquisitions both through creation of a conservation burial ground, Spirit Sanctuary Split Rock, and enrollment in The Nature Conservancy's carbon sequestration program. Champlain

Area Trails (champlainareatrails.org) is raising support for protecting Split Rock Wildway through providing sensitively placed footpaths to scenic highlights and creating a hamlet-to-hamlet system of trails.

Thanks to local officials and sporting interests, as well as conservationists, the lowest dam on the Boquet River was recently removed, reopening spawning habitat for Landlocked Atlantic Salmon and other fish that depend on Lake Champlain and its tributaries. Since that dam removal about two years ago, salmon have been reported returning to historic spawning grounds on the North Branch of the Boquet River in Split Rock Wildway.

Thanks to NWT, Eddy, CATS, Adirondack Land Trust, and other partners, and in welcome contrast to much of the world, the wildlife corridor linking Lake Champlain with the Adirondack High Peaks is growing a little wilder year by year. Trackers in Split Rock Wildway trained by Susan Morse of Keeping Track (keepingtrack.org) commonly find prints of such focal species as Bobcat, Fisher, River Otter, Mink, and Coyote—but not yet of those much-missed top carnivores, Puma and Wolf.

Moving westward across the 6 million-acre Adirondack Park (nearly half of which now is state Forest Preserve land enjoying Forever Wild constitutional protection, thanks to heroic land-saving work by Adirondack Land Trust, Adirondack Nature Conservancy, Adirondack Council, Protect the Adirondacks, and other conservation groups), a Moose would enter the A2A connection, being championed by the Algonquin to Adirondack Collaborative (a2acollaborative.org). Here part of the needed work is identifying areas where animals are trying to cross busy roads—especially the major east-west highways just north of the Canadian border—and convincing transportation and wildlife officials to support wildlife crossings for these places. The A2A Collaborative is also exploring the feasibility of an A2A International Scenic Trail linking the two great parks, to build support for better protection of the wildlife corridor. A2A held a highly successful biological symposium April 11, 2019, where conservation leaders discussed biological attributes and conservation priorities for this globally important habitat connection. There biologist Roland Kays gave an inspiring talk and slideshow on using wildlife cameras not only to track the movements of our wild neighbors but also to enlist more citizens, including school kids, in protecting wildlife habitat.

Despite much good land-saving work in Split Rock Wildway, A2A, the central Adirondacks, and elsewhere, the northeastern United States and southeastern Canada continue to be starved of their top carnivores, and thus suffer from over-browsing and related trophic cascades. As noted in previous *Rewilding Earth* reports, Puma recolonization of the East seems unlikely in the near term—given all the roads and guns between the nearest viable populations westward and the abundant potential habitat in the Adirondacks and Northern Appalachians. Eastern Coyotes, which have interbred with Gray Wolves in the Northeast and Red Wolves in the Southeast, are playing some of the role of top dog, but not nearly all of it, for they are a smaller and more opportunistic predator, only occasionally preying on White-tail Deer (more often scavenging deer carcasses, from hunters' bullets or road-kill) and seldom taking Moose.

Rewilding efforts, though, sometimes may be most successful if they are incremental, starting with less controversial species (as Tompkins Conservation, tompkinsconservation.org, is showing in its species reintroduction work in Iberá Argentina). Partly for this reason, rewilding proponents in Adirondack Park are exploring the possibility of planting disease-resistant American Chestnut and American Elm trees and helping bolster Brook Trout, Landlocked Atlantic Salmon, and American Eel populations, even as they build support for Puma and Wolf reintroductions.

Wildway Rambles

Occasional opinionated update or peripatetic field notes from *Rewilding Earth* editor, executive director, and wildways scout, **John Davis**.

Wildlife Crossings in the Adirondacks

By Kevin Webb

Part One: Exploring the Role of Wildlife Crossings in the Adirondacks

A mere three-hour drive from the buildings, people, and frenzy of New York City are the Adirondacks, one of the largest, most dynamic experiments in the history of conservation. Formed in 1885, Adirondack Park was the first state preserve of its kind in the United States, and today its 6 million acres are a roughly even mixture of public and carefully managed private lands.

Centered around the Adirondack mountain range, Adirondack Park houses the world's largest intact temperate deciduous forest, as well as rivers, lakes, wetlands, and a range of other attractive habitats for New York's native wildlife. Its 130,000 permanent human residents live in towns and cities scattered throughout the park, with primary economic activity including social services, tourism, and retail trade. Every year, 7-10 million visitors come to commune in some fashion with nature.

Adirondack Park's history of serving the needs of both humans and wildlife makes it a global model for ecological refuges that, for political or economic reasons, must account for human habitation as well. While humans and nature are not incompatible, many of the hallmarks of modern life can be extremely disruptive to wildlife. Among our worst impacts is environmental fragmentation, where manmade structures such as roads, cities, farmland, or dams divide ecosystems. These divisions prevent animals from finding food, evading predators, reacting to seasons, pursuing genetically diverse mates, and increasingly, adjusting to changing climate patterns.

For this reason, the Adirondacks may prove to be an ideal location to build and test "wildlife crossings." Modeled after over- and underpasses erected in Banff National

Black bear © Sheri Amsel. Despite their fierce reputations, predator attacks on humans are so rare as to be individually listed in Wikipedia. Over the past century, black bears, wolves, mountain lions, and coyotes have combined killed fewer Americans than lightning strikes, drowning in bathtubs, or being crushed under falling vending machines. Their protection is vitally important to the flourishing of a healthy natural ecosystem.

Park in Alberta, Canada, these crossings would safely connect animal populations that are currently separated by highways. If built and maintained, these crossings would suggest a future, better balance with nature, where the needs of humans and those of wildlife are both critical design considerations.

Human-Wildlife Conflicts in the Adirondacks, and a Role for Crossings

The Adirondack Park's balance between ecological conservation and economic needs is of course not without tension. Since 1970, the forest preserve has been enlarged by over 400,000 acres, and nearly 800,000 acres of private land have been protected under state-held conservation easements

(Long and Bauer). Meanwhile, as with many rural areas in America, the Adirondacks' human population is gradually aging, college-educated adults of childbearing age have not moved in at replacement rates, and its manufacturing sector has suffered employment declines. Some critics have thus blamed the erosion of manufacturing, particularly forestry, on a perceived excess of environmental protections.

Compared with other rural regions, however, the Adirondacks have been comparatively resilient economically, which may in fact be attributed to the region's environmental appeal to tourists (Long and Bauer). Indeed, tourism and hospitality-related services are the second biggest employer in the region (12.4%), following education, health care, and social work (27%) *(Adirondack Park Economic Profile)*.

In addition to humans, the Adirondacks are home to 53 mammalian species, including black bears, bobcats, fishers, coyotes, white-tailed deer, moose, and beavers; 220 species of birds; and 35 species of amphibians and reptiles. Now extirpated, wolves, mountain lions (cougars), lynx, elk, and Eastern wood bison inhabited the larger region prior to European arrival.

Many of the most direct conflicts between humans and wildlife today stem, in part, from the loss of keystone predator species in the region, which has led to an increased presence of herbivores like white-tailed deer. These herbivores, in turn, wander across major roadways (an issue for drivers), they over-browse early successional forests (an issue for foresters), and they harbor large volumes of unwanted parasites like ticks (an issue for public health). Though counterintuitive, erecting wildlife crossings may help on all fronts.

Animal-Caused Traffic Incidents

From the decade spanning 2009 to 2018, animals were implicated in over 40,000 police-reported accidents throughout the 12 counties of the Adirondacks. Roughly 6.5% of these incidents resulted in personal injury or death to the driver or passenger; and while these data are not reported, undoubtedly a far higher percentage resulted in the death of the animal. Animal-related accidents exceeded the next highest cause of accident, speeding, with nearly 32,000 police-reported incidents *(New York State County Crash Summary, 2009-2018)*.

Although information about which species were responsible for these accidents is not available, most accidents occurred near forests and waterways, suggesting that wild, rather than domestic, animals were likely the primary cause. Further, only a small number of wild species in the park are large enough to cause major vehicular damage: moose, black bears, white-tail deer, and coyotes. Assuming even probabilities of highway crossings, their relative population densities strongly suggest that white-tailed deer are, by far, the primary culprit in causing accidents.

In addition to harm to wildlife and inconveniencing people, animal-caused collisions result in adverse economic impacts. While less dangerous than other collisions due to the frailty of animals relative to vehicles, they can easily total vehicles traveling at speed, and may result in traffic jams and drains on highway patrol time. A 2008 FWHA report to Congress estimates that an average cost per vehicle collision with deer is $1,840, while collisions with elk and moose resulted in damages of $3,000 and $4,000, respectively (Trentacoste). Conservatively assuming all reported accidents with wildlife were with deer, the 12 counties of the Adirondacks saw nearly $75 million in animal-caused vehicular damage from 2009-2018. Assuming an economic value of $1,250 per head of white-tailed deer, this would translate to further losses of up to $50 million from wildlife-vehicle collisions.

If Banff's highway crossings are indicative, constructing wildlife crossings with fencing along highways would prevent many of these needless accidents.

Disease Burden

With shortening winters, arthropods like ticks and mosquitos are extending their ranges northward and into mountains, and they are remaining active longer into the year. Ticks, which carry Lyme disease (LD), are of particular note, as LD can have particularly severe health consequences, and its incidence has roughly doubled since 1991 *(Lyme Disease: Data and Surveillance)*. Ticks depend on many factors throughout their lives for ideal growing conditions, but one of the strongest correlations involves their access to reservoir species like white-tailed deer, which can feed many ticks simultaneously and facilitate rapid reproduction. It remains unclear whether the increased frequency of tick-borne illness throughout the Northeast is due to environmental fragmentation, the increase of white-tailed deer numbers, the growth in human presence near forests, climate change, or increased interest in outdoor activities; quite possibly, all factors have contributed.

Economically, LD presents several risks to Adirondack visitors and tourists alike. A recent literature review suggests that in the US, treatment for one LD patient entails nearly $4,300 in direct costs, with nearly $7,500 in indirect future costs. Diagnosis too is expensive; in one cited study, seven laboratories were paid $566 million to test 3.4 million samples from Connecticut, Maryland, Minnesota, and New York (Mac et al.). While these costs are typically borne by insurers, or by consumers paying out-of-pocket, the risks of LD do appear worse for retirement-age citizens, which means the burden of costs may largely fall to federal and state healthcare programs.

These direct expenses of LD do not account for the disease's societal impacts, as it can lead to significant losses of productivity. Further, if likelihood of contracting LD continues to increase, there may be a downward trend in outdoor tourism in coming years.

Constructing wildlife crossings could potentially help control Lyme disease through two mechanisms: first, the reconnection of different habitats would better link the gene pools of deer and other reservoir species, thereby preventing inbreeding-related disease susceptibility. Second, wildlife crossings would benefit predators, which could then more effectively control herbivore populations.

Predator Competition

A primary reason why mountain lions and wolves were hunted to local extinction was the perception that they consumed important domestic animals, or that they were competition in hunting for game species like deer and elk. Today, these fears remain, as evidenced by New York State Department of Environmental Conservation mandates around desired regional bear population levels, which range from a high of "Maintain generally moderate population level" to lows of "Incompatible for bears" and "Bears infrequent—keep it so" *(Black Bear Harvest Summary 2018)*.

Despite their fierce reputations, though, predator attacks on humans are so rare as to be individually listed on Wikipedia. Over the past century, black bears, wolves, mountain lions, and coyotes combined have killed fewer Americans than have lightning strikes, drowning in bathtubs, or being crushed under falling vending machines. Indeed, the most recent reported black bear attack in the Adirondacks was in 2018, when a man hospitalized from crashing his all-terrain vehicle lied and said he had fought off a bear (Figura).

While attacks on humans are exceptionally unusual, predators have critical roles to play in ecosystem integrity. Unlike humans, they tend to hunt weaker animals—the young, the old, and the sickly. These are the animals most likely to harbor disease; with weakened immune systems, they become ideal reservoirs for fleas and ticks. Perversely, hunting by humans—which prizes taking the healthiest animals—may select against traits that make animals more resistant to disease.

Indeed, in a recent study Stanford researchers reported that after a decade of monitoring Jasper Ridge Biological Preserve (in the foothills near Santa Cruz, California), with camera traps, scat samples, and DNA analysis, the return of mountain lions to the preserve was directly correlated with drops in white-tailed deer numbers and in substantial changes to deer and coyote behavior. Both deer and coyote shifted their waking hours to daylight, when mountain lions were dormant, and pack-hunting coyotes began traveling as individuals. Lowered deer population in turn led to changes in the successional patterns of young forests (Leempoel et al.).

Within the Adirondacks, the largest predators are currently the Eastern coyote (which also has wolf and dog genes from past hybridization), the black bear, and the bobcat. While these species may occasionally target juvenile deer, they tend to prey upon smaller mammals like snowshoe hares and beavers. Should managers wish to better control deer population, they may be wise to cautiously facilitate the return of larger predators like mountain lions and wolves.

No matter the species, though, predators are some of the most critical beneficiaries of wildlife crossings. With lower population densities than herbivores, predators tend to require far larger territories to find sufficient food. Linking currently separated habitats would enable them to reach new prey, maintain large and diverse gene pools, and better adjust to changes in weather or climate.

Wildlife Crossings, a Recap

For all these reasons, ecologists, epidemiologists, and conservationists increasingly realize the importance of contiguous stretches of habitat for living things, with biologist E. O. Wilson famously proposing that to preserve biodiversity into the future, humans should plan to leave fully half of Earth's lands and waters in a wild state. Where such wilderness is impractical, though, it seems that manmade wildlife crossings can achieve some of the same objectives.

Part Two: Scouting Locations for Wildlife Crossings in the Adirondacks

Key Lessons from Banff

Dissecting the Rockies and Canada's Banff and Yoho national parks is the Trans-Canada Highway (TCH), an east-west roadway that fragments important north-south migratory routes for deer, bison, elk, bears, wolves, and more. In the late 1970s, plans began to "twin," or add second lanes to, much of the highway to accommodate increased traffic levels; already, Banff saw over 100 accidents per year caused by deer and elk, and designers were concerned that with increased traffic this would worsen, and might further interfere with the animals' migratory behaviors.

Because the TCH is managed within the parks by Parks Canada, which includes wildlife welfare and visitor experience as core mandates, planners secured funding to build wildlife-exclusionary fencing along the highway through the parks, along with a series of underpasses and overpasses to facilitate animal movement. Construction began in 1983, and, as of 2013, there were 6 overpasses and more than 40 underpasses, all of which have seen use by animals. These crossings have become miniature corridors that connect habitats on both sides of the highway.

Over the past century, black bears, wolves, mountain lions, and coyotes combined have killed fewer Americans than have lightning strikes, drowning in bathtubs, or being crushed under falling vending machines.

With over 30 years' experience in building and testing these new wildlife crossings, conservationists from Banff are now consulted globally for their expertise. The following highlighted learnings are drawn from published articles and personal correspondence with Trevor Kinley, an environmental assessment scientist with Parks Canada's Highway Engineering Services (Clevenger et al.; Dickie; Kinley; Bissonette et al.).

Prioritize East-West Highways

By focusing on east-west highways, planners can typically see a higher conservation return on investment (ROI), as these highways bisect natural seasonal migrations. Facilitating movement in a south-north direction will also help animals adapting to warming climates.

Build Fencing Fully

A hard lesson has been the need to construct fencing fully between over- and underpasses; animals are often wary of these new means of crossing highways, and may choose to run across highways wherever they see a break in fencing. This becomes particularly dangerous to animal and motorist alike when they panic; should they flee back from the road, they will often be too confused and stressed to be able to navigate back through the fence.

Further fence-related precautions at Banff now include a top-mounted wire, to better ensure the fence stays upright when trees are downed in inclement weather, and adding chain link fence belowground to prevent digging by carnivorous animals. Generally, fences should be located as close to roadways as possible, to ensure animals can see and smell the other side of the road.

Build Underpasses and Overpasses

Cheap and unobtrusive, underpasses do the majority of work in Banff, and are the preferred crossings for black bears, mountain lions, and smaller animals like reptiles and amphibians. They can be assembled relatively quickly using prefab concrete culvert materials.

Overpasses, meanwhile, are underpasses' charismatic, costlier cousins. Built in much the same way a bridge might be, they can be planted with natural vegetation which helps lessen the noise from the highway below. They are the preferred path for ungulates and grizzly bears, which seem to prefer clearer sightlines.

Use Features of the Land

A key mistake for designers is over-optimizing locations of corridors for where animals presently attempt to cross roads or where vegetation suggests an ideal site. Instead, designers should focus on "constructible" sites, where building an overpass or underpass is facilitated by the characteristics of the land. An overpass, for example, is simpler to build and more likely to be used where a road already runs beneath land on either side; an underpass may be better installed where a roadway is already elevated. Many locations are poorly suited for either type of construction, but animals in Banff will dependably move to reach a crossing site.

Prepare for Maintenance

In Banff, securing financing for new projects, particularly underpasses, has been relatively straightforward, as these projects tend to be popular and the public safety benefit is fairly clear. Maintenance, however, remains an ongoing concern; with these projects, highway workers must maintain miles of fencing against poor weather, animals, and

Piseco Lake from Abby's Lookout © Bill Amadon

car accidents, as well as overpasses that must work both as manmade projects that ensure driver safety and as wildlife-friendly corridors.

Some Needed Wildlife Crossings in the Adirondacks

In this report, we highlight and discuss three potential highways within or near New York's Adirondack Park that could be suitable for the construction of wildlife crossings. This assessment is based on police-reported, animal activity-caused traffic accident data for the twelve counties that make up the Adirondacks. Municipality-level data were combined for the 10-year period from 2009-2018 to yield a very rough approximation of where human-animal collisions were most frequent and where they were most likely to result in personal injury or death *(New York State Crash Data by County and Municipality. Crash Contributing Factors: Animal Action. 2009-2018. Counties of Clinton, Essex, Franklin, Fulton, Hamilton, Herkimer, Lewis, Oneida, Saratoga, St. Lawrence, Warren, Washington).* Data were then mapped using QGIS open-source software. As might be expected, these stretches tend to fall in between desirable habitats, and where humans are likely to drive at sufficient speeds to cause damage. Notably, all three target highways have more wildlife-vehicle collisions per year than Banff did when construction began there.

Target Site 1: I-87

Assigned in 1957, Interstate 87 is one of the most trafficked highways in America, and it serves not only as the entry for most visitors to the Adirondacks but as the primary economic thoroughfare between New York City and Montreal. It serves approximately 80 million people throughout New York, the mid-Atlantic states, and Montreal (Harbour).

Although I-87 is a south-north route, the Wildlands Network has nonetheless identified the Southern Lake Champlain Valley to its east as a key linkage to create a wildlife corridor that stretches from Florida to Maine. By connecting New York's Adirondack Park to Vermont's Green Mountains and to other forests of the Northeast, it could become easier for species like moose to move between regions (Davis).

One key thematic benefit for the I-87 route is its prominence; with the creation of wildlife overpasses, civic planners could showcase the Adirondacks' "Forever Wild" shared landscape values with all who pass underneath. Logistically, due to its location near New York City, the movement of construction materials could be relatively inexpensive compared to the other sites considered.

Construction around I-87 could initially focus on the 55-mile stretch from just north of Albany to the southern end of Lake George, which would encompass the sites of Queensbury (526 animal-caused traffic incidents reported between 2009-2018), Wilton (411), Saratoga Springs (493), and Malta (385). Some of these cities also touch US Route 9, which is a smaller highway running roughly parallel with I-87 and a second source of road mortality. Ideally, construction of safe wildlife crossings would eventually continue northward to Lake Champlain and beyond.

The selection of this southerly portion of I-87 would bring with it drawbacks. As the largest, most trafficked highway of any of those proposed, construction is likely to be disruptive, and manufacturing will be made more expensive by the need to span 6 lanes, rather than two or four. Indeed, even if built, this long width may prove a deterrent for wild animals who might otherwise consider crossing. Further, due to its close parallel with US 9, it may become necessary to build crossings along that highway as well. Lastly, the higher frequency of collisions with animals in this region may owe more to the higher amount of traffic on this leg of the highway than to the ecological value of wildlife crossings there. For maximal ecological impact, it may be wise to instead erect crossings and fencing on the stretch of I-87 within park boundaries, even though fewer collisions would be prevented there.

Target Site 2: US Route 11

Designated in 1926, US Route 11 hugs New York's northern boundary, where wildlife may seek to cross from near the St. Lawrence River, before hooking southwest as it moves toward the state's border. A potential project could focus on a 44-mile stretch from De Kalb Junction through Moira. This would transect three of the most accident-prone sites in the studied region, per data from 2009-2018: Canton (734 reported animal collisions), Potsdam (853), and Stockholm (479). Extended 21 miles further east to Burke, the project could also include Malone (434 animal-caused collisions).

As a lower-trafficked site, this highway may present advantages in ease of construction, and importantly, this stretch corresponds with where there are only presently two lanes, which would reduce cost of construction and present shorter, more attractive paths for animals to migrate from one side to the other. Because the route moves east-west, it would be well-suited for aiding animals' natural migration patterns north-south, as well as facilitating new climate-related movements.

Commerce advocates from the region have discussed replacing or supplementing US 11 with a larger highway to support industry in the region, which has sometimes been referred to as Highway 98 or the Rooftop Highway. While the construction of such a project would doubtless interfere with animal crossings, and is opposed by most wildlands proponents, it may if approved present an opportunity to include wildlife crossings as part of its scope, similar to how the construction of Banff's crossings were tied to new road twinning. More modest plans to add passing lanes to parts of US 11 (an alternative preferred by conservationists) could similarly be coupled with adding under- or overpasses, along with fencing.

Drawbacks of this site include its far-northern placement, which would increase transportation and construction costs, and which may make finding construction workers more difficult. Additionally, it receives fewer tourists than the other two sites, which may reduce the cultural value of construction.

Target Site 3: Interstate 90

Along the Adirondacks' southern border is Interstate 90, a 386-mile highway that connects from Pennsylvania to Massachusetts. A potential stretch suitable for adding fencing and crossings is the 33 miles from Oneida to Mohawk. This would include Verona (635 animal-caused accidents between 2009 and 2018), Westmoreland (611), Whitestown (414), and Frankfort (394).

While this proposed stretch could be lengthened with time, future capital near the proposed I-90 site may be better spent on adjacent State Routes, as nearby cities with larger accident rates include Rome (645), New Hartford (524), Trenton (570), and Marcy (425). Taken together, it seems that wildlife travels southwest to northeast toward the Adirondacks, and that the larger human population outside the Park increases the probability of accident.

Ecologically, this site is valuable for its east-west alignment, and for connecting the Adirondacks to the interior of New York, where activities like hunting are a significant regional pastime. However, its proximity to larger populations of humans may make it unlikely to add biological diversity to the Adirondacks, and it may increase human conflicts with species like coyotes and bears.

Economically, its shorter length, four lanes, and access to larger cities and thus potential workers may make construction costs somewhat moderate compared to other proposals. Its location between neighboring states, and above larger rural populations to the south, may ultimately yield some of the cultural value of I-87's proposal.

In a fragmented world, wildlife crossings are becoming an increasingly important conservation tool to maintain biodiversity, without forfeiting human economic needs.

Drawbacks include its potentially lowered ecological value, the need to work on additional nearby state routes, and the risk of unwanted, increased human-animal interactions.

Other Possible Locations for Safe Crossings

In addition to entire stretches of highway, we should consider specific sites where animals are crossing roads. Regional wildlands advocates like John Davis have identified, but not yet thoroughly studied, specific places in and around Adirondack Park where busy roads fragment key habitats and thus need wildlife crossings (including modified culverts). These include:

- I-87 where it fragments Split Rock Wildway, particularly where it passes over the North Branch of the Boquet River
- Route 3 in the northwest Adirondacks, where it bisects the Algonquin to Adirondack (A2A) connection
- I-90 and I-88 where they cross over Schoharie Creek, which may be the least fragmented link between Adirondack Park and Catskill Park to the south
- Route 12 and other major roads that bisect the Adirondack to Tug Hill link
- Route 22 and other roads that bisect the Southern Lake Champlain Valley link between New York's Adirondacks and Vermont's Green Mountains.

High Rock on the Oswegatchie River © Kevin Raines

For some road stretches, Adirondack Nature Conservancy, AuSable River Association, Wildlands Network, and other conservation groups have already had some success at working with departments of transportation on road and culvert modifications that enhance permeability for wildlife. In general, though, New York has not done nearly enough to make its roads safe for the wildlife that need to cross them.

Anticipated Overall Benefits and Drawbacks of Crossings

With any of the above potential locations, there could be several additional benefits, as well as unwanted consequences, to the ecology and economy of the region. Among these are:

Innovation

In a fragmented world, wildlife crossings are becoming an increasingly important conservation tool to maintain biodiversity, without forfeiting human economic needs. While Banff remains the global leader in implementing crossings, more expertise and innovation are needed to reduce costs of construction and increase the structures' appeal to wildlife. With one of the world's largest concentrations of architects, academics, and outdoor experts, New York is well-positioned to pilot approaches and structures that could, in turn, be used globally. There may be opportunities to employ tools from civil engineering projects in New York City, such as used tunnel boring machines, to make construction minimally disruptive. Ultimately, the Adirondacks region could build on its environmental legacy to become a globally important center of building for the needs of humans and animals alike.

Economic Activity

As with any major infrastructure project, construction along any of these sites would lead to new jobs for designers and laborers, as well as ongoing jobs focused on maintenance, research, and public outreach. There would also likely be a benefit to the local tourism economy, due to the novelty of the structures, and to any resultant increase in wildlife density and diversity, which could make the region more enticing to visit. For hunters, preventing the needless loss of wildlife will mean healthier populations of deer, elk (if reintroduced), moose (though so far their numbers in New York are too low to allow hunting), and other prey species. Lastly, as a rural region with an aging population, any source of new economic activity could help slow or reverse demographic trends.

Reintroduction of Predators and Ecological Benefits

With larger, more connected habitats, the Adirondacks would become even more hospitable to predator species than it already is, which may facilitate the natural or human-assisted reintroduction of keystone predators like mountain lions or wolves. If allowed to return to their historic ranges, these species would prey on weaker, more disease-prone herbivores, which could in turn reduce numbers of ticks and improve the health of forests. Reductions in the incidence of tick bites would reduce the costs of diagnosing and treating Lyme disease, which would have a positive economic impact for residents and tourists alike.

Adverse Consequences

As with any plan, construction of highway crossings would come with tradeoffs and drawbacks. Most significantly, any construction project of this scale would incur significant expense at its outset, as well as on ongoing costs for maintenance. While there are economic benefits to curtailing accidents, the expense of corridor construction would be borne by the taxpayer, while the costs of accidents are generally borne by the individual. Additionally, success of this plan may lead to an increase in unwanted human-animal interactions, which could negate the positive population impacts of connecting habitats. Lastly, there could also be a loss in aesthetic value along highways, as these projects would require miles of wildlife-exclusionary fencing.

Conclusions

Wildlife crossings are a well-studied concept, but we still have much to learn about how best to create and maintain them. In the span of centuries, Americans have completely reshaped our landscape and broken up historically connected ecological regions. No wildlife crossing should be expected to undo these actions. Yet, if there is any place to experiment with how we can build infrastructure to serve the needs of humans and wildlife alike, it just may be New York's Adirondack Park and surrounds. With a high incidence of human-animal collisions, rising rates of Lyme disease, and tourism as a primary economic source, the expense of constructing wildlife-exclusionary fencing and over- and underpasses is easier to justify here than elsewhere. Perhaps more importantly, though, such projects would reflect in concrete the true ethos of this ecologically distinct region, which has spent over a century balancing the needs of humanity with those of nature.

Works Cited / Works Referenced, Part One

Adirondack Park Economic Profile. Adirondack Park Agency, Mar. 2012, https://apa.ny.gov/Economy/index.html.

Black Bear Harvest Summary 2018. New York Department of Environmental Conservation, 2018, p. 16. Zotero, https://www.dec.ny.gov/docs/wildlife_pdf/bbrpt2018.pdf.

Climate Change Indicators: Lyme Disease. EPA, Aug. 2016, https://www.epa.gov/climate-indicators/climate-change-indicators-lyme-disease.

Figura, David. "Man Made up Story of Bear Attack in Adirondacks to Cover ATV Crash, DEC Says." *NYup.Com*, 18 Oct. 2018, https://www.newyorkupstate.com/outdoors/2018/10/dec_adirondack_bear_attack_story_doesnt_match_the_evidence.html.

Leempoel, Kevin, et al. *Return of an Apex Predator to a Suburban Preserve Triggers a Rapid Trophic Cascade.* preprint, Ecology, 1 Mar. 2019. DOI.org (Crossref), doi:10.1101/564294.

Long, James McMartin, and Peter Bauer. *The Adirondack Park and Rural America - Economic and Population Trends 1970–2010.* Protect the Adirondacks, 2019, https://www.adirondackalmanack.com/2019/04/peter-bauer-the-adirondack-park-and-rural-america.html.

Lyme Disease: Data and Surveillance. CDC, 15 Feb. 2019, http://www.cdc.gov/lyme/stats/index.html.

Mac, Stephen, et al. "The Economic Burden of Lyme Disease and the Cost-Effectiveness of Lyme Disease Interventions: A Scoping Review." *PLOS ONE*, edited by Giampiero Favato, vol. 14, no. 1, Jan. 2019, p. e0210280. DOI.org (Crossref), doi:10.1371/journal.pone.0210280.

New York State County Crash Summary, 2009-2018. Institute for Traffic Safety Management and Research, https://www.itsmr.org/tssr/. Accessed 8 May 2019.

Trentacoste, Michael F. *Wildlife-Vehicle Collision Reduction Study.* US DOT, Aug. 2008, https://www.fhwa.dot.gov/publications/research/safety/08034/08034.pdf.

Works Cited / Works Referenced, Part Two

Bissonette, John A., et al. *Evaluation of the Use and Effectiveness of Wildlife Crossings.* National Academies Press, 2008. DOI.org (Crossref), doi:10.17226/14166.

Clevenger, Anthony P., et al. Banff *Wildlife Crossings Project: Integrating Science and Education in Restoring Population Connectivity Across Transportation Corridors.* Parks Canada Agency, 11 June 2009.

Davis, John. "Eastern Wildway - The Essential 16." *Wildlands Network*, https://wildlandsnetwork.org/wildways/eastern/the-essential-16/.

Dickie, Gloria. "As Banff's Famed Wildlife Overpasses Turn 20, the World Looks to Canada for Conservation Inspiration." *Canadian Geographic*, Dec. 2017, p. 7.

Harbour, Parsons-Clough. *I-87 Multimodal Corridor Study.* New York State Department of Transportation, May 2004.

Kinley, Trevor. *Planning Wildlife Crossings in Canada's Mountain Parks.* International Association for Impact Assessment, 13 May 2013.

New York State Crash Data by County and Municipality. Crash Contributing Factors: Animal Action. 2009-2018. Counties of Clinton, Essex, Franklin, Fulton, Hamilton, Herkimer, Lewis, Oneida, Saratoga, St. Lawrence, Warren, Washington. Institute for Traffic Safety Management and Research, https://www.itsmr.org/tssr/. Accessed 8 May 2019.

Something Wicked This Way Comes: The Menace of Deep-Sea Mining

By Eileen Crist

The Set-Up

A new chapter of Earth pillage is in the works: the commercial venture of deep-sea mining. The deep sea lies 200 meters below sea level into the abyssal depths and comprises roughly 65 percent of Earth's surface (Danovaro et al., 2017). It is being encroached by a nexus of nation-states and industries slavering over its "mind-boggling quantities of untapped resources" (Mengerink et al., 2014: 696).

According to official discourse—and apparent consensus—it is not about whether the deep sea will be mined, but about how, by whom, and when. In fact, deep-sea mining has already started, with the industrial-scale commercial show coming soon to a theatre far away from you. Same as it ever was.

Deep-sea mining has gotten quietly underway since the turn of the century (and with gathering speed in recent years), with concessions granted for exploring mineral resources and testing mining techniques. As of 2018, twenty-nine exploratory contracts for the high seas have been conceded to nation-states and the mining industry by the International Seabed Authority (ISA), covering at least 1.2 million square miles (IUCN, 2018; Kim, 2017; Wedding et al., 2015). Companies and states have been granted leases, for both national and international areas, for exploratory mining of hydrothermal vents for deposits of sulfides, seamounts for cobalt crusts, continental margins for phosphates, and seabed for polymetallic nodules (Mengerink et al., 2014). These areas of the deep sea harbor a rich, endemic, and largely unknown biodiversity, yet they are currently being wrecked by mining machinery—even though deep-sea mining commercial regulations are not yet in place. "We are operating in the dark," Director of IUCN's Global Marine and Polar Programme, Carl Lundin states. "Our current understanding of the deep sea does not allow us to effectively protect marine life from mining operations. And yet, exploration contracts are being granted even for those areas that host highly unique species" (IUCN, 2018).

The ISA was created in 1994 by the United Nations Convention on the Law of the Sea (UNCLOS) with the mandate to regulate "all solid, liquid, and gaseous mineral resources in the Area [the high seas] or beneath the seabed" (quoted in Van Dover et al., 2018: 25; Wedding et al., 2015). In other words, the operative assumption has long been that the deep-sea will be mined, so the ISA was vested with the authority to regulate extraction operations in areas beyond national jurisdiction. At the same time, exploratory mining contracts for national waters have been granted to companies by nation-states. (For example, Papua New Guinea to Nautilus Minerals.)[1] No surprise there: nation-states (de jure) own marine territories 200 nautical miles offshore; in the typical pomposity of human-supremacist speak, these areas

---

1   Fortunately, that relationship has run into political and economic controversy, forestalling or derailing mining plans, though Nautilus Minerals continues to hold the deep-sea mining license from the government of Papua New Guinea (*The Economist*, 2018; Heffernan, 2019).

The Loggerhead Sea Turtle Caretta Caretta. © 2019 Angela Manno, 7"x 9"x 1" *Egg Tempera and Gold Leaf on wood, angelamanno.com/icon/endangered.php*

how depraved the old one was. The new venture is not only for gold, but for other metals and minerals like silver, copper, cobalt, nickel, manganese, zinc, rare earths, and yttrium. Enough to make the hungry ghosts—governments and corporations—line up for filching stuff useful for making cellphones, iPads, PCs, kindles, batteries, LED bulbs, flat screen TVs, fuel cells, and not to mention "essential parts of advanced military technology," like missile guidance, laser targeting, and radar surveillance (Kato, 2017).

We should have no doubt about the obscenity of what is in process, nor about its significance. If commercial deep-sea mining goes ahead, the destruction of life—in a part of the ecosphere that harbors millions of mostly undiscovered life forms—will be enormous (Koslow, 2007; Heffernan, 2019). Our time is the long-due time to put down the weapons of warring against Earth, seeking instead to downscale humanity's presence, cease our invasions into the natural world, and pull out of large-scale portions of the ecosphere. At precisely this time of mass extinction, imminent climatic chaos, and global toxification—what do we see? We see the hungry ghosts gearing up to reel out more death and extinction in exchange for "natural resources."

In case you have never heard the term "hungry ghosts," they are archetypal beings with extremely narrow

are called "Economic Exclusive Zones" (EEZs). Fishing, extractive, and other activities in the EEZs have devastated marine life there, as one would expect from such a naming.

There has been no public discussion or debate about deep-sea mining. Just a well-planned, technologically-ready, new raid on Earth about to be fast-tracked into business as usual. Deep-sea mining is blithely touted as "the new gold rush," as though it is not common knowledge throats and obese bellies, so that no matter how much they eat they never get enough. Never enough. Forever hungry. "Always encroaching," in the words of Native American Shawnee Chief Tecumseh (quoted in Waters, 1972: 278).

The Main Targets: Hydrothermal Vents, Seamounts, and Seabed Polymetallic Nodules

Piling on the cheap cliché of "the new gold rush," the deep sea is proclaimed "the last resource frontier." That resource frontier is neither. The deep sea is filled with beautiful life, amazing adaptations, abiding mystery, and primordial being. Scientists believe there are millions of species in the deep sea, Earth's largest biome, yet we know next to nothing about deep-sea biodiversity (University of Oxford, 2017; Deep Sea Conservation Coalition). The places targeted for violation—the hydrothermal vents, the seamounts, and the abyssal seabed—are filled with life and, importantly, also largely created by life. The destruction of life forms and habitats will be all the more severe, given that these environments are a poster case of "out of sight, out of mind."

There has been no public discussion or debate about deep-sea mining. Just a well-planned, technologically-ready, new raid on Earth about to be fast-tracked into business as usual.

Hydrothermal active vents are extremely rare habitats on Earth and shelter endemic and largely unknown species. To the best of our knowledge, life originated in hydrothermal vents (Van Dover et al., 2018). Besides their unique microbial communities, hydrothermal vents are also inhabited by larger organisms, including tubeworms, mussels, crabs, lobsters, limpets, different kinds of worms, fish, and octopus. As scientist C.L. van Dover and colleagues state, "hydrothermal vent ecosystems are natural wonders of the ocean… oases of vibrant and exotic life" (Van Dover et al., 2018: 20). Each vent site has its own cast of species and combination thereof, with less than 5 percent of species overlap across vent sites.

If deep-sea mining proceeds, hydrothermal vents are destined for rubble, as mining machines gouge ore that lies 20 to 30 meters beneath the seafloor to extract sulfide deposits, containing copper, gold, and other metals (Wedding et al., 2015). The mining will thus "cause severe if not total loss of biodiversity" (Van Dover et al., 2018: 21). Every single active hydrothermal vent on this planet is an invaluable singularity, yet the industry will have to "bulk-mine" them, as well as mine "multiple sites," in order to make their ventures profitable. The ISA has already approved exploration contracts for vent mining in the Atlantic and Indian oceans, which means that a portion of hydrothermal-vent life has already been destroyed. Given the high endemism of vent life forms, undoubtedly mining-driven extinctions have already occurred.

Seamounts are underwater mountains that rise 1,000 feet or more from the seafloor. They harbor enormous deep-sea biodiversity. Life has set up home on seamounts and life has also crafted the surfaces of seamounts as habitat. According to the Deep Sea Conservation Coalition, seamounts "are home to cold-water coral reefs and forests, sponge beds and hydrothermal vents, as well as the many millions of species dependent on these… Virtually every study finds [seamount] species that were previously unknown and are endemic… meaning unique to that area." Seamounts harbor huge amounts of phytoplankton and extraordinary fish diversity, and are spawning grounds for pelagic species. They are also critical as stopovers for a cosmopolitan citizenry of dolphins, whales, sharks, tuna, sea turtles, and others. The mining industry describes seamounts as "cobalt-rich ferromanganese crusts," verbiage to grease the wheels of seamount gouging for cobalt, rare earths, and other minerals (Wedding et al., 2015). Many seamounts (and continental shelves) and their species around the world have already been devastated by industrial-fishing trawlers (a fact unknown to most people)—giving precedent for more of the same.

Strewn over vast stretches of the seabed lie polymetallic nodules that range from pebble- to potato-sized. It takes millions of years for them to grow a few millimeters at a time. How they form is still largely unknown, and whether the process is strictly chemical or mediated by life (biogenic) is also debated (Koslow, 2007: 164). Not until the mid-1980s did scientists discover the existence of "a unique ecological community contained in the universe of nodules" (Koslow, 2007: 163). Polymetallic nodules are gems of the deep, found over 70 percent of the deep seabed, and abyssal life loves them well: there is twice more life in the stretches where these nodules lie than where they do not (Vanreusel et al., 2016). Nodules add habitat heterogeneity so life likes to swirl about them. They also form hard substrate, so tiny sessile animals can attach to them and eat food that currents waft by (Vanreusel et al., 2018; Koslow, 2007). Like much of the biota of hydrothermal vents and seamounts, nodule-dependent seafloor life is only recently discovered and of mostly unknown composition. The mining-industry looters and their nation-state accomplices—or is it vice versa?—plan to scarf up the polymetallic nodules for the copper, cobalt, nickel, manganese, etc. they contain (Vanreusel et al., 2016).

The hungry ghosts speak with a silver tongue. "It makes sense to explore this untapped potential in an environmentally sustainable way," states the CEO of Nautilus Minerals, "instead of continually looking at the fast depleting land resources of the planet to meet society's rising needs" (quoted in Carrington, 2018). "Explore," here, is a stand-in for mine; the "untapped potential" that Nautilus Minerals would tap into in an "environmental sustainable way" is hydrothermal vents off the coast of Papua New Guinea. The sustainable way involves giant crawling machines grinding up rock (containing copper, zinc, and gold), pumping the slurry up at a rate of 3,000 tons a day, and dumping the water back into the sea contaminating the water column and smothering life (see Carrington, 2018). In other words, the sustainable way involves death, extinction, suffering, and destruction of habitat that will not recover in human timescales. We live in a time, however, where words are cheap, sustainability babble plentiful (one seabed mining recent start-up calls itself "DeepGreen" [Heffernan, 2019]), and pseudo-noble sentiments for humanity abounding. As one company representative of deep-sea mining equipment told *The Economist*, they are in the business of developing "resources that are absolutely necessary for the future prosperity of humankind" (*The Economist*, 2017).

Humanity's "Common Heritage"

In 1982, UNCLOS declared the area beyond national jurisdiction—called "the Area" and also known as the high seas—"the common heritage of mankind." Let's bring that one up to speed with current language-use decorum. UNCLOS surely meant "the common heritage of humankind," as contemporary reports are rectifying (see, for example, Jaeckel et al., 2017). That one raises no eyebrows. On the contrary, it is avowed a principle— one "generally understood to require access and benefit-sharing arrangements, especially for developing [nation]-states" (Jaeckel et al., 2017: 150). The common heritage of humankind raises the dutiful mission to ensure that the benefits of "deep-sea mining are equitably shared among all states on a nondiscriminatory basis," and applied toward "alleviating poverty" (Kim, 2017). "UNCLOS recognizes," as the same idea is echoed elsewhere, "the right of all states to access marine resources in the area beyond national jurisdiction" (Danovaro et al., 2017). Some assurance of environmental protection is deemed part of the ISA's mandate in regulating deep-sea use as humanity's "the common heritage." Such protection is lagging while mining contracts are being shelled out and environmental protection does not include the prevention of extinctions—which any amount of deep-sea mining guarantees. Moreover, the question of whether to mine the deep sea at all has never been on the table.

> *In 1982, UNCLOS declared the area beyond national jurisdiction— called "the Area" and also known as the high seas—"the common heritage of mankind." Let's bring that one up to speed with current language-use decorum.*

How is it that calling the high seas "the common heritage of humankind" pulls the wool over so many eyes? An ancient living landscape that preexists Homo sapiens by millions of years is our common heritage? Instead of denouncing such bunk, in response to imminent industrial scale deep-sea mining, well-meaning scientists and analysts are scrambling for damage control—calling for "preservation reference zones," "remediation obligations," "collaborative governance," "balancing tradeoffs," "environmental impact assessments," "mitigation strategies," "baseline data," "holistic management of deep-sea use," and so forth. The very political-economic establishment that is destroying the ecosphere and endangering so much of humanity forces such genuflecting compliance that observers cannot bring themselves to stand against it and say what needs to be said: We are mad as Hell and we are not going to take more Earth desecration anymore!

The colluding alliance of nation-states and industry is consummately skilled in securing near-universal submission. It has a two-tiered mode of operation: one discursive, another operational. The discursive one is the longstanding appropriation of Earth as human property, ensuring the embezzlement of all geographical space for human use and control. In the specific case of the high seas, this core brainwash spins out in their "declaration" as humanity's common heritage. People hesitate to call out such drivel for fear of being labelled foolish, idealistic, or radical. Instead, they abide pliantly with the official discourse, and do their best to make the "inevitable" deep-sea mining a little less destructive.

The second strategy by which the hungry-ghost coalition secures submission is operational: Just do it. Which is exactly what has happened—deep-sea mining is underway. (If you call it "exploratory" apparently no public deliberation is needed.) What's more, most nation-states are already involved since the UN created body, the ISA, consists of 168 nation representatives; the technologies are already developed and deployed; and the rules and regulations to dress it all up as "sustainable" are being ironed out.

The cognitive schema of human Earth-ownership and the operational schema of human Earth-looting work together. Planetary ownership licenses getting a head-start on the looting operation—nothing untoward in doing what you want to your own property. Then, once the operation is already happening, it invites more of itself: it is already begun, certain players are more involved than others, and when it comes to politically-correct Earth-ravaging everyone in the posse needs to get their turn. To mirror the vulgarity of deep-sea mining and its squalid skulk, it's like this: spitting into the soup is the surest way to ensure you get to eat it. How fitting for the hungry ghosts.

The Ecocentric Response

Not only should deep-sea mining be immediately halted, but the high seas (the Area) should be put off limits to all extractive activity: for fish, fossil fuels, and metals and minerals. The Area needs to be renamed "the common heritage of all Life," in order to reflect what it actually is. Human presence in the high seas must be limited to the lightest of impacts for the elevated purposes of witnessing, learning about, and teaching our children the marvels with whom we share the ecosphere. With the Area as a whole designated as Marine Protected Area (MPA), marine life abundance will be able to rebound and cope (and help humanity cope) with climate-change upheaval and ocean acidification (see Roberts et al., 2017). Coastal seas and continental shelves (critically endangered and endangered, respectively [Jackson 2008]) are inherently life-rich, so robust MPA networks need to be globally created for them as well. Ocean protection could thus achieve 70 to 80 percent overall levels. Today is the time to stop new modes of Earth destruction from coming online and also to halt established ones: specifically, industrial trawling, longline fisheries, and deep-sea oil and gas drilling are among the most atrocious activities ever unleashed on Earth and they need to be banned. The humungous amount of scrap from that technological arsenal can be recycled for better uses.

Along with setting vast areas of the ocean free to preserve and recover their living abundance, we must turn the spotlight on the high-tech industry—the one poised to most benefit (if profiteering counts as "benefit") from deep-sea mining. The high-tech industry needs to change fundamentally and clean up its act, rather than trying to buy another century's worth of time for its wasteful, dollar-hungry workings. First, engineering, innovating, investing, and public policy must focus resolutely on recycling metals and minerals. At the moment, recycling rates hover between modestly low and abysmally low. For example, thirty-two percent of copper is recycled and just 1 percent of rare earths (Kim, 2017). The focus of turning an extraction industry into a recycling one will not only give Earth a rest, it will force governments and industry to quit dumping their e-waste on the disempowered—human and nonhuman. Second, the high-tech industry must put an end to the profligate production of ever-more devices, to be replaced by ever-more new lines, ad nauseum. (The same applies for the production of other commodities like cars and appliances.) Instead, the high tech industry—calling here on any conscientious leadership therein—needs an immediate paradigm shift toward the durable: stuff must be made well, made to last, and made to use not flaunt (McKibben, 2007). Devices can indeed be long-lasting, made to be repairable if they malfunction, and only upgraded when hugely meaningful increases in efficiency, or changes in energy sourcing, warrant "new generations." Finally, civil society has to figure out how to create a culture of sharing this stuff.

One last response to the specter of deep-sea mining is to raise a question: If this planned violation of Earth's ocean does not reveal the imperative to achieve a lower global population, what does? The global middle class—the clientele of high-tech products—is growing by leaps and bounds. The middle-class population is projected to reach 5 billion before midcentury (Kharas, 2017). All these people will want (inter alia) cellphones, PCs, flat-screen TVs, hybrid cars, solar panels, etc. Making materials recyclable, durable, and shareable is critical, but it will only get us so far. Design changes and behavioral shifts will not offset the commodity-supply surges that the growing global middle-class population portends. Therefore, we must ramp up without further delay the human-rights campaigns—for women's equality, state of the art family planning, and comprehensive sexuality education for all—that will stabilize the human population and steer it in the direction of 2 billion (Engelman, 2016; Kaidbey and Engelman, 2017; Crist et al., 2017; Crist, 2019).

We cohabit living Earth with countless Earthlings we know and more we have still to meet. Are we awake yet?

References

Carrington, D (2017). Is deep sea mining vital for a greener future—even if it destroys ecosystems? *The Guardian*. 4 June. Available at: https://www.theguardian.com/environment/2017/jun/04/is-deep-sea-mining-vital-for-greener-future-even-if-it-means-destroying-precious-ecosystems

Crist, E et al. (2017). The Interaction of Human Population, Food Production, and Biodiversity Protection. *Science* 356: 260-264.

Crist, E (2019). *Abundant Earth: Toward an Ecological Civilization*. Chicago: University of Chicago Press.

Danovaro, R et al. (2017). An ecosystem-based deep-ocean strategy. *Science* 355 (6324): 452-454.

Davidson, H and Doherty, B (2017). Troubled Papua New Guinea deep-sea mine faces environmental challenge. *The Guardian*. 11 December. https://www.theguardian.com/world/2017/dec/12/troubled-papua-new-guinea-deep-sea-mine-faces-environmental-challenge

Deep Sea Conservation Coalition. http://www.savethehighseas.org/

Engelman, R (2016). Nine Population Strategies to Stop Short of 9 Billion. In Washington, H. and P. Twomey eds. *A Future Beyond Growth: Toward a Steady State Economy*. London: Routledge, pp. 32-42.

Heffernan, O (2019). Deep-Sea Dilemma. *Nature* 571: 465-468.

IUCN (2018). Draft mining regulations insufficient to protect the deep sea—IUCN report. 16 July. https://www.iucn.org/news/secretariat/201807/draft-mining-regulations-insufficient-protect-deep-sea-%E2%80%93-iucn-report

Jackson, J (2008). Ecological Extinction and Evolution in the Brave New Ocean. PNAS 105(1): 11458-11465.

Jaeckel, A et al. (2017). Conserving the Common Heritage of Humankind—Options for the Deep-Seabed Mining Regime. Marine Policy 78: 150-157.

Kaidbey, M and Engelman, R (2017). Our Bodies, Our Future: Expanding Comprehensive Sexuality Education. Chapter 15 in *EarthEd: Rethinking Education on a Changing Planet*.

State of the World 2017. The Worldwatch Institute. Washington D.C.: Island Press.

Kato, Y (2017). Deep-sea mud in the Pacific Ocean as a new mineral resource for rare-earth elements. https://www.pecc.org/resources/environment-1/1923-deep-sea-mud-in-the-pacific-ocean-as-a-new-mineral-resource-for-raw-earth-elements/file

Kharas, H (2017). *The Unprecedented Expansion of the Global Middle Class: An Update*. Brookings Global Economy & Development, Working Paper 100. https://www.brookings.edu/wp-content/uploads/2017/02/global_20170228_global-middle-class.pdf

Kim, RE (2017). Should Deep Seabed Mining be Allowed? *Marine Policy* 82: 134-137.

Koslow, T (2007). *The Silent Deep: The Discovery, Ecology, and Conservation of the Deep Sea*. Chicago: University of Chicago Press.

McKibben, B (2008). *Deep Economy: The Wealth of Communities and the Durable Future*. St. Martin's Griffin.

Mengerink, K et al. (2014). A Call for Deep-Ocean Stewardship. *Science* 344: 696-698.

Niner H et al. (2018). Deep-sea mining with no net loss of biodiversity—an impossible aim. *Frontiers in Marine Science* 5 (53): 1 March.

Roberts, C et al. (2017). Marine Reserves Can Mitigate and Promote Adaptation to Climate Change. PNAS. http://www.pnas.org/content/pnas/early/2017/05/31/1701262114.full.pdf

Teske, Sven (2017). Renewable energy and deep-sea mining: supply, demand and scenarios. Institute for Sustainable Futures. http://dscc.hifrontier.com/wp-content/uploads/2017/03/Teske_Sven_ISF-Kingston-11-July-2016.pdf

The Economist (2017). Deep-sea mining could transform the globe. https://video.search.yahoo.com/yhs/search?fr=yhs-pty-pty_maps&hsimp=yhs-pty_maps&hspart=pty&p=deep+sea+mining+youtube#id=1&vid=2fe8a99fb-94538f3abc2b70847a8e3ce&action=click

The Economist (2018). Deep Trouble. (December 8): 63-64.

University of Oxford (2017). Shocking Gaps of Knowledge of Deep Sea Life. http://www.ox.ac.uk/news/2017-08-21-shocking-gaps-basic-knowledge-deep-sea-life-3

Van Dover, C et al. (2017). Biodiversity loss from deep-sea mining. *Nature Geoscience*, 10(7): 464-465.

Van Dover, C et al. (2018). Scientific rationale and international obligations for protection of active hydrothermal vent ecosystems from deep-sea mining. *Marine Policy* 90: 20-28.

Vanreusel, A (2016). Threatened by mining, polymetallic nodules are required to preserve abyssal epifauna. *Scientific Reports*, 6: 26808. Available at: https://www.ncbi.nlm.nih.gov/pmc/articles/PMC4887785/pdf/srep26808.pdf

Waters, Frank (1972). *The Book of the Hopi*. New York: Penguin Books.

Wedding, L.M. et al. (2015). Managing mining of the deep seabed. *Science* 349 (6244): 144-145.

POETRY

You are the Last Whale

By Gary Lawless

I spent the summer of 1980 volunteering for a small museum in southern Labrador, a summer of wind, icebergs, codfish, seal, and whale. One day I was traveling a shore road in northern Newfoundland, just across the Strait from Labrador. I saw several vehicles parked along the beach, so I stopped to see what was happening. People were standing around a male humpback whale, still alive, washed up on the edge of the beach. I wasn't sure what was proper behavior in this situation. We humans have ceremonies for dying and death, but often we let the doctors and priests attend to it. We don't have many ceremonies for the dying of other species, and not only the dying but the extinction of other species. How do we say goodbye? How do we wish them well? How do we express our sadness, our sense of love, and loss? As a poet, I thought that I would try to keep the memory of this whale alive, in a poem, and also to allow this whale to help me think about, and speak about, extinction as a larger issue. I was feeling lonely and sad at the loss of these larger friends before we ever came to really know them, but how do you say that in human language and how, other than the way we behave and act, do we express our love and loss to other humans and other sentient beings on this earth? And back then, in 1980, I wanted to end the poem somehow on a hopeful note. I'm not so sure that I would choose to do that now, but I still try to live with hope.

> You are the last whale,
> washed up on a far beach.
> The waves are pushing against you,
> pushing against you.
> Your brothers and sisters are gone.
> The light is too bright for your eyes.
> You cannot breathe.
> Small children are throwing rocks and laughing,
> climbing onto your body.
> You die alone,
> your ears full of wind.
>
> You are the last buffalo.
> the sun is setting, over the plains.
> You stand alone, enormous,
> heavy with fur, lonely,
> you are tired of running,
> tired of running.
> All of your friends have gone.
> It seems even the earth
> has turned against you.
> There is no one to say goodbye.
> You rest,
> listening to the wind.
>
> When the time is right,
> the spirit of the wolf returns.

Humpback Whale © Susan Morgan

Northeast Woodland © Shelby Perry. Big old trees like this one at Hersey Mountain in New Hampshire play a critical role in sequestering and storing carbon. This land is protected as forever-wild by Northeast Wilderness Trust. As the forest rewilds, its maturing trees will play a role as a natural climate solution.

Wild Carbon

By Mark Anderson and Jon Leibowitz

We find ourselves not at the edge of a precipice, but beyond it. Climate change is altering the world as we know it, no matter how quickly we act to reduce our collective carbon footprint. But the worst impacts are still avoidable with natural climate solutions. Permanently protecting forests and allowing them to grow in landscapes free from direct human manipulation is proving to be one of the most effective and cost efficient methods available to address the climate crisis. While wild nature has a right to exist simply for its intrinsic value, recent science is shedding peer-reviewed light on the exceptional carbon storage capacity of unmanaged land and its equally important benefits for safeguarding biodiversity. In this short synthesis, ecologist Mark Anderson summarizes recent studies which demonstrate that in our fragmented, fast-developing world, wilderness offers the earth and its community of life the precious gift of time.

—Jon Leibowitz, Executive Director, Northeast Wilderness Trust

A Synthesis of Recent Findings, by Mark G. Anderson, PhD

A long-standing debate over the value of old forests in capturing and storing carbon has prompted a surge of synthesis studies published in top science journals during the last decade. Here are five emerging points that are supported by solid evidence.

1) Trees accumulate carbon over their entire lifespan. Plants absorb carbon dioxide from air and transform it into carbon-rich sugars. These are then converted to cellulose to create biomass (trunk, bark, leaf) or transferred belowground to feed the root-fungal networks. Over the long lifespan of the tree, large amounts of carbon are removed from the air and stored as biomass. Growth efficiency declines as the tree grows but corresponding increases in the tree's total leaf area are enough to overcome this decline and thus the whole-tree carbon accumulations rate increases with age and size. A study of 673,046 trees across six countries and 403 species found that at the extreme, a large old tree may sequester as much carbon in one year as growing an entire medium size tree (Stephenson et al. 2014). At one site, large trees comprised 6 percent of the trees but 33 percent of the annual forest growth. Young trees grow fast, but old trees store a disproportional amount of carbon.

2) Old forests accumulate carbon and contain vast quantities of it. Old-growth forests have traditionally been considered negligible as carbon sinks. Although individual trees experience an increasing rate of carbon sequestration, forest stands experience an "S-curve" of net sequestration rates (e.g. slow, rapid, slow). The expected decline in older stands is due to tree growth being balanced by mortality and decomposition. To test the universality of carbon neutrality in old forests an international team of scientists reviewed 519 published forest carbon-flux estimates from stands 15 to 800 years old and found that, in fact, net carbon storage was positive for 75 percent of the stands over 180 years old, and the chance of finding an old-growth forest that was carbon neutral was less than one in ten (Luyssaert et al. 2014). They concluded that old-growth forests are usually carbon sinks, steadily accumulating carbon and containing vast quantities of it. They argued that carbon-accounting rules for forests should give credit for leaving old-growth forest intact. This is important globally, as old forests in the tropics have acted as long-term biomass/carbon sinks but are now vulnerable to edge effects, logging and thinning, or increased mortality from disturbances (Brienen et al. 2015, Lan Qui et al. 2018).

3) Old forests accumulate carbon in soils. The soil carbon balance of old-growth forests has received little attention, although it was generally accepted that soil organic carbon levels in old forests are in a steady state. In 2017, Guoyi Zhou and colleagues measured the 24-year dynamics of the soil carbon in an old-growth forest at China's Dinghushan Biosphere Reserve. They found that soils in the top 20-cm soil layer accumulated atmospheric carbon at an unexpectedly high rate, with soil organic carbon concentration increasing from about 1.4 percent to 2.4 percent and soil carbon stock increasing significantly at an average rate of 0.61 metric tons of carbon per hectare per year (Zhou, G et al. 2006). Their result directly challenges the prevailing belief in ecosystem ecology regarding carbon budget in old-growth forests and calls for further study.

4) Forests share carbon among and between tree species. Forest trees compete for light and soil resources, and competition for resources is commonly considered the dominant tree-to-tree interaction in forests. However, recent research made possible by stable carbon isotope labeling indicates that trees interact in more complex ways, including substantial exchange and sharing of carbon. In 2016, Tamir Klein and colleagues applied carbon isotope labeling at the canopy scale, and found that carbon assimilated by a tall spruce was traded with neighboring beech, larch, and pine trees via overlapping root spheres. Aided by mycorrhiza networks, interspecific transfer accounted for 40 percent of the fine root carbon totaling roughly 280 kilograms per hectare per year tree-to-tree transfer (Klein et al. 2016). In a subsequent study, Morrie et al. (2017), found that mycorrhiza soil networks become more connected and take up more carbon as forest succession progresses even without major changes in dominant species composition.

5) Forest carbon can help slow climate change. There has been debate about the role of forests in sequestering carbon and the role of land stewardship in achieving the Paris Climate Agreement goal. In 2017, Bronson Griscom and colleagues systematically evaluated twenty conservation, restoration, and improved land management actions that increase carbon storage and/or avoid greenhouse gas emissions. They found the maximum potential of these natural climate solutions was almost 24 billon metric tons of carbon equivalent per-year while safeguarding food security

It is now clear that trees accumulate carbon over their entire lifespan and that old, wild forests accumulate far more carbon than they lose through decomposition and respiration, thus acting as carbon sinks.

Bobcat © Sheri Amsel

and biodiversity. About half of this could be delivered as cost-effective contributions to the Paris Agreement, equivalent to about 30 percent of needed mitigation as of 2030, with 63 percent coming from forest-related actions. Avoided forest conversion had the highest carbon potential among the low-cost solutions (Griscom et al. 2017). New research suggests this strategy is the most cost-feasible option by a large margin (Busch et al. 2019) and it should receive high priority as a policy consideration in the U.S. (McKinley at al. 2011). An analysis of 18,507 forest plots in the Northeast found that old forests (greater than 170 years) supported the largest carbon pools and the highest simultaneous levels of carbon storage, timber growth, and species richness (Thom et al. 2019). In addition to carbon, old forests also build soil, cycle nutrients, mitigate pollution, purify water, release oxygen, and provide habitat for wildlife.

Conclusion

Recently published, peer-reviewed science has established that unmanaged forests can be highly effective at capturing and storing carbon. It is now clear that trees accumulate carbon over their entire lifespan and that old, wild forests accumulate far more carbon than they lose through decomposition and respiration, thus acting as carbon sinks. This is especially true when taking into account the role of undisturbed soils only found in unmanaged forests. In many instances, the carbon storage potential of old and wild forests far exceeds that of managed forests. We now know that the concept of overmature forest stands, used by the timber industry in reference to forest products, does not apply to carbon. In the Northeast, a vigorous embrace of natural climate solutions to mitigate global overheating does not require an either/or choice between managed and unmanaged forests. Conserving unmanaged wild forests is a useful, scalable, and cost-effective complementary strategy to the continued conservation of well-managed woodlands.

[Since completing this important paper, Northeast Wilderness Trust has launched a Wild Carbon conservation program, to help get Forever Wild protection on more private lands and help stabilize climate. Go to newildernesstrust.org *for details.*

Additional images and other graphics included in the original version can be seen at:

rewilding.org/wild-carbon-a-synthesis-of-recent-findings/ *—Rewilding Earth* editors]

References

Stephenson et al. 2014. Rate of tree carbon accumulation increases continuously with tree size. Nature 507, 90–93. doi:10.1038/nature12914

Luyssaert et al. 2008. Old-growth forests as global carbon sinks. Nature 455, 213–215. doi:10.1038/nature07276

Zhou, G. et al. 2006. Old-Growth Forests Can Accumulate Carbon in Soils. Science 314 (1) 1417.

Morrie et al. 2017. Soil networks become more connected and take up more carbon as nature restoration progresses. Nature Communications 8:14349.

Klein et al. 2016. Belowground carbon trade among tall trees in a temperate forest. Science 352, Issue 6283, pp. 342–344.

Griscom, B.W., Adams, J., et al. 2017. Natural Climate Solutions. PNAS 114 (44) 11645–11650.

R. J. W. Brienen, R. J. W., et. al. 2015. Long-term decline of the Amazon carbon sink. Nature 519, 346–347.

Lan Oje et al. 2017. Long-term carbon sink in Borneo's forests halted by drought and vulnerable to edge effects. Nature Communications 8: 1966.

Busch J, et al. 2019. Potential for low-cost carbon dioxide removal through tropical reforestation. Nature Climate Change 9, 463–466.

McKinley, D.C. et al. 2011. A synthesis of current knowledge on forests and carbon storage in the United States. Ecological Applications 21(6) 1902–1924.

Thom et al. 2019. The climate sensitivity of carbon, timber, and species richness covaries with forest age. Global Change Biology 25:2446–2458.

Requested Citation for this Article

Anderson, M.G. 2019. Wild Carbon: A synthesis of recent findings. Northeast Wilderness Trust. Montpelier, VT USA.org.

Profile of the Northern Forest Atlas Project

We introduce The Northern Forest Atlas Project (NFAP), an organization we greatly admire for their contribution to the protection of these vital forests. This profile is drawn from the NFAP website, northernforestatlas.org. Field guides, plant charts, blogs, and photos from NFAP are all state-of-the-art works, directed by botanist Jerry Jenkins, sharing biological wonders and important tools to build support for protecting the Northern Forest. —Rewilding Earth *editors*

From eastern Maine and the Maritimes to the prairie's edge in Minnesota and Manitoba, the Northern Forest in northeast North America is a standard of great forests, large, diverse, and surprisingly continuous. As the NFAP website states, "In a world in which much forest has been lost or damaged, and where natural carbon storage is critical to the future of the planet, the Northern Forest is very important." Its continuing importance depends upon its integrity and health.

The Northern Forest Atlas Project was created to protect that integrity and health by documenting the current biology of the forests and providing tools for the next generation of naturalists and conservationists who will study and protect them. Conservation philanthropist Ed McNeil and biologist Jerry Jenkins conceived the Atlas in 2011 to: "create a library

Northeast old-growth © Larry Master, MasterImages.org

PROFILE OF THE NORTHERN FOREST ATLAS PROJECT

Avalanche Lake, High Peaks, Adirondack Park © Bill Amadon

of photos and air videos showing the landscapes, plants and animals of the northern forest; to create photographic and diagrammatic atlases, both paper and digital, for plants and landscapes; and to design and produce a series of modern field guides to plants and ecology."

The project's vast work can be found on their website which includes approximately 5,000 photos and videos and makes available a dozen atlases and charts. The imagery currently focuses on woody plants, mosses, sedges, and landscapes. Grasses, herbs, forest ecology, and mammals will follow. Their first charts and digital atlases are for mosses and landscapes. Their first book is a field guide to woody plants; sedge and moss field guides will soon be available.

An index of their products, which includes Charts and Posters, Decorative Products, Digital Atlases, Field Guides, Graphics for Download, and Photographic Guides can be found at northernforestatlas.org. Their website also includes a "Quick Guide to Northern Forest Landscapes" and introductions to photographic technique. This is all accomplished by exceptional board, staff, and collaborators (whom you can also learn about on the NFAP website).

Thoughts from a New Hampshire ex-pat on the *Rewilding Earth* editorial team: Conservation of any natural area requires deep knowledge of what is being protected and support from enough people informed of what is at stake who will rally to the cause. These are educational challenges, and the Northern Forest Atlas Project is tackling them head-on. It aims to document and present in accessible detail the beauty and biodiversity of what is left of this important biological community in the 21st century. What remains of the Northern Forest in the heavily settled northeastern North America, is likely to continue to shrink in the face of human population growth and development unless someone steps up to make very clear what is to be gained by conservation or lost by exploitation. The Northern Forest Atlas Project is a key part of stepping up to the challenge.

Box Creek Biodiversity

By Christopher R. Wilson, Conservation Ecology LLC

Beginning around 2010, a private land conservationist named Tim Sweeney began purchasing and protecting important properties across North Carolina. By 2017, he'd acquired over 10,000 acres in the Blue Ridge Mountains, 20,000 acres in the South Mountains, and another 10,000 acres in the Piedmont. Many of these lands are now actively managed for biodiversity and have been placed under the North Carolina Natural Heritage Program's Registered Heritage Areas program, a voluntary agreement to protect outstanding examples of natural diversity in the state. Many have been transferred to public or private conservation organizations for permanent protection and management, including the largest easement donation in the state's history. This high-profile conservation work has been widely celebrated among conservationists, and, indeed, much has been written about Tim's remarkable land protection efforts. But a lesser-known story is his support for one of the most intensive biological inventories of a natural area in the state's history.

When done in support of a land protection project, biological inventories tell you what plants, animals, and habitats are on the property and what types of protection and management are needed to preserve these features in the long-term. But more importantly, the work reveals what makes the property a special place for biodiversity and why we should care, which generates the vision, enthusiasm, and support needed to make a meaningful conservation project happen. Some species are elusive and require lots of survey effort to find, many are only detectable in certain seasons, and others require highly specialized experts to find them. When done right, a biological inventory engages teams of professional zoologists, botanists, natural community ecologists, and taxonomic specialists to survey the property on multiple occasions over different seasons using a variety of techniques. Unfortunately, in the real world, this level of effort is seen as too expensive and perhaps unnecessary, so it rarely happens, particularly on voluntary private land protection projects. But Tim Sweeney saw things differently.

Tim Sweeney is Founder and CEO of Epic Games, creators of the smash hit video game Fortnite, among others. Fascinated with biodiversity, Tim hired a team of field naturalists to systematically inventory the natural features of all his conservation properties over a 5-year period. Conducting surveys year-round, these "boots-on-the-ground" biologists were able to document hundreds of locations of rare species tracked by the North Carolina Natural Heritage Program (NCNHP), which maintains a database of the state's rarest species and their locations. These biologists also classified and mapped fine-scale natural communities, vegetation types, and habitats across tens of thousands of acres. But it all started and reached its highest intensity on a property known as the Box Creek Wilderness located in the South Mountains of McDowell and Rutherford counties, about 30 miles east of Asheville.

Incited by a proposed 100-ft wide powerline condemnation through the heart of the property and the ensuing legal fight to stop it, Tim wanted to document every possible species that was under threat. A local consulting ecologist and conservation advocate named Kevin Caldwell of Mountains-to-Sea Ecological was hired to begin the work. Kevin quickly assembled a team of biologists to scour the property for rare natural features and included regional taxonomic experts, volunteer BioBlitz members, and another local consulting botanist named Lloyd Raleigh of Helia Environmental. In the race up to a potential legal showdown, managing the inventory project became daunting, and soon Kevin convinced me to join the Box Creek effort. I had worked for wildlands philanthropists and land conservancies around the country for years yet had almost never heard of a private individual protecting this much land this fast and insisting on biological inventories, restoration, and management. So, in the spring of 2013, I took a position with Unique Places (a firm administering Tim's land management at the time) as Director of Conservation Science to lead the ecological inventories on Tim's lands. Together, Kevin, Lloyd, and I would form the core biological team for Box Creek and the rest of Tim Sweeney's lands across the state.

The Box Creek Wilderness is a 7,000-acre property located within a large continuous matrix of private and public conservation lands that make up roughly 53,000 acres and include the South Mountain State Park and Gamelands. It provides part of a linkage between the South Mountains to the east and the larger Blue Ridge Mountain province to the west. NC Natural Heritage Program biologists first visited Box Creek back in the mid-2000s and these brief surveys documented around 10 natural communities and 25 rare species. By 2015, after our intensive surveys, the documented natural communities on Box Creek expanded to 34 (included 23 global and state imperiled communities), and the rare species count ballooned to nearly 130. State threatened and endangered species included Dwarf Chinquapin Oak, Rough Blazing Star, Divided Leaf Ragwort, Virginia Spiderwort, and Allegheny Plum. In all, about 1,100 plant and animal species were documented on the property. Kevin remarked, "Before our first survey season had really begun, we were joking that whoever didn't find rare species that day was a loser." But the real excitement came from new discoveries for science.

During the natural community mapping work, Caldwell and Raleigh noticed that several communities on Box Creek didn't match the classifications available in the latest NCNHP *Guide to the Natural Communities of North Carolina*. So, they consulted the author Michael Schafale, who visited the property and suggested these could be new and undescribed communities: a Dry Basic subtype of Montane Oak-Hickory Forest, a Low Elevation Basic Glade, and a Headwater Stream Forest. All certainly rare and likely state- and globally-imperiled. Caldwell and Raleigh also documented four natural communities common elsewhere but never before found in the South Mountains, as well as hundreds of acres of unlogged old growth. But the new discoveries didn't stop there.

Dwayne Estes, Associate Professor of Biology at Austin Peay State University, conducted botanical surveys in the glades at Box Creek. He was instantly struck by a few species that "didn't look right." After closer inspection and consultation with other regional experts, he realized he had discovered what appear to be two plant species new to science—a new spiderwort (*Tradescantia*) species and a new fameflower (*Phemeranthus*) species. Upon returning down the mountain from the glades, Dwayne remarked, "I felt like I was Asa Gray up there!" Just prior to our surveys, a biologist named David Campbell discovered the state's first and only known record of Allegheny Plum on the property.

Bo Sullivan, a Research Associate of the Smithsonian Institution, recorded 373 moth species on the Box Creek land, including 3 new-to-science or undescribed species, 2 species never before recorded in the state, and 10 rare species tracked by the NCNHP. One of the new state records was previously unknown east of Arkansas. One moth was not just a new species to science, but was also an entirely new genus. It was formally described by Bo and his colleague as the "Hillcane Borer" moth (*Cherokeea attakullakulla*) [Quinter, E. L. and J. B. Sullivan 2014. A new

Mole salamander © Larry Master, MasterImages.org. Mole salamanders (genus Ambystoma*) are mid-sized, stout-bodied with large flattened heads, endemic to North America, found throughout the Coastal Plain and in scattered populations of the Piedmont.*

apameine genus and species from the southern Appalachian Mountains, USA (Lepidoptera, Noctuidae, Noctuinae). ZooKeys 421: 181–191]. Bo commented, "These results reflect the rich woodlands at Box Creek. Had the study occurred for the full season, the number of species would probably have exceeded 650, making Box Creek one of the more diverse sites in the state."

The Southern Appalachian Mountains are well known as a hotspot for salamander diversity, and Box Creek did not disappoint. The South Mountain Gray Cheek Salamander, a globally imperiled local endemic known mostly from the South Mountains State Park to the east, was found on the property further west and at lower elevations than previous records. Within small floodplain pools on the property, I found the first county record of the Mole Salamander and, in nearby mossy seepage areas, the first county record for the Four-toed Salamander—both state rare species.

Interesting wildlife findings didn't stop there. One day a neighbor walked up to a group of the biologists with a plastic bucket containing an interesting turtle he had found. It turned out to be the first county record of a Gulf Coast Spiny Softshell Turtle, another state rare species. On a property immediately adjacent to Box Creek, also owned by Sweeney, my camera traps captured photos of the Eastern Spotted Skunk, a declining and understudied rare species with few recent observations in the state at that time. Two biologists from the NC Wildlife Resources Commission, Steve Fraley and T.R. Russ, conducted stream surveys on the property and found the Fantail Darter, Broad River Crayfish, and Carolina Foothills Crayfish—all state rare species. My acoustic surveys for bats, using an arsenal of automated ultrasonic recorders placed throughout the property, as well as mist-netting and acoustic surveys by consultant Gary Libby, detected or captured a number bat species including the state rare Little Brown Myotis, Tricolored Bat, and Northern Myotis (Northern Long-eared Bat). The Northern Myotis was recently listed as Threatened under the federal Endangered Species Act and the Tricolored Bat was recently petitioned for listing under the ESA.

Kevin and I did extensive bird surveys throughout Box Creek and found abundant populations of many species considered high conservation priorities by the Appalachian Mountain Migratory Bird Joint Venture Program, Partners in Flight, the US Fish and Wildlife Service, NCNHP, and others. These species included Acadian Flycatcher, Louisiana Waterthrush, Swainson's Warbler, Sharp-shinned Hawk, Worm-eating Warbler, and Wood Thrush. Based on these results, and additional data sources, Audubon North Carolina is considering expanding the current South Mountains Important Bird Area to include the Box Creek property.

At the completion of our surveys, an astounding 386-point occurrences of rare species were documented on Box Creek. Based on these findings the NCNHP designated the Box Creek Wilderness as a state recognized Natural Area (a site of special biodiversity significance) and gave it the highest possible significance rating, placing it in the top one percent of nearly 2,500 Natural Areas in the state. In the end, our biological survey findings and NCNHP's recognition of the property's significance helped convince the US Fish and Wildlife Service to accept a donation of a conservation easement on the property (the largest easement donation by a private landowner in the state's history), which permanently protected Box Creek and put an immediate stop to the proposed powerline condemnation.

Summed up well by Misty Franklin, Director of the NC Natural Heritage Program, "The Box Creek Wilderness project is a perfect example of how public-private partnerships can achieve the best conservation outcomes. After the area was originally highlighted in the Natural Heritage Inventory of Rutherford County, Tim's team of biologists logged hundreds of hours gathering additional information about the species and natural communities there. They shared this information freely with the Natural Heritage Program and collaborated with taxonomic experts to identify new species and natural communities and document the incredible richness of the site. Thanks to their hard work and expertise, this site was recognized as one of the most important sites for conserving North Carolina's natural heritage, and, most importantly, the Box Creek Wilderness is being protected through a variety of voluntary conservation agreements."

But rather than just put our report on a shelf and call it good, Tim chose to use the biological findings to guide management and restoration. Our biological team worked with his forestry staff to prioritize locations for prescribed burns on Box Creek and other properties, and we returned the following growing seasons to monitor the results. In some community types, we saw dramatic increases in the cover of rare herbs after the burns. In other stands, we saw dramatic increases in invasive species. So, we adjusted the burns accordingly the next time around. Other restoration activities included treating hemlocks for wooly adelgid infestations, doing crop tree release for Butternut trees and Allegany Plum, and working with the American Chestnut Foundation to plant stands of blight resistant American Chestnuts.

The Box Creek Wilderness project is a perfect example of how public-private partnerships can achieve the best conservation outcomes.

As a conservation scientist, the Box Creek project is everything I like to see. It's full of rare and endemic species, it's big and wild, and it's connected to a large surrounding landscape of protected lands. The experience shows how turning loose a diverse team of passionate field biologists can lead to incredible discoveries on a property whose true significance for biodiversity would otherwise have been overlooked. It shows how biological surveys can generate enthusiasm, support, and collaboration for a land protection project, which can lead to opportunities in the deal-making process that might not have been available before. It also shows how biological inventory data can lead to a more informed and meaningful outcome for biodiversity conservation. One might think, "but of course, this was a well-funded project." But in my experience, these lessons are not limited to projects like Box Creek. I have seen time and time again where even brief surveys by knowledgeable biologists can make all the difference to good conservation. Simply put, biodiversity conservation needs more boots-on-the-ground field biologists: people who live and breathe this stuff and have the experience to know when "something doesn't look right." I thank Tim Sweeney for having the vision to see that and supporting the work and for all he has done for biodiversity in NC.

Acknowledgements In no particular order, the following biologists, not already mentioned above, contributed to the surveys on Box Creek: James Padgett, Shawn Oakley (NC Natural Heritage Program); Lori Williams, Alan Cameron, Gabriel Greater (NC Wildlife Resources Commission); Sue Cameron (US Fish and Wildlife Service); BioBlitz volunteers from NC Partners in Amphibian and Reptile Conservation coordinated by Jeff Hall and Ed Corey; Dave Beamer and his students (Nash Community College); volunteers from the Carolina Vegetation Survey; Bill Moye, botanist; Lee Echols and Peter Smith (North American Land Trust); Karin Heiman, consulting botanist; Josh Kelly and Bob Gale (MountainTrue); Becky Hardman, herpetologist; and Merrill Lynch, lepidopterist. The biological work was a massive collaboration and included many volunteers not individually mentioned here. Please know your work is appreciated.

The Librarians

By Robert Michael Pyle

There is a golden walnut tree outside
and a spider, dropping bit by bit on her way to work
like a lineman cinching down a cable, or a climber
rappelling. There are people
who do no harm from one day to the next. They spray
no poisons, drop no bombs, pave no meadows.

There are deep colors in this glass of ale,
and pools of liquid light on its surface
like ponds in Cumbria, or the second eyelids
of a seabird. There are people
who glow softly through the garish tumult. They make
no waves, launch no rockets, claim no fame.

Is this a genetic condition, to withstand
the no-tax morons, beat back the dunderheads, flail
the philistines with nothing more than the love of books and reading?
or is it a matter of life and death?

The walnut will drop its leaves, and one of these nights
the spider will freeze. Books too will die,
they say. But don't believe it.
Not until the last librarian is gone
will I give up.

[Originally appeared in Evolution of the Genus Iris, *Lost Horse Press, 2014. Reprinted by permission of the author and Lost Horse Press.*—Rewilding Earth *editors]*

Spider © Susan Morgan

Drifting from Rewilding

By Mark Fisher

The level of hyperbole in the promotion of a Dutch concept of nature conservation, and its confusion with rewilding, risks reducing the meaning of rewilding to a thoughtless, simplistic equation. The undermining in Europe of the principles of rewilding is helped by media that give little acknowledgement to its original meaning, nor any evidence of the sound ecological understanding from which it was derived.

The Dutch concept is Nature Development—*Natuurontwikkeling*. It started as a means of maintaining conservation reliant species by livestock grazing, but it has been turned by Rewilding Europe and private foundations in the Netherlands into an ideology with a bizarre hatred of native structural vegetation. At its zenith of realisation, this ideology is easily recognised as Aldo Leopold's observations on the killing off of predators leading to overpopulation of the Kaibab Plateau by deer and in John Terborgh's documentation of the ecological meltdown that occurred in the vegetation of predator-bereft islands in a Venezuelan impoundment.

Trophic ecology, the interaction between all trophic levels in complete food webs, is not somehow different depending on which continent you are on, and thus it's ecologically illiterate of proponents of this ideology to claim that rewilding is different in Europe, that it is achieved with the actions of domesticated livestock enclosed by fencing. There are strictly protected public lands in the national protected area systems of Europe, often connected through national ecological networks. Contrary to popular assumption, Europe does have areas with wilderness characteristics—with self-willed land. Thus, rewilding here, too, should always be about restoring ecological and evolutionary processes, including natural disturbances, and with freely living native species, especially ecologically effective populations of highly interactive species.

I wrote a manifesto in 2003 for rewilding the UK based on the principles I had seen in *Wild Earth* and The Wildlands Project. I circulated it widely, but perhaps its lack of impact was because I was acting alone, and I made the mistake of citing the Wilderness Act when wilderness is such a contested concept in the United Kingdom. Shortly afterward, I set up an advocacy website (self-willed-land.org.uk) and, having learnt my lesson, called it Self-willed Land. Every year since then, I have had to counter the drift in meaning of rewilding while making the case for it in the UK and the rest of Europe.

I have tracked the ecological illiteracy of Frans Vera's plaything at the Oostvaardersplassen in the Netherlands for many years, documenting that his theories on shifting woodland creation driven by herbivory had no support in the literature, and watching the landscape there deteriorate toward an ecological meltdown on the back of well over 10,000 domesticated animals dying of starvation behind the fencing. Vera does not label it as rewilding, but the media and many other commentators, including academics, do. I have described this maniacal *experiment* in Dutch nature development as a zombie idea in ecology, an idea that should be dead but isn't. The deliberate trophic imbalance created by Vera, and the devastating consequences it has had for landscape vegetation, make the project not about ecology but about human agency. The population expansion and the inability of animals trapped by fences to migrate to other food sources finally upended the experiment, when the Province of Flevoland implemented the recommendations of the Van Geel commission on reducing herbivore numbers to well below food-limited carrying capacity, with the aim of sparking a regeneration in vegetation.

I was present at the conference in Brussels in 2010 when the Wild Europe Field Program was launched, which shortly afterward renamed itself Rewilding Europe. It takes a bit of experience to look behind the syllogisms perpetrated by this private Dutch foundation to understand that its explanations of its approach are generalised and superficial at best, and entirely misleading at worst. The Dutch foundation continually massages science to suit its purpose, a primary thrust being to assert that the outcome of its actions creates the original natural landscape, which it portrays as being open and savannah-like in the future visualizations of the landscapes of its project areas. This foundation's actions, the equivalence of maintaining farming pressure, do create and maintain open landscapes; but it's a leap of faith, or a particularly wanton agenda, to believe that this is the original natural landscape. The key, as always with Rewilding Europe, is that their approach is also nature development and involves dumping lots of domesticated herbivores into their fenced-off project areas, often in places where there are no large carnivores. It doesn't stop there, as Rewilding Europe seeks to push changes in policy and even national legislation to their own advantage when it argues for its back-bred, domestic cattle to be accepted as wild animals and thus be released to free living. Rewilding Europe advocates likewise argued that Przewalski's horse is a genuine wild horse so that there should be no legislative bar on introducing it to free living—even though it has been shown by genetic analysis to be a feral descendant of horses herded at Botai in the Central Asian steppes. I am reminded of what Michael Soulé wrote about this, as he saw that maintaining or restoring ecological processes by use of surrogate species could not be justified, as it was not the same as putting back the native community. Dave Foreman was later to write that without native species, the land is domesticated or feral, not wild, that a land without native species is not a wilderness, but a wasteland.

A pseudo-intellectual gloss is given to another aspect of this continual shift in rewilding by calling it *trophic rewilding*, an orchestration of functional traits behind fences rather than restoring wild ecosystems. Rewilding Europe chooses to disregard paleo-ecological evidence for the distribution of European bison by aligning with researchers who claim that bison are a refuge species in woodland, that their true habitat is open countryside. This assertion is really cover for a justification for dumping bison behind fences in the Netherlands and watching them clear the landscape of its woody vegetation. Another exasperating example was a modelling of *trophic rewilding* through enlisting the predatory behaviour of wolves in reducing the number of Red deer in Scotland, but this would take place within a fenced enclosure to avoid conflict with people. I had a ghastly vision of the reaction people would have when they saw a wolf pack chase and manoeuvre a Red deer into the fence so that its further escape was blocked, and its fate inescapable. This is why the Standards of Modern Zoo Practice in the UK do not allow predator and prey to be in the same enclosure, nor do they allow live feeding in front of the public. Zoo standards aside, what really angers me about this is its demeaning of wolves in expecting them to perform a function, when this is really dewilding through constraining the freedom of their lives by the fences removing their autonomy.

Planted Trees © Mark Fisher. Trees planted on South House Moor amongst grasses, heather, and sedges grown taller in the absence of sheep grazing on this moorland in Yorkshire.

To my indignity, the scourge of nature development infected rewilding in the UK too, linked as it has been to an intolerable absence of any critical evaluation of Frans Vera and his crackpot ideas and to the influence of Rewilding Europe, which is similarly uncritiqued. The high-profile example is Knepp, the farm owned by the Chairperson of Rewilding Britain, and which drew its approach of roaming domestic livestock behind fences from Vera as its advisor. However, there is a spatial anomaly in the autogenic development of scrubby tree growth on the farm, the main driving force for increasing diversity in UK landscapes. What becomes clear about the anomaly is that the area of the farm that has the most scrubland cover was ungrazed for a number of years, whereas the area that has the least has been under continuous grazing. The claim, though is that rewilding at Knepp is *process-led* conservation based on the grazing function of the cattle, the implication being that any change in the state of landscape vegetation was determined by and took place under the influence of grazing. This is the Vera theory of woodland development, but the area of greater development of scrub at Knepp is where it took place in the absence of livestock grazing. It would not likely have developed to the extent that it has if grazing of that area had been implemented earlier.

At issue in the UK is the lack of willingness of the shifting rewilders to learn, a pedagogical challenge that would first need a clear-out of the false prophets of rewilding. It's not for want of trying. I was asked what I would do with 140 hectares (346 acres) of degraded moorland in the Cambrian Mountains of Wales, this being the putative core area of Rewilding Britain's *big idea* for landscape scale rewilding. The site had not been grazed for six years, and the intention was to plant scattered groups of native trees, a necessary recourse in upland landscapes trapped as they are in a tree-less state from centuries of overgrazing so that there is no seed source for autogenic recovery. It seemed to have the potential for the initiation of new trophic processes based on the in-migration of small mammals like field voles, wood mice, and common shrews attracted to the taller, ungrazed vegetation and predatory birds then attracted to the small mammals. This has been seen at similar upland locations after cessation of grazing and tree planting. I looked at species records within migration distance of the location—predators like the fox, weasel, and badger, predatory and insectivorous birds like buzzard, kestrel, woodpecker, thrushes, and owls, the herbivorous small mammals and invertebrates, omnivorous birds, and the shrubby and herbaceous plant species—so that a rough capacity for harbouring those species could be calculated, and then I constructed a potential trophic pyramid as a means of assessing outcome and evaluating barriers to progress, once its natural vegetation was on a trajectory of restoration. I put a large question mark at the apex of the pyramid, representing our lack of large carnivores in the UK and how their absence creates a trophic imbalance if large herbivores are unthoughtfully introduced. Given that it was planned to introduce grazing by horses relatively soon at this location, I cautioned that six years in the absence of grazing at an upland location wasn't long enough to see the benefits that have accrued at similar upland locations in terms of ground layer regeneration and return of mammal and bird species, and that tree establishment would face difficulties without an elaborate system of physical protection. The dogma of nature development won out and, within months, six allegedly *wild* Konik horses were introduced.

Wolves are now present in every country in Continental Europe as a result of their voluntary reinstatement westward, a sign of their innate behaviour on population expansion to redistribute into new home territories. The UK and Ireland still lack wolves only because of their separation from the continent. Dietary studies show that once settled, the wolves are predominantly consumers of wild species. Countries on that expanding edge, like Germany, Denmark, the Netherlands, and Luxemburg, developed their national wolf plans in anticipation of their arrival, adjusting legislation to give strict protection and developing educational programs and mitigation plans for livestock predation. This was the mature response, underpinned by requirements of the Bern Convention and European Union legislation. I don't see that nature development has anything to offer when this real rewilding is taking place in Europe, unconfined by fencing and through a trophic interaction with free-living, native species.

Rewilding isn't something different, ecology isn't something different, just because it is taking place in Europe. Rewilding is a global issue and must not be put into confusion by those who seek to shift its meaning.

Rewilding isn't something different, ecology isn't something different, just because it is taking place in Europe. Rewilding is a global issue and must not be put into confusion by those who seek to shift its meaning. The global context is that it is one of the urgent steps listed in the World Scientists' Warning to Humanity: a second notice. As well, the Intergovernmental Science Policy Platform on Biodiversity and Ecosystem Services report on land degradation sees rewilding as a means to reverse that degradation, and Nature Needs Half gives us an over-arching strategic goal that must have rewilding as the means for its achievement.

[Mark Fisher backs his controversial critique of the drift in the meaning of 'rewilding' with extensive research and citations, available on his website: self-willed-land.org.uk. *This* Rewilding Earth *anthology includes two favorable views of European rewilding, by visitors from the U.S. –Rewilding Earth editors]*

Rewilding Scotland

By Kenyon Fields

The name "Scotland" conjures a medley of images both clichéd (bagpipes, kilts, *Braveheart*) and more enchanting (lochs, highlands, and mist). But an association not typically made with "Scotland" is "wild"—at least, not as defined by the typical North American ecologist or conservation activist. Over the past two summers my wife and I have mucked about in our Wellies from the outermost reaches of the Outer Hebrides to the most remote of the Northwest Highlands, playing connect-the-dots between remnant stands of ancient forest and climbing mossy mountains. And while true that Scots have denuded nearly every hectare of native forest and extinguished nearly every native creature larger than your rubber boot, the simple fact remains that much of Scotland still simply *feels* wild. It's for good reason that *rewilding* is not a foreign term there. In fact, in Scotland it could be said that nature conservation is synonymous with rewilding.

I am by no means an expert on Scotland, but I offer a few impressions on rewilding Scotland. First, a condensed history. After the last ice age, beginning 9,000 years ago and peaking around 6,000 years ago, oak and Caledonian pinewoods (Scots pine) became established through most of Scotland, and all but the most wind-shorn islands had significant temperate rainforest cover akin to Alaska's Tongass. But soon after reaching its geographic peak, forest cover thinned due to a changing climate, and by 4,000 years ago the metal tools of the Bronze Age took their toll. Smelting ore required continuous supplies of charcoal, and that ore produced ever more effective tools for felling trees, and on the cycle went. Continuing changes in climate increased the acreage of moorland (peat bogs), and agriculture and population experienced extensive growth. By the Viking era, many of today's most remote outer coastal sites were heavily logged for the shipbuilding Norse populating the shore. By the Middle Ages, the great majority of the island of Britain's original forests were gone, and the pattern of small copses of woods surrounded by agricultural land that you see today was established. By the late 17th century, gone too were predators such as wolf, lynx, and bear, and soon after moose ("elk" in their terms), boar, beaver, and more.

Today's Scotland has but a scattering of stars—pockets of remaining historical jewels that are not even fairly called "forests," but rather, copses or groves, often the size of city parks. Yet to bounce one's way on the carpet of drenched mosses amidst the fog-shrouded Fanghorn-inspired old-growth remnant Caledonian pinewood is one of the most enchanting experiences a forest ecologist can savor in life. A close second is a walk amongst the chest-high bracken fern that form dense understories beneath whimsically corkscrewing limbs of enormous ancient sessile oak, clad in epiphytic liverworts, lichens, and mosses. Elsewhere, pedunculate oak, wych elm, rowan, ash, hazel, holly, and alder may each be featured in isolated vivacious green corners left abandoned by the ages.

"Ancient" woodlands in Scotland are typically those persisting since 1750, though examples of much older individual trees or pockets of coppiced hazel (sometimes thousands of years old) certainly exist. These woodlands generally share in common a remote and difficult location, typically of poor soils. The growth of human population and of forest clearings in Scotland was not a free-for-all of entirely unplanned exploitation—plenty of evidence suggests planned forest management as far back as the Bronze Age. But it certainly did not favor old wizened forests. And unfortunately, "modern" forest management in Scotland, beginning in the early 19th century, recognized the problems of mass deforestation and set out to solve it with the planting of non-native conifers.

Today, the traveler is often surprised by the high volume of tree cover in Scotland, but even the most untrained eye will recognize these are unnatural plantations of largely American Sitka spruce and Norwegian spruce. A complex system (or "scheme" as they say) for afforestation in recent decades has encouraged—often with subsidies—farmers to plant these conifers for tax benefits, carbon credits, "shelter belts" for wildlife, and ultimately profit for felling the

Remnant Oak Stand © Kenyon Fields, kenyonfieldsphoto.com. Trees For Life and other Scottish NGOs have been working for years to rewild the Highlands, with extensive planting of native trees and reintroductions of extirpated wildlife.

plantations. More controversially, grants are available for "restocking" after felling plantations, even though owners are legally required to restock. Regardless, in nearly every case I witnessed, these plantations are ecologically valueless "doghair" stands of tightly packed non-native trees, typically fenced to prevent deer browsing, which serves to concentrate their nibbling on native broadleaf trees elsewhere.

But now it's time for a little hope. Opening the summer issue of *Rural Matters*, a free Scottish publication, after an article or two about the benefits of tree plantations and forestry grants, there is an article entitled "Back to the Wild," about the benefits of *rewilding*. It spoke specifically of efforts being made by large sporting estates (which vaguely play the role of a Western ranch in the USA) to remove non-native local organization or school to raise awareness of the rewilding challenge facing this beautiful country. Copses of old oak or Caledonian pine, some smaller than your local drugstore, will be proudly announced by a road sign and interpretive signage along a short trail. It's not uncommon to see huge piles of dead, hand-removed rhododendron—a wildly successful non-native shrub that overtakes everything else in these northern Atlantic woodlands. Debates on rewilding are printed in the country's most prominent newspapers. One of the more rancorous debates concerns billionaire philanthropist Paul Lister's publicly stated desire to reintroduce wolves onto his private guest-lodging estate, which he has been using as a grand rewilding experiment (where you can attend conservation seminars after your yoga or survival lessons).

> *While we in North America are concerned with saving what's left, it's not terribly exaggerated to say that the Scots have a nearly blank canvas from which to begin to create anew.*

While we in North America are concerned with saving what's left, it's not terribly exaggerated to say that the Scots have a nearly blank canvas from which to begin to create anew. Fortunately, although one cannot escape the touch of humanity anywhere in Scotland, there remains plenty of room to work with, and wide-open spaces are easily found; not depopulated Wilderness, but quiet and largely empty. Once beyond the reach of the Glasgow, Edinburgh, and Aberdeen metro areas, where the bulk of Scots live, population density is often very low. True, you can climb over two mountain ridges to reach a blank spot on the map and you'll surely descend to find a cottage along the shore replete with baying sheep all about—but it ain't no Walmart.

Rewilding might not yet be a household word in Scotland, but it's catching on. Little oaks are growing behind protective fences, and the odd wildcat is seen roaming the hills. After their first reintroduction trials in 2009, Scottish beavers received protective status the winter of 2019, and now even have their own website. Not all hope is lost in the world!

References

The Rainforests of Britain and Ireland, Clifton Bain.
Rural Matters, The Galbraith Group, Summer 2019.
treesforlife.org.uk

conifers, reintroduce native species, more closely manage where sheep may roam, and so forth. My point here is that this is a publication one might find lying about anywhere, from a laundromat to a grocery store, and it is not alone in heralding the benefits of a rewilding approach.

Trees For Life and other established Scottish NGOs have been working for years to rewild the Highlands, with extensive planting of native trees and reintroductions of creatures. But the concept has clearly broadened out to a wider audience, and it is not rare to stumble across a new effort by perhaps a

European Experiments in Rewilding: Elbe River Biosphere Reserve

By David T. Schwartz

The last official act of the East German government (DDR) before dissolving in 1990 was to enact the proposal of a renegade biologist-turned-bureaucrat named Michael Succow. Knowing German reunification was imminent, Succow persuaded the outgoing politicians to adopt a sweeping proposal to set aside 7 percent of all land in the DDR for nature preserves and nature parks, a move that he knew would be binding on the government of a unified Germany. Hence was born a vast network of national parks and reserves, including the Flusslandschaft Elbe Biosphere Reserve, the largest nature reserve in Germany.

Part of UNESCO's Man and the Biosphere Program, the Flusslandschaft Elbe Reserve covers 340,000 hectares of ecologically diverse habitat along the Elbe River in northern Germany. The Elbe-Brandenburg section of reserve, which I visited earlier this year, encompasses 53,000 hectares of sensitive flood plain along a section of the Elbe that once served as the border between East and West Germany. While many of Europe's great rivers have been thoroughly tamed, the Elbe is one of Germany's most 'natural' remaining rivers, sustaining great biodiversity and providing habitat for numerous threatened species. In addition to its natural value, Flusslandschaft Elbe is also incredibly rich in cultural significance. Its role in the Cold War is a mere blip when one considers that the region has supported human civilization since Neolithic times, or about 8,000 years.

My tour of the reserve began on a brisk May morning in the company of Jan Schormann, Biosphere Deputy Director. Our first stop was the largest and perhaps most successful restoration project in the reserve's history, a massive dike relocation near the town of Lenzen. While the old dike generally protected nearby towns from flooding, its close proximity to the riverbank meant that only a small strip of land benefited from the rejuvenating cycles of natural flooding. Floodwaters could not reach most of the natural floodplain, making it impossible for the waters to nurture wetlands and rejuvenate depleted soil. After much negotiation with skeptical local citizens, work began in 2003 on a new dike further inland. After ten years of work, a new dike was in place and large cuts made into the old dike so that floodwaters could pass through to the new barrier. The result has been not only a larger and healthier floodplain but also better flood protection. Jan explained that a bad 2003 flood nearly breached the old dike, requiring the German military to haul in 2 million sandbags to prevent catastrophic flooding. After the dike relocation, an even worse flood in 2013 needed no such intervention. The local skeptics were won over.

A closer look at an odd building reveals it to be an abandoned East German watchtower, revealing that the old dike ran precisely along the old border between East and West Germany. Said another way, thirty years ago we would have been shot for just standing on this spot!

While the science and engineering aspects are formidable, Jan says the most challenging aspect of his work is often more personal—persuading local citizens to go along with the Reserve's various projects and proposals. For example, for several years Jan and his team have been hoping to restore a large natural moor in the area. Critical to storing carbon and reducing greenhouse gases, 35 percent of moors, bogs, and other such wetlands worldwide have been lost to human development, according to a recent U.N. Climate Report. The moor in Elbe has been damaged

Stork in Trees © David Schwartz. The Biosphere Reserve supports the storks' migration by providing technical and financial assistance to local citizens so they can keep nest sizes manageable and repair any structural damage to buildings.

by humans draining off water so that the land can support grazing cattle. The practice dates back centuries, but it was ramped up exponentially by the East German government in the 1980s to increase food production. When water is extracted from a moor, the underlying peat breaks down (releasing its carbon into the atmosphere) and the land slowly sinks. While restoration is technically possible, the Elbe Reserve has so far been unable to persuade local farmers to sell their land to the Reserve to begin the process. Interestingly, the resistance seems grounded more in cultural tradition ("we've done it this way for centuries") than economics, as most of the cattle are being raised for a hobby, not a livelihood.

While the Reserve has political authority to seize the moor by eminent domain, Elbe officials refuse to use such heavy-handed tactics. Not only do they view seizure as morally suspect, they also believe persuasion is the only real route to changing long-term environmental attitudes. After 45 years of totalitarian control, the locals are in no mood for top-down, imposed solutions. Some of this resistance goes back to how the Biosphere Reserve was created in the first place—imposed by an act of the East German government with no local input. As local critics were fond of saying at the time, "We want jobs, not owls." In a role that he describes as 'rural diplomat,' Jan hopes to show that they can have both.

Traditional rewilding advocates may well ask, "Why allow people to farm here at all? Why not take such sensitive land out of service and do a complete restoration?" While understandable, this reaction reveals a fundamental difference in philosophy between traditional rewilding and the UNESCO mandate. Whereas traditional restoration often aims to erase the human footprint entirely, the Man and the Biosphere Program views human culture as a legitimate element of a region's landscape ecology.

An example of this philosophy can be seen in the Elbe Reserve with the annual migration of white storks. Each spring a colony of white storks makes the 7,000 mile journey from South Africa, arriving in March and residing here until their return trip south in August. Rather than hiking through remote forest or wetlands to see such beautiful birds, I was able to observe them from the comfortable balcony of a restored warehouse in the small town of Rühstädt, which bills itself as the stork capital of Germany. Jan described the storks as "culture followers," a fascinating term for animals whose life is intimately tied to cultural landscapes. In fact, the storks' entire migration pattern has been adapted over centuries to take advantage of human habitation. For the storks, living near humans means an abundance of freshly mowed hayfields, where worms and other foodstuffs are much easier to find than in wild landscapes or forests. It also means the safety and security of nesting and brooding high on the rooftops of barns, houses, and other human structures. This nesting behavior has developed over centuries, with storks often returning to the exact same nests each year. In fact, conflicts often break out if storks return to find an interloper on their 'property.'

Like any other conservation organization, the Elbe Reserve works to ensure that the storks' migration patterns continue into perpetuity. But unlike nature preservation efforts that seek to erase the human footprint, here the goal is actually to maintain the human footprint upon which the storks' migration depends. For example, because these nests can weigh over a ton, they can damage or even collapse a roof or barn if not actively managed. The Biosphere Reserve supports the storks' migration by providing technical and financial assistance to the local citizens so they can keep the nest sizes manageable and repair any structural damage. With this kind of support, the locals are more willing and able to allow the storks to live on their property while in Germany. The result is obviously good for the storks, and it also pays dividends to the local economy through eco-tourism. Thousands of tourists flock here each year to take in this amazing sight. Jan explained that a stork's first priority is always maintaining control of the nest. They will sometimes opt to change mates rather than lose a nest. Because preserving property seems to come before all else, he thinks that at heart the storks may be capitalists!

Whereas traditional restoration often aims to erase the human footprint entirely, the Man and the Biosphere Program views human culture as a legitimate element of a region's landscape ecology.

Nothing says rewilding more than wolf reintroduction, and the Elbe Biosphere Reserve has that, too. Yet unlike the wolves reintroduced by humans into Yellowstone National Park in the 1990s, these wolves are reintroducing themselves! Extirpated from much of Western Europe in the 20th century, wolves are slowly migrating back into Germany, France, and even the Netherlands from less populated countries such as Poland and Russia. There are two breeding wolf packs in the Elbe River Biosphere Reserve alone, and dozens more have been documented across the German state of Brandenburg.

While many Germans (mostly in large cities) are ecstatic about the return of the wolf, others (mostly in rural areas) see wolves as a menace to their livelihood and family. From exaggerated stories about wolves killing livestock and even abducting children, critics argue that tolerating wild wolves is a step too far in environmental activism. In fact, on the very day I arrived in the Elbe Reserve a bill was introduced in the German Bundestag to ease prohibitions on hunting and killing wolves. Until now, official government policy toward wolves has essentially been one of toleration—farmers received compensation for lost livestock, but the wolves themselves could not be harmed.

While the tolerance policy has obvious advantages for the wolves and for rewilding efforts generally, it is expensive financially and politically. Besides the public funds needed to compensate farmers for livestock losses, many farmers now feel compelled to buy canine protection for their animals. Bred and trained in the Balkans specifically to guard livestock from wolves, these dogs are expensive to buy and to maintain, adding to the farmers' economic woes. While specialized wolf-fencing may seem like an obvious alternative, it is not a panacea. Besides being costly to build, wolf-fencing has environmental drawbacks. Because it requires installing electrified wires much closer to the ground than traditional cattle fencing, wolf-fencing unintentionally blocks the passage of numerous other species (mostly small mammals) integral to ecosystem health. Thus, with no easy technical solution at hand and anxieties running high, 'rural diplomacy' may again be the best hope for encouraging local farmers to tolerate this 'new' wild neighbor.

Reflections

While Flusslandschaft Elbe Biosphere Reserve is an experiment in rewilding, it is experimental in a different sense than projects such as Oostvaardersplassen preserve in the Netherlands. Here in the Elbe Reserve there is no speculative hypothesis about European ecology being tested, nor anything as technologically aggressive as back-breeding proxies for extinct herbivores. In fact, the Elbe Reserve isn't even a nature reserve in the traditional sense, as only a small percentage of the total land area (the 3-5% inner core zone) is absolutely protected from human development.

The Elbe Reserve is experimental not in its science but in its philosophy. Choosing not the wilderness paradigm that protects nature by sequestering it from human influence, the Elbe Reserve stresses the fundamental inter-connectedness of nature and culture. It takes seriously the insight that nature is something humans live *within*, not something we manage from afar as if a garden or zoo. This is one reason so many of its projects concern the various ways humans have historically interacted with the land—especially agriculture. From working with local farmers to improve feeding practices to awarding prizes for the preservation of historical farm structures and their related crafts, Elbe is slowly mapping what it might look like for humans to live beyond the traditional nature/culture dichotomy. They are experimenting with new ideas and approaches whereby wildness might thrive not only in wilderness but also in the midst of human culture.

Elbe is also something of a political experiment. By rejecting practices such as eminent domain in favor of 'rural diplomacy,' the Reserve seeks to harness the power of democratic deliberation to help identify a sustainable environmental future. In this way, it reminds me of efforts such as the Valle de Oro Wildlife Refuge near Albuquerque, New Mexico, which has worked closely with local citizens to envision how environmental restoration can also serve the interests of local citizens, including the traditionally underserved.

While promoting democratic participation is good in itself, there may also be a distinctly environmental benefit of this approach. In his work on the ethics of restoration, philosopher Andrew Light argues convincingly that technical restoration alone will not address our environmental challenges. Restoration must also focus on revitalizing "the human culture of nature." Rather than thinking of nature as something we use up and then try to repair, long-term restoration requires learning to live less destructively in the first place. By engaging local citizens in the quest for solutions rather than imposing solutions from on high, the work at Elbe Reserve seems committed to the kind of cultural shift Light has in mind.

[This article originally appeared in Rewilding Earth *on December 31, 2019. To see additional beautiful photographs taken by David T. Schwartz, not included here, go to:*
rewilding.org/european-experiments-in-rewilding-elbe-river-biosphere-reserve/ —*Rewilding Earth editors]*

POETRY

Historic bison bones, photograph in the public domain

How to Bring the Bison Home

By Susie O'Keeffe

Take a million tears
in each salty jewel slip
the dust of a red man
his starved children, his raped wife
string the glimmering spheres
along frozen prairie grasses

Pray for 120 years

Gather the 300 bison ancestors

Build a pen   Cut the grass   Offer the grass

Give the survivors
a cold Montana corner (for now)

Carve white men
into their sacred mountains
(no rock climbers permitted)

Give one hill for worship
(rock climbers come anytime)

Offer their great, great grandchildren
crystal meth   suicide   diabetes

        Wait

Sing the bones
(60 million bison)
dance the slaughter
(700,000 wolves)
chant the loss
(12 million people)

Drum, drum, drum
on the cold gym floor
the fire water fight

Open the gates

Days of Fire

By Stuart Pimm

Fly from the USA to Rio de Janeiro and choose a day-time flight. Reject all demands to lower your window shades. You must not miss the view. One heads southeast, crosses Cuba, and makes landfall near Caracas, Venezuela. The next two and a half hours are a planetary spectacular, while the final three are apocalyptic.

The transect from Caracas to Manaus on the Amazon shows vast, unbroken tracts of forest. I've done this on crisp, clear days and, on magical ones, when the tepuis rise above low-lying mist. They inspired Arthur Conan Doyle's *The Lost World*. I don't think undiscovered dinosaurs live there, but undiscovered species? Bet on it.

At Manaus, the black waters of the Rio Negro, coming in from the north, meet the coffee-coloured ones from the Andes. From the plane, I see they refuse to mix for a long way downstream. Unbroken forest returns—but not for long. Soon, there will be huge columns of smoke rising to the height of the plane, their plumes trailing downwind for as far as we can see. All too soon, thick grey smoke will completely cover the ground below. It will continue for most of the rest of the journey.

No other journey tells me what wonderful places we still have of our planet—and how we might lose them in a generation.

July and August are the burning season, the driest time of year, and when fires are at their worst. And this year, under the administration of President Jair Bolsonaro, they have been worse than for a decade. So, what do we need to know? And what do we need to do?

Are There More Fires Under Bolsonoro?

Bolsonaro initially claimed that the increase in damage to the Amazon was "lies" and sacked the director of INPE, Brazil's National Space Agency who publicly criticised him.[1] This has an unfortunate resonance to US President Trump, who has a similar disregard for science that one can confirm quickly and independently. There are many places to check, but the easiest one is online at Global Forest Watch.[2] Click on the link at the top left of the page for "Forest Change" then switch on the "Fire Alerts."

The map I produced for the last week of August 2019 was a broadly similar pattern to what I saw from the plane years earlier, in that the fires are south of the Amazon.

It takes only a little more effort to compare fire maps from different years. They confirm that Bolsonaro's administration has encouraged a massive surge in destruction.

The thing about fires is that they literally glow in the dark—especially so in the infrared. So, as satellites spin around Earth, their infrared sensors pick up hot spots letting us know each night where fires are or have recently burned. In short, there's good science.

What a difference a decade makes! Ten years ago, I interviewed Carlos Minc, then Brazil's environment minister.[3] He was announcing data from INPE that showed that Brazil had reduced annual deforestation in the Amazon by close to 80% over previous levels. When I asked him about how Brazil had achieved that, his first answer surprised me: "good science." He also went on to say "Federal Police are now fighting crime—illegal timber cutting and illegal ranching—so that people will not get wealthy from crime. It's a matter of tracking cattle… making sure that they are not raised in

---

1   *The Guardian*, "Brazil Space Institute Director Sacked in Amazon Deforestation Row"
    https://www.theguardian.com/world/2019/aug/02/brazil-space-institute-director-sacked-in-amazon-deforestation-row
2   Global Forest Watch https://www.globalforestwatch.org/
    map?map=eyJjZW50ZXIiOnsibGF0IjoyNywibG5nIjoxMn0sImJlYXJpbmciOjAsInBpdGNoIjowLCJ6b29tIjoyfQ%3D%3D
3   *National Geographic*, "Brazil's Major Victory in Reducing Greenhouse Gas Emissions"
    https://blog.nationalgeographic.org/2009/11/24/brazils-major-victory-in-reducing-greenhouse-gas-emissions/

illegal areas, such as national parks…and working with supermarkets to make sure they are not selling illegal beef." In short, it isn't a matter of sending in firefighters, as Bolsonaro has suggested. It's a matter of law enforcement.

Money from Norway and more recently from others in the international community comes from the international consensus (the Trump Administration, excepted) that global climate disruption is bad business. Stopping burning tropical forests is the lowest hanging fruit: about 10% of global carbon emissions come from that source. And over a decade ago, Brazil was the third largest emitter (after the USA and China).

Many international companies are now suggesting boycotts. They may be small in terms of their total purchases and investments, but telling for Brazil's economy, which has been in recession.[4]

Where Are The Fires?

There are more fires in the south and east than in the north and west. That's because in the former the forests are drier—there's less rainfall—and more flammable. They are also nearer Brazil's population centres in São Paulo and Rio de Janeiro—the markets for agricultural produce.

The Global Forest Watch site allows a close inspection of where the fires burn. Most fires are in areas already partly deforested—landscapes where previous deforestation has left a mix of cattle pastures and forest fragments. Many fires are a consequence of past deforestation.[5] So should we worry?

Fire Aftermath © Stuart Pimm. This year—under the administration of President Jair Bolsonaro, who shares Trump's disregard for science and declared that reports citing an increase in damage to the Amazon were "lies"—fires have been worse than for a decade.

A fire is a fire is a fire. Wherever the fires are, this upswing in their numbers means that more carbon dioxide is going into the atmosphere. That disrupts the climate globally. At the time of writing this (Sept. 1, 2019),

---

4   The Guardian, "Corporations Pile Pressure on Brazil over Amazon Fires Crisis" https://www.theguardian.com/world/2019/aug/30/corporations-pile-pressure-on-brazil-over-amazon-fires-crisis

5   Mailchimp, "Seeing the Amazon Fires with Satellites" https://mailchi.mp/amazonconservation/maap-seeing-the-amazon-fires-with-satellites-3128007?e=a922307878

low-lying coastal counties in North Carolina are expecting yet another major hurricane, Dorian. They have barely recovered from Florence (2018) and Matthew (2016). Local politicians may share President Trump's denial of climate disruption, but insurance companies read the science and understand that warmer oceans mean more major hurricanes. Premiums rise and deny already low-income families the chance to cover their losses.

It's About Biodiversity

The Amazon is rightly famous for its exceptional species diversity. Maps—produced by my Brazil based colleague, Clinton Jenkins, available at biodiversitymapping.org, show the concentrations of bird, mammal, and amphibian species.[6] The fires convert so many species to ash.

It's Also About People

The Amazon is not uninhabited. Most of the green areas on the fire maps are indigenous reserves. And most of the fires are not within them. Of those that are, lightning causes some.[7] But many are set. The spread of fires and deforestation to the boundaries of and sometimes inside indigenous reserves reflects Bolsonaro's alarming views of indigenous peoples:

> "Pena que a cavalaria brasileira não tenha sido tão eficiente quanto a americana, que exterminou os índios."

> "It's a shame that the Brazilian cavalry hasn't been as efficient as the Americans, who exterminated the Indians." (Correio Braziliense newspaper, April 12, 1998).[8]

He reflects his party's base that views the Amazon as some immensely rich resource, waiting to be exploited for agriculture, minerals, and other resources. If only the international community would stop interfering!

My experiences in several parts of the Amazon suggest that the deforestation has caused nothing but misery—even for the colonists who have moved in from poor areas of Brazil to clear forests and the peoples that once lived in them. The deforestation is often a long way from the nearest main road, which itself is not surfaced and is impassable for the rainy season. Markets are a very long, expensive trip away.

My experiences in several parts of the Amazon suggest that the deforestation has caused nothing but misery—even for the colonists who have moved in from poor areas of Brazil to clear forests and the peoples that once lived in them.

Like Trump who boasts he "digs coal," the long-term economic prospects for cattle ranching in much of the Amazon aren't any better than for coal in Appalachia. (For the record: I grew up in sight of a coal mine. My friends worked in them and understand better than most the desperation of extractive industries than cannot be economically sustained.)

So What Can You Do?

First, this is indeed an international problem. It matters to us here in economic terms, albeit indirect ones. Encouraging international action—both from politicians and the private sector—is essential.

Second, it's an ethical, indeed religious issue. As Pope Francis says about the destruction of biodiversity in his Laudato Si—"we have no right".[9] The very real and implied threats to indigenous peoples, as well as to wildlife species, are truly appalling.

Third, we need to stop deforestation, but we must also go on the offensive and plant trees! Reforestation with native trees is what we do at Saving Nature savingnature.com—and in Brazil, too, though in coastal forests, not the Amazon.

[Excellent graphics to document this article may be seen online at rewilding.org/days-of-fire/. —Rewilding Earth editors]

---

6   https://www.biodiversitymapping.org
7   Adeney JM, Christensen Jr NL, Pimm SL. https://journals.plos.org/plosone/article?id=10.1371/journal.pone.0005014
8   Survival International, "What Brazil's President, Jair Bolsonaro, has said about Brazil's Indigenous Peoples" https://www.survivalinternational.org/articles/3540-Bolsonaro
9   Pope Francis' encyclical on the environment and human ecology https://laudatosi.com/watch

Alaska adventurers with Representative Jared Huffman (CA), sponsor of HR 1146 to protect the Arctic Refuge from oil development. © Brad Meiklejohn

Will You Join Us in Defending the Arctic Refuge?

By Brad Meiklejohn

This is what love of wild places looks like.

Luc Mehl, Roman Dial, and I recently traveled to Washington D.C. to tell Congress why we care so deeply about the Arctic National Wildlife Refuge. The 3 of us represent nearly 100 years of wilderness exploration, and collectively we have touched every wild corner of Alaska.

I've been visiting the Arctic Refuge since 1981 because it is one of the few big, wild, and intact places left on the planet. Each visit rewards me in surprising ways, whether it is the deep silence, witnessing thousands of caribou give birth outside my tent, the network of animal trails etched over thousands of years, or the timeless feel of original America.

That this place might be converted into an oil field is wrong for many reasons. Alaska sits on the front lines of climate change, yet we are hellbent on making the problem worse. Alaska is a drug addict who can't help herself. Alaska doesn't know what's best for the Arctic Refuge, she just wants another oil fix.

I'm pleased to report that we have many friends who are intervening to stop our mindless plunge. Congress will soon take up HR 1146, a bill to reverse the theft of the Arctic Refuge.

Luc, Roman, and I would rather spend our time exploring the wilds than defending them in D.C. But this is personal for each of us. The Arctic Refuge is one of the last wild remnants of our crowded planet.

Will you join us in defending the Arctic Refuge?

Tongass National Forest Alert

By Andrew Thoms, Sitka Conservation Society

Tongass National Forest occupies almost the entire Southeast Alaska Panhandle. It is one of the few temperate rainforests left on Earth that has not been lost because of human actions. The Tongass is the largest National Forest in the country. It is comprised of 17 million acres of rugged mountains, glaciers, ice-fields, wetlands and estuaries, lakes and rivers, and beautiful moss-laden forests with Sitka Spruce, Western Hemlock, and Red and Yellow Cedar trees.

The trees of the Tongass have long been the target of the timber industry. There is a long history of short-sighted timber extraction on the Tongass and a tragic, depressing, and shameful history of land management. The political dynamics of National Forest management and Alaska's Congressional delegation's obsession with short-sighted exploitation over long-term ecological protection and economic and social development have combined to make the Tongass one of the continent's most entrenched environmental conflicts.

Luckily, citizen activism—and the pure ruggedness of the landscape—have kept some of these great forests standing. The Clinton-era Roadless Area Conservation Rule laid out protections and ensured that any National Forest areas where no roads had already been built would remain without roads, without timber sales, or timber access roads. The Roadless Rule currently keeps over 9 million acres of the Tongass wild, protecting clean water sources and critical fish and other wildlife habitat.

Listen to Andrew's interview on Episode 32 of the Rewilding Earth Podcast!

That would change if the Trump Administration, Alaska's governor, and the Alaska Congressional delegation get their way. They are pushing for a full exemption from the Roadless Rule on the Tongass, and they seek to increase the levels of old-growth logging and to prop up a timber industry that needs tens of millions of dollars a year in subsidies to keep it afloat. This is happening despite Alaska Native tribes' opposition and scoping comments from thousands of Alaskans who urged the Forest Service not to touch the 2001 Roadless Rule.

The Tongass is a national issue. It is a National Forest and is owned by all Americans.

This conservation roll-back is being pushed despite the fact that after 60 years of logging the best of the old-growth timber, very little left is economic to harvest. Timber sales are being put up by the Forest Service that cost them $4 million for planning and road building, while being offered for minimum bids of $120,000. Some of these sales, such as the North Kuiu timber sale, receive no bids at all and constitute a total loss for the American taxpayer. Acres are clear-cut for just a handful of spruce trees that have the vertical tight grain that is wanted by piano and instrument makers or for a couple of Red Cedar logs that are of sufficient grade for suburban fencing and patio furniture.

The Tongass is a national issue. It is a National Forest and is owned by all Americans. Forest management decisions should not be made because of a Senator's father being old-buddies with the people who were big in the logging heydays, and who, as a result of this friendship, have unprecedented access to the Senator's ear. These old-school timber industry folks are able to use their connection to the Senator's family to exert political influence. They push the narrative that "if we can just get access to more acres on the Tongass, we can get back to the good-old days of widespread clearcutting and economic prosperity"—even though this supposed economic prosperity never extended past the pockets of a few well-connected mill owners and timber operators. Unfortunately, this corruption is the

Long the target of the timber industry and at risk again, majestic old-growth trees in the Tongass National Forest have been subject to short-sighted timber extraction and a tragic and shameful history of land management © Crossroads Photography for Sitka Conservation Society

current reality, and especially with Trump as president, this sort of thinking is encouraged.

Today, the Tongass National Forest is recognized as a wild salmon producer where most of the salmon on the West Coast spawn. It is a place that gets millions of visitors and is becoming more affordable to visit. Old-growth forests are among our continent's most important and stable carbon sinks. The Forest Service is increasingly recognizing these facts, but they need Congress to give them the mandate to manage the Forest for these values—rather than keeping up the failed paradigm of "getting out the cut."

How You Can Help the Tongass

1. Write a letter to the Secretary of Agriculture telling him that you support keeping the 2001 Roadless Rule in place on the Tongass. The Secretary has the final decision-making authority in this process. His address is:

   Sonny Perdue
   Secretary of Agriculture, USDA
   US Department of Agriculture
   1400 Independence Avenue, SW
   Washington, DC, 20250

2. Call your Representatives and Senators and tell them you support the 2019 Roadless Area Conservation Act Rule and want to see it codified into law and say it must include the Tongass. Tell them you don't want old growth clear-cut logging on the Tongass.

3. Follow our organization and other environmental groups that work on Tongass issues like the Sitka Conservation Society, Alaska Wilderness League, and Trout Unlimited by subscribing to our newsletters or finding us on social media.

4. Sign up for our action alert newsletter (at sitkawild.org) so that you can learn more about the Tongass and voice your concerns about keeping the Roadless Rule.

Citizen Scientist: Searching for Heroes and Hope in an Age of Extinction
By Mary Ellen Hannibal

Reviewed By John Miles

Mary Ellen Hannibal is a science writer, journalist, and gifted storyteller. Rewilders will recognize her as the author of *Spine of the Continent* (2012) in which she described the project of linking protected areas from the Yukon to Mexico that stems largely from the visionary work of Dave Foreman and Michael Soulé. In this book she succinctly defines citizen science as "the widening practice of noncredentialled people taking part in scientific endeavors." Long a participant in citizen science projects in California where she lives, concerned about such threats as global climate change and extinction, she wondered if the volunteer efforts of amateurs like her would really make any difference in addressing such monumental threats. Many conversations with scientists collaborating with "citizen scientists" convinced her that these dedicated amateurs, working with scientists, are cause for hope.

Hannibal here offers what she calls a "double narrative," an inquiry into science and history.

> *Extinction is a world from the realm of science, but it isn't about science. It's about history—what happened on the land and in the water, and why. History is based on storytelling, on narratives. The Spanish priests who established the missions here [in California] thought they were creating something—and they were—but they were also destroying something. They told themselves one story but they were living another one at the same time. Two things going on—so it is today. We get in our cars and we go to work, and we work to fulfill ourselves to support ourselves and our families, and on a certain level we think, I am creating. But we are destroying.*

She goes on to observe that we humans assume "that while our history changes in hundreds of years, the geographical environment changes only over millions of years." We think there is one short history and one long history, and they rarely intersect, but this separates history from nature. In fact, she contends as she looks out at the Santa Cruz Mountains, "Human history has made ecological history, and vice-versa – people, other species, geology, water, and weather have made this view, and they have done it together."

Hannibal concludes that, more than anything, we need new stories to confront such huge challenges as climate change and extinction, and she finds such stories in the work of citizen scientists. The story that she tells again and again is of innovative credentialed scientists working with teams of citizen volunteers to compile huge data sets that when analyzed with cutting-edge technique and technology, reveal what is happening in time and space. Their work helps us understand what can be done to address big problems. For instance, she notes that "One of the most effective and well-run citizen science projects in the US, Vital Signs, connects researchers who are grappling with the impacts of invasives on land and water with citizens (often students) who essentially do their field work for them." These citizens are also providing "an early warning system for natural resources managers" who can take action before the problems get out of hand.

Another example, in which Hannibal participated, was a three-year project under the direction of vegetation ecologists to measure grasses, wildflowers, and shrubs in part of the Marin Municipal Water District. The project was formed under the auspices of the Water District and the California Academy of Sciences which had a collection of plant specimens collected on the site over decades between 1890 and 1949 by Alice Eastwood, who was a botanist with no college degree and therefore herself a citizen scientist. The aim was to determine what changes in vegetation might have occurred on a part of Mt. Tamalpais important to the watershed. The results of the citizen team's work were impressive.

There's a big difference between drawing a circle around a piece of earth and counting up all the species you find in it, and doing that again at a later date, and, alternatively, counting up just the species you find in a certain life stage—budding, blooming, or dying ... Williams and Klein designed our surveys to capture these stages of growth, and they set up species lists for us to find. In the three years of the survey, we collected more than 1,137 plants comprising more than 550 species. Adding photographic observations where no plant was collected, those numbers are 2,075 observations and more than 650 species. Logging more than 2,600 hours, 185 volunteers helped uncover 93 species not previously known to live on Mt. Tam, including three grasses.

Beyond the impressive numbers here is the fact that such a project would have been impossible without volunteer help, and that is a central rationale for citizen science. Projects that involve monitoring over long periods and construction of large sets of data gathered in the field would be prohibitively expensive without citizen science contributions. Hannibal writes that "As the business school adage goes, if you can't measure it you can't manage it. And managing vegetation on land sustaining a municipal water supply is important indeed." Measuring the data to define and address problems in the Marin Municipal Water District required big data, and the citizen scientists impressively helped gather it.

This book is chock full of examples of how citizen scientists are contributing today to projects that are gathering data on migrations, responses to climate change, invasive species, the impact of wildfire on natural systems, and many other phenomena that require intensive long-term effort. Such projects always involve trained and credentialed scientists, but the legwork is largely done by volunteers. Hannibal delves into the history of citizen science, including such notables as Thomas Jefferson, Lewis and Clark, Rollo Beck of the California Academy of Sciences, Alice Eastwood, and Ed Ricketts. Aristotle, Leonardo, and Darwin "are trotted out as original 'citizen scientists,' and so they are, in the definition of one who explores the world of causality from the perspective of the amateur." Hannibal also describes institutions, like the California Academy of Sciences, that were instrumental in the history of citizen science. Citizen science as a movement, engaging many people, is a relative recent development but has deep roots.

Citizen Scientist is rich in detail about projects in which Hannibal is a participant, revealing how projects such as the Pacific Rocky Intertidal Monitoring Program and Hawkwatch are conducted and how citizens play a part. She provides deep historical background on these and many other projects that include citizen science. She profiles the key players in the stories, including both scientists and citizen volunteers. As she participated in projects, she lost her father, which led her to include a personal dimension as she realized how much her citizen science work added to her life. What seem to be tangents as she describes the emergence of citizen science at the California Academy of

Prospective citizen scientists study pine bark beetles in the North Cascades. © John Miles

Sciences or the contribution of Ed Ricketts always lead to insights about the nature of citizen science. The depth of her reporting results in a lengthy and rewarding read.

The recent efflorescence of citizen science is at least in part the result of the ever-increasing ability to analyze large data sets. Hannibal offers many examples of how this is so, profiling scientists who have launched projects, supported by advancing technology, to analyze large-scale changes in nature. Among them are the Breeding Bird Survey, the North American Bird Phenology Program, Frogwatch, eBird, and Hawkwatch. She profiles scientists contributing their technology savvy to projects. One is Rebeca Moore, a computer scientist and expert in bioinformatics who used her technical expertise to help block a logging proposal by the San Jose Water Company. Landing at Google, she led development of Google Earth Outreach and Goggle Earth Engine which are great tools for communities (citizens) to take action against damaging industry proposals like that of the Water Company.

Another "guru of citizen science" she profiles is Sam Droege. Among his many projects is Monitor Change. The website monitorchange.org explains that "The concept uses little more than a camera phone and a stout piece of bent steel to start." Droege's idea is to use photo-stitching software and repeat images of bracketed sites to record change over time. For example, Hannibal writes, "Droege has proposed placing brackets all along the Adirondack trails and challenging hikers to put their smartphone and camera in them while trekking past, take a photograph, and send it in to a central repository. With the georeferencing utility provided now by virtually every phone and camera, hikers would be providing a piece of scientific evidence of what was going on when and where." The platform for this is still in development in 2019, and the site states it will serve as "an open source community for collaborative development of change monitoring systems, tools, and applications. People can do this right now, using existing materials at single sites or they can organize networks of camera stations at scales of parks, cities, watersheds, counties, states, countries, or the world." It continues, "This is a presentation of an idea. Anyone can modify this in any way they like and implement it at any scale. No copyrights, no permission needed. Just Do It."

This book is full of exciting examples of scientists like Moore and Droege developing tools and approaches that citizens, with a modicum of training, can participate in. The compelling new story presented in *Citizen Scientist* is that every concerned citizen can participate in the projects of sustaining and restoring the natural world upon which all depend, not just an elite group of scientists. My first encounter with the *idea* of citizen science came when I was introduced to the *idea* of adaptive management. A policy would be developed and implemented to manage forests or wildlife, the results of the policy would be monitored, and the policy would be adapted to improve the likelihood of achieving the management goal. In the 1990s when this approach was being applied, the problem was that there was usually not sufficient money or people to do the monitoring, which was quite labor intensive. One solution to the monitoring challenge might be, some said, to recruit and train volunteers to do this work under the guidance of scientists and managers. The accounts of the many citizen science projects Hannibal describes in this book add up to the new story that citizens can, and must, help understand how the world is changing and what it means for all living things.

Hannibal's approach to telling the story in *Citizen Scientist* is deeply influenced by the work of writer and mythologist Joseph Campbell who found a pattern in the world's indigenous stories that he called the hero's journey. Campbell came to see Myth as "nature talking" and believed that the hero's journey is universal, and in Hannibal's words, "unites humankind across races, cultures, geography, and time." The hero's journey, for Campbell, was "the pathway to personal identity." Hannibal observes that Aldo Leopold, in his classic definition of a land ethic, connected what must be a new pathway to citizenship when he called for changing "the role of *Homo sapiens* from conqueror of the land community to plain member and citizen of it." Such would be a new and essential Myth, in Campbell's sense of it, and Hannibal sees citizen science as an important contribution to it.

Much more might be said of this remarkable book which should be read by all of us engaged in conservation and rewilding, efforts that at times seem overwhelming in their immensity. Hannibal searches for heroes and hope and finds them. The heroes are not only the trained scientists working to understand and sustain nature, but all the citizen scientists who are dedicated to these vast goals. Hannibal sums up the story and the significance of citizen science in her preface:

> *Some people like to call citizen science "participatory research." This comes out of a decades-long unfolding of thought in the humanities in which researchers began to grapple with the very unpleasant insight that they were treating their subjects as inferior objects, that it is impossible to take a "me expert, you study subject" view that is not condescending, incomplete, and more or less self-serving. With some horror, researchers looked in the mirror and saw themselves reiterating colonial control of indigenous and economically underserved people. A full-on identity crisis ensued. How are we gathering information and creating knowledge, and what are we using it for? Basically, the cure for the dominator approach is to insert the word I into the narrative. We can't remove bias completely, but we can state our position as honestly as possible, declare our self-interest, our subjectivity. If the researcher is also a subject, and the subject is also a driver of the research project, then maybe we can get some equity here, and "co-create" knowledge. So here is I.*

Insights like this make *Citizen Scientist* a book everyone who would rewild at any scale must read.

[*Citizen Scientist was published on September 6, 2016, by The Experiment.* —Rewilding Earth *editors*]

POETRY

White Birds of Winter

By Saul Weisberg

On the delta of the Skagit River
There are flocks of snow geese 10,000 strong:

    wing-strong
        wind-strong,

rising, then settling
on silent fields.

The sun melts into the ocean,
Waves cast shadows on the beach,
Everything stands still.

Six swans,
The ones that flew over our tent last night,
Settle in the lagoon behind the dunes.

[Originally appeared in Headwaters: Poems & Field Notes, Pleasure Boat Studio, 2015. —Rewilding Earth editors]

Snow Geese pictured here in the Skagit River Watershed summer in Alaska and on Russia's Wrangell Island. © John Miles

A Tale of Three Weasels

By Paula Mackay

Marten © David Moskowitz, Cascades Wolverine Project. Martens once roamed the Olympic Peninsula. Today, researchers are trying to determine whether a viable population still exists there.

Wildlife sightings in the North Cascades are a gift from nature. You can roam the backcountry for a week and return home with little to report beyond gray jays and ground squirrels, or maybe a mule deer and her fawn grazing a mountain meadow. There are countless other rewards, of course—the craggy summits, the solitude, the tranquility of the trail—but when it comes to actually *seeing* a storied carnivore, you're better off visiting Yellowstone.

So I was as surprised as anyone when the stars aligned one July afternoon in 2014 while I was taking a lunch break with my two companions—my husband and field partner, Robert, and a friend—next to a sublime alpine lake near North Cascades National Park. We had been out there alone for days deploying wildlife cameras; there was still too much snow in the shadows for most summer-loving campers.

As I contemplated the snowfield across the lake, I uttered something aloud that I'd thought to myself a hundred times before: "I always hope I'm going to see a wolverine in a setting like this." Just then, and I mean *just* then, I turned around to face a steep avalanche chute behind me. And there it was, not 200 yards away: a large animal loping low to the ground, its formidable form a masterpiece of wildness on a pure white canvas. The wolverine was gone within seconds, disappearing into the chute-side rocks and vegetation before our friend could zero in on its location. Fortunately, Robert saw it, too, or he would have thought I was dreaming. In the not-too-distant past, he probably would have been right.

Wolverines and their smaller cousins, Pacific fishers and Pacific martens, were decimated by Northwest trappers in the late 1800s and early 1900s—the latter two killed for their fur, the former mostly persecuted as trap-raiders. With habitat loss and widespread poisons for predator control dealing additional blows to already severely diminished populations, wolverines and fishers were eliminated from the Washington Cascades, and fishers were also extinguished from the Olympic Peninsula (where wolverines never occurred). Martens suffered a more complicated fate, having been left intact in the Cascades but perhaps on the brink of extinction in the Olympics.

Regional scientists are now using innovative technologies, diverse partnerships, and hiking boots on the ground to study these little-known mustelids (members of the weasel family) and try to assist them in their recovery. "Each suffered similar fates historically, but each has a very different status currently, resulting from divergent conservation stories," says Keith Aubry, emeritus scientist at the US Forest Service's (USFS) Pacific Northwest Research Station and global expert in mustelids.

Aubry is passionate about connecting the dots between the past and the present for rare mustelid populations so that we can better understand their needs moving forward. "You can't know where you want to get to if you don't know where you've been with these species."

WOLVERINES WERE GENERALLY ABSENT from Washington for much of the twentieth century. There was a small rash of confirmed accounts in the 1960s—possibly wolverines who went on walkabout from Canada when their prey cycled high—but the species didn't take root again until the mid-1990s. Then, Aubry and colleagues began to see a significant rise in verifiable records from the North Cascades, and in 1997, a female wolverine was struck and killed by a vehicle. The road-killed juvenile was wandering well west of the Cascade crest and outside of predicted wolverine habitat. Wolverines were definitely on the move, but where were they coming from, and were they finally here to stay?

Intrigued by the wolverine's resurgence, Aubry and fellow USFS wildlife biologist Cathy Raley launched a collaborative wolverine telemetry study in 2005. "At that time, we didn't know if there was a resident population—didn't even know if there were more than occasional sightings," Raley says. Over the next decade, Aubry and Raley worked closely with other agency biologists to trap and collar 14 wolverines in the North Cascades, allowing them to track these animals' cross-country travels via satellite technology.

One snapshot of data collected from a collared male named Special K shows he walked 11 straight-line miles through rugged Cascades terrain in a six-hour period; over a stretch of nine months, his wanderings covered a remarkable 1,000 square miles. I got to meet this tenacious solo climber once, while visiting a live-capture site in 2015. I'll never forget his lion-like roar as he exited the log trap, or the massive, claw-clad paws that enable him to float across the frozen landscape and dig into its depths for a refrigerated meal.

Satellite data indicates that it might also have been Special K we'd seen at the lake in 2014 when we were out testing methods to monitor Washington's wolverine population. Some researchers study wolverines by hanging a tantalizing piece of bait above a small wooden platform positioned opposite a motion-triggered camera. When the animal climbs onto the platform and looks up at the bait, it exposes its uniquely identifiable chest pattern to the camera. The problem is, two-legged access to Cascadian wolverine habitat in winter can be difficult, dangerous, or downright impossible at the scale necessary to replenish baits scattered throughout the wilderness. And during summer, wolverines apparently have better places to be than at survey stations— or better things to eat than a rotting beef bone. We needed a way to attract wolverines to our camera sites during the winter without having to get to them ourselves.

Imagine an IV-type bag that drips stinky liquid instead of medication. Now imagine this bag, a miniature pump, and its electronic controller stored in a bear-proof metal box secured to a tree 15 feet from the ground—high enough to remain above snow line even when it snows *a lot*.

In his role as a senior scientist with Seattle's Woodland Park Zoo, Robert partnered with engineers at Microsoft and a state biologist from Idaho to create an automated scent dispenser for wolverines. The dispenser is programmed to release a tiny amount of lure (think: *eau de skunk* blended with anise) daily, eliminating the requirement to rebait camera sites in winter. This new technology has already been a game-changer for detecting wolverines in the North Cascades, increasing our detection rate more than tenfold during our pilot study in the winter of 2016-17. The dispenser was also used effectively in a multi-state wolverine survey conducted across Montana, Idaho, Wyoming, and Washington.

As Robert and his co-developers continue to tweak the scent dispenser's design and Woodland Park Zoo strategizes

A TALE OF THREE WEASELS

Winter Sentinels © Evan Cantor

to make this tool more widely available to researchers, wolverines are further expanding their range in Washington. Given genetic data and other available information, Aubry thinks these newcomers likely dispersed from the Coast Mountains of British Columbia. At least a few wolverines have even ventured south of Interstate 90 (I-90), the major east-west highway that bisects the Cascades near the center of the state. In early 2018, cameras deployed by biologist Jocelyn Akins photographed two kits near Mount Rainier National Park at the third reproductive den to be documented statewide (the first two were found in the North Cascades in 2012). Sadly, only a few months later, a 37-pound male wolverine met his demise trying to cross the same interstate, serving as a tragic reminder that people are still a threat to wolverines, even if over-trapping is a thing of the past.

Indeed, wolverines face a new suite of hazards from human activities, some of them presented by people who love wilderness. A recent study in the Rocky Mountains found that wolverines avoided areas of motorized activity (e.g. snowmobiles) *and* non-motorized winter recreation, such as skiing. Lead researcher Kim Heinemeyer and her co-authors speculate that "the potential for backcountry winter recreation to affect wolverines may increase under climate change if reduced snow pack concentrates winter recreationists and wolverines in the remaining areas of persistent snow cover." I've heard Raley express similar concerns for the North Cascades, where a growing number of people want to live and play in the remote places wolverines need to survive.

Researchers have also predicted that climate change will reduce the spring snowpack that wolverine females in the Cascades and elsewhere rely upon for their reproductive dens. In 2010, this prediction and its dire implications compelled the US Fish and Wildlife Service to propose listing wolverines in the lower 48 states as threatened under the Endangered Species Act. The decision is still being batted about in the courts.

In the short-term, wolverines represent a best-case scenario for carnivore restoration, as they were able to return to Washington on their own and they're finding what they need to thrive there. Fingers crossed, conservation efforts to promote habitat connectivity in the Cascades, including wildlife crossing structures on I-90, will enhance the wolverine's chances of long-term recovery. Pacific fishers, on the other hand, needed a little more help.

"THIS NEVER GETS OLD." It's a damp December morning in 2018, and Jeff Lewis, a wildlife biologist with Washington Department of Fish and Wildlife (WDFW), is clearly elated as he welcomes the more than 100 people who have traveled to North Cascades National Park to witness the first-ever release of fishers into the surrounding forest. Lewis has worked on behalf of fishers for much of his career, having spent years studying them in California and Oregon prior to co-authoring Washington's status report for this species in 1998. Today's release marks the launch of the third and final phase of the fisher recovery effort he's helped bring to fruition, with reintroductions having already been carried out in the Olympics and the southern Washington Cascades. Lewis sums up the project's mission with heartfelt humility: "All you've got to do is bring them back, because the habitat is there."

The solution sounds simple enough, but the task of ecological redemption is a long and windy road. WDFW's recovery plan for fishers, also co-authored by Lewis, was published in 2006, eight years after the state listed the species as endangered. Like wolverines, fishers were thought to be gone from Washington. Unlike wolverines, however, the semi-arboreal fisher lives only in forests, and there wasn't a source population close enough to naturally recolonize forested habitats in the Cascades or the Olympics. The fisher's distribution in other Pacific states had been reduced to small, disjunct populations, and its range in southern British Columbia was contracted as well. The recovery plan's conclusion? "A self-sustaining fisher population is not likely to become re-established in the state without human intervention."

To advance fisher recovery, Lewis and others created a core team of project partners consisting of WDFW, the National Park Service, and Conservation Northwest (CNW), a regional conservation group that had initiated and helped fund the feasibility assessment for a reintroduction. Dave Werntz, CNW's Science and Conservation Director, felt the timing was right for the fisher's return. "We had worked really hard for years to protect old-growth forest habitat, and we prevailed in that," he says. "As we were looking toward now rewilding these habitats—bringing back species that were once here but had been extirpated for various reasons—we wanted to start with fishers, to get familiar with the process we needed to go through."

Ironically, as part of this process, the fisher's historical foe would become one of its saviors. With operational support provided by CNW, the project recruited Canadian trappers to help them source live fishers for translocation to Washington. Between 2008 and 2010, 90 fishers were moved from central British Columbia to Olympic National Park. The translocated animals hit the ground running, with at least three females giving birth in 2009. Fishers in search of new territory turned up in a variety of terrains, from mountainous forest to coastal plains. One motivated male, released in 2008, meandered all the way to the northwest tip of the Olympic Peninsula, traversing some 55 miles across a mix of federal, state, and private lands before arriving on the Makah Reservation at Washington's Neah Bay.

Ironically, as part of this process, the fisher's historical foe would become one of its saviors.

The Makah Tribe agreed to help track the collared male with radio telemetry and later became engaged in more extensive fisher monitoring on tribal lands and neighboring forests. "We've always been supportive of fishers and the whole reintroduction," says Shannon Murphie, Wildlife Division Manager for the tribe. "We were just curious to know what was really out there." Partnering with Olympic National Park and the US Geological Survey, the Makah Tribe created the Makah Fisher Density Estimate Project in 2017. Tribal staff and volunteers set out 86 stations consisting of cameras and hair-snagging cubbies (for DNA), detecting seven individuals over a two-year period.

"The tribes were integral partners," says Patti Happe, Wildlife Branch Chief at Olympic National Park. Based on data collected by federal, tribal, and state field biologists, she's cautiously optimistic about the population's future, although she's careful to say that fishers are not yet fully recovered. Happe is concerned about the fishers' genetic diversity and wants to be sure that not just a few females are doing all the breeding—in which case, biologists would potentially need to bring in more animals to avoid inbreeding depression (a reduction in survival and fertility rates resulting from mating between close relatives). "We just need to get over this genetic hurdle, if there is one. Or, just give them time," she says.

Meanwhile, the success of the fisher reintroduction on the Olympic Peninsula precipitated similar efforts in the Cascades. With a broad host of partners from the US and Canada, the core team released 73 fishers between 2015 and 2018 into central Washington's Mount Rainier National Park and the Gifford Pinchot National Forest. Then, in late 2018, the project progressed to the North Cascades, where Lewis and his collaborators ushered their audience from the national park's auditorium to the nearby release site. There, the team freed six fishers one by one from wooden crates, allowing them to re-enter a wild scene they'd been written out of almost a century before. Those animals have now been joined by 20 more. Ultimately, the researchers plan to reintroduce a total of 80 fishers into this portion of the recovery area.

Lewis says it's too soon to say how the fishers will fare in the Cascades, although preliminary results are positive.

"We'll know a lot more once we complete our long-term monitoring effort in three to five years." By then, he hopes the hand-picked pioneers and their offspring will have begun to fill a niche that has been vacant for far too long.

NORMALLY, BETSY HOWELL WOULD BE THRILLED to see a Pacific fisher captured on one of her motion-triggered cameras. A veteran USFS wildlife biologist in the Olympic National Forest, Howell knows these animals are very rare, and she is well-versed in the important role they have to play in forested ecosystems—by preying on small mammals, for example, and distributing berry seeds after consuming the fruit. But Howell's disappointment is palpable as we scroll through our photos after a six-hour hike into the Mount Skokomish Wilderness. Coyote. Gray jay. Black-tailed deer. The camera's memory card reveals the usual suspects. Then, "fisher!" I exclaim, as a brown, elongated animal—almost half bushy tail—pops up on our viewing screen. "Always good to see a healthy fisher," Howell replies, her good-natured tone reflecting a glass half-full. Yes, fishers are an exciting find, but our quarry is the Pacific marten, much rarer on the Olympic Peninsula than the reintroduced fisher. If wolverines look a bit like bear cubs and fishers can be compared to a hefty housecat, martens might be thought of as the fisher's cute, feisty kitten. Weighing in at only 1 to 3 pounds, these compact carnivores are nonetheless capable of taking care of themselves in the forest. In his classic 1949 monograph, *Mammals of the Olympic National Park and Vicinity*, Victor B. Scheffer tells of a regional trapper who found feathers, rabbits, mice, squirrels, and spotted skunks in the stomachs of martens.

Historically, Scheffer writes, martens occurred throughout the coniferous forests of the Olympic Peninsula, "from salt water to timberline." Recent genetic research conducted by Keith Aubry and colleagues suggests that martens in the Olympics originated from the Cascades thousands of years ago and then became isolated by geographical barriers. Although martens in the Cascades occupied mostly the high country, where they presumably enjoyed some protection from trappers, their ancestors in the Olympics inhabited a broader range of elevations. Those living down low disappeared with the fishers; Aubry thinks they were probably gone by the end of the Great Depression. "Once populations were impacted by over-trapping and habitat loss, it makes sense that they would retreat to their primary habitat in high-elevation forests where deep snowpacks form," says Aubry.

Fast forward almost a century, and those high-elevation retreats may be all the martens have left. Since the late 1960s, there have been only 11 reliable marten detections on the Olympic Peninsula—all but the first two were above 2,000 feet—including a juvenile female found dead in 2008 on Mount Rose, in the southeastern corner of the peninsula. Aubry points out that this discovery was particularly important because it showed that martens were reproducing in the area a decade ago. Genetic analyses confirmed that the Mount Rose female was a remnant of the original population.

In 2017, Robert and I began a collaboration with Howell, Happe, and other agency biologists to help determine if a viable marten population still exists in the Olympics. As part of this research, we paired motion-triggered cameras with the scent dispenser initially designed for wolverines in hopes that we could detect rare and reclusive martens over the winter. Thus far, the project has photographed two martens in the upper Hoh River drainage, deep within Olympic National Park. This is the only place on the entire peninsula where previous camera surveys yielded detections as well, one in 2015, another in 2016.

Each photographic image is a glimmer of hope, but many questions remain about the status of martens in the Olympics. "I'm really concerned about how many are left and if there is enough genetic diversity for a healthy population," says Happe, who acknowledges that a targeted augmentation (adding new individuals to a sparse population) may eventually be required to maintain martens on the peninsula. But for now, we will keep on trying to gather more information. As Aubry put it, we can't know where we want to get to if we don't know where we've been.

Nor can we achieve our conservation goals without opening our hearts and minds to the animals themselves. Martens, fishers, wolverines—in their own unique ways, these animals are telling us that to rewild broken landscapes with our scientific prowess, we must also internalize the life lessons we learn along the way. About teamwork. About resilience. About paying careful attention to the past.s article:

[This article was originally published in Earth Island Journal, *Summer 2019.* —Rewilding Earth *editors]*

Riverscape © Susan Morgan

The River I

By Tim McNulty

Along the south bank of the McKinley,
close to dark:
the fresh tracks of what look to be
       A young caribou,
     And following, over them,
          The larger track of the wolf.

Clouds deepen the mountain night;
a hawk owl circles the stones.

I build a cairn to mark our crossing.
It stands
like a man who has waited too long for something.

By morning
only the river is left singing.

The River II

By Tim McNulty

Who live here speak footfall and wind.
Caribou, belly-deep in willow,
lifts his antlers and drifts away.
Ptarmigan flutter tails in fright.

Grizzly has led her children up a ravine:
she rests now, almost sleeping.
The tips of her fur shine with icelight.

Downriver, Raven draws circles
around a story his uncle left unfinished.
Already the small hoofed feet are dancing
far over the tundra.

[Poems originally appeared in In Blue Mountain Dusk, *Pleasure Boat Studio, 1992.* —Rewilding Earth *editors]*

Rio Mora Seasons

By Brian Miller

Introduction

Phenology is the study of patterns in nature that repeat themselves periodically through seasons. For example, when does a particular species of flower bloom, or when does a given species of migratory bird arrive in the spring to build nests and lay eggs? By noting the timing of concurrent events, an observer of nature can know that by seeing one event, he or she should be able to predict and search for another event happening at the same time. My upcoming book, *Spirit of Nature in Northern New Mexico*, is a phenology and natural history for Rio Mora National Wildlife Refuge and the surrounding region. I've written this book for the interested lay person who wants to get some mud on his or her shoes while working to restore land health.

Although the base area for this book is the Rio Mora National Wildlife Refuge, it also reflects the sequence of events elsewhere on the high plains of northeastern New Mexico. Altitude and latitude affect phenology. For every 100-meter increase in altitude, the temperature decreases by one degree Celsius. Latitude is the distance of a given location from the Equator. When a location is farther from the Equator, it receives less solar energy. Because the Earth is round, the angle of sunlight hitting the Earth changes as you move away from the Equator. At the Equator, solar energy strikes the Earth at a nearly perpendicular angle, and the shorter distance sunlight travels through

Picuris Bison Bull © Anabella Miller. Rio Mora's partnership with the Pueblo of Pojoaque tribe is strong and unique in the National Wildlife Refuge system. The herd provides ecological restoration on the land and cultural restoration for the tribe.

the atmosphere means that heat is concentrated. As you get nearer to the poles, the angle grows acute, and solar energy must travel a longer distance through the atmosphere to arrive. Thus, heat is lost as it travels through the atmosphere. The direction of a slope can also create microclimates. A south-facing slope will receive more solar energy than a north-facing slope.

The Rio Mora National Wildlife Refuge is located on the high plains near the foothills of the Southern Rockies. The Refuge is located between 6,700 feet and 7,000 feet. It is the center of a U.S. Fish and Wildlife Service Conservation area covering 952,000 acres of the Mora River watershed. The Mora River starts on Osha Mountain in the Sangre de Cristos range. It begins at 10,000 feet of altitude, then flows eastward to enter the Canadian River at approximately 4,500 feet of altitude. Your location along the Mora River will affect phenology sequences, but the heart of this book is the Rio Mora National Wildlife Refuge, which is midway between the start and finish of the Mora River.

Landscape Around Rio Mora NWR

Rio Mora National Wildlife Refuge's main habitat types are shortgrass prairie, riparian, ephemeral natural catchments, and perennial seeps/springs/marsh wetlands, piñon/juniper/oak woodlands (*Pinus edulis-Juniperus* spp.-*Quercus* spp.), and ponderosa pine (*Pinus ponderosa*) forests. The Refuge includes the Mora River, which is a sub-basin in the Canadian Watershed. The main tributaries feeding the Mora River are the Sapello River and Coyote Creek. The Mora River starts in the Rincon Mountains north of Chacon (at about 10,000 ft.) and enters the Canadian River near the tri-county border of Mora, Harding, and San Miguel Counties. The river covers a distance of 116 miles.

Audubon has designated the Refuge (when it was the Wind River Ranch) as an Important Bird Area. Important Bird Areas are sites that provide essential breeding, migrating, or wintering habitat for birds and/or they support one or more high-priority species, large concentrations of birds, exceptional habitat, and/or have substantial research value. Designation as an Important Bird Area confers no regulatory authority.

Habitats within the Mora River watershed provide important life cycle needs for a wide variety of neo-tropical migratory birds and many other riparian, grassland, woodland, aquatic, and wetland dependent species. The Migratory Bird Program in the USFWS Southwest Region has identified at least 18 species from the Birds of Conservation Concern list (U.S. Fish and Wildlife Service 2008) that utilize the area during migration or for winter stopover habitat.

The Refuge lies on the high plains east of the Sangre de Cristos Mountains. This is the southern end of the Rocky Mountain chain, a discontinuous series of ranges.

The elevation transition between the Great Plains and the Sangre de Cristo Mountains, the juxtaposition of two ecoregions, and the riparian habitats in this arid part of the West all enrich the species diversity of the area.

The entire Rocky Mountain chain extends from central New Mexico to northern Canada.

The elevation transition between the Great Plains and the Sangre de Cristo Mountains, the juxtaposition of two ecoregions, and the riparian habitats in this arid part of the West all enrich the species diversity of the area. The location of the Rio Mora National Wildlife Refuge in the heart of this transition provides remarkable species diversity. We have documented close to 200 bird species, close to 30 amphibian and reptile species, and close to 50 mammal species on the Refuge.

About 140 million years ago, during the Cretaceous, eastern New Mexico was flooded by a shallow sea. This sea left thick deposits of shales and sandstones. About 80 million years ago, the Laramide Orogeny began fault-lifting Pre-Cambrian rocks upward to start the New Mexican part of the Rocky Mountain chain; the upward faulting continued into the Cenozoic Era. Along the east edge of the faulting, sedimentary layers bent upward to form the present-day hogbacks.

Erosion from the mountains was heaviest during the Pleistocene Epoch of the Cenozoic Era because of continued uplift combined with Ice-Age precipitation. Dakota sandstone and Pierre shale still lie on the basin east of the mountains today. The dark, gray Pierre shale was deposited as mud on the floor of the shallow sea. The Dakota sandstone, however, is a beach and shore deposit, and like beach sand it is porous and permeable. Thus, the soil-covered sandstone serves as an aquifer throughout the east side of the Sangre de Cristos Mountains. Various layers of soil cover this sedimentary base, with topsoil averaging about four inches thick. Dominant soils are loam and clay.

Until about 25 million years ago, there were palms as far north as Montana. During the Miocene, from 25 million years ago until 12 million years ago, a drier climate forced the neotropical vegetation south and nearctic vegetation north, and the grasslands emerged in between. During the Pleistocene, there were 17 ice ages. Vegetation moved south ahead of ice, then moved north as the ice later melted—at least as a generalization of the time.

At the end of the last Ice Age, the Clovis Culture arrived in New Mexico. The Clovis points were exquisitely beautiful as art and extremely deadly as weapons. Following human entry into North America, 70% of large animal species (averaging above 100 pounds full-grown) disappeared. A distant exception was the mammoth, which continued life on Wrangel Island, of what is now southeastern Alaska, until 4,000 years ago. That is when humans arrived on the island, and mammoths then went extinct. Bison and the other animals we associate with the grasslands came about after the loss of the megafauna approximately 12,000 years ago. The specialized Clovis and Folsom cultures were then replaced by a more generalized approach to life in the Southwest. About 7,000 years ago, the Altithermal period produced a 2,000-year drought that depopulated the lowland areas.

Ancient Pueblos lived in complex, multi-storied buildings constructed of stone, adobe, and wood. The culture has existed for more than 5,000 years. People often talk about places like Santa Fe and Jamestown being old settlements, but the Pueblo communities are far older. Both the Acoma Pueblo and Taos Pueblo have been consistently occupied for nearly 1,000 years.

About 1,200 years ago, Navajos and Apache arrived in the Southwest from the north. The Rio Mora NWR was once part of Jicarilla Apache lands and Pueblo lands. The Mora River offered a travel route for Pueblos coming down to the plains and plains tribes going up to the Pueblo villages to trade or raid. In addition to northern Pueblos and Apache, other tribes like the Comanche, the Navajo, the Ute, and Kiowa also passed through the Rio Mora area, particularly after the arrival of the horse.

When the Spanish arrived, they subjugated tribes, but the Spanish were thrown out of Santa Fe by the Pueblo Rebellion of 1680. Popé, who was from the Ohkay Owingeh, united the Pueblo tribes, and they attacked the Spanish with 2,500 warriors. The Spanish returned in 1692 to retake Santa Fe. The meadows where Las Vegas, NM, is today had been given to Luis C. de Baca as a Spanish Land grant in 1821, shortly before Mexico became independent of Spain (*vegas* means *meadows* in Spanish). The C. de Baca Land grant was used for grazing but was later abandoned. The Las Vegas Land Grant from Mexico founded the town of Las Vegas in 1835. The area now in Rio Mora NWR was part of the Mora Land Grant from Mexico in 1835. By this time the Santa Fe Trail was bringing U.S. settlers into the area. In 1848, the Mexican-American war ended and the United States took control of New Mexico. Tribal Wars continued with the U.S. government. The Apache Wars, Navajo Wars, and Comanche Wars were the most famous.

In the 1700s and 1800s, the grasslands of New Mexico were still very rich in quantity and quality. Journals from cavalry officers, freighters, and stockmen noted abundant grama grasses from north to south on the Great Plains of New Mexico. Soldiers and stockmen cut grama grasses for hay and claimed it was superior to the best clover or timothy (*Phleum pratense*) hay. Reports from the Diné lands on the west side of the Rocky Mountains noted knee-high grasses.

Today the grasslands are very deteriorated and would be unrecognizable to someone from several hundred years ago. Following 1870, the bison (*Bison bison*) were replaced with cattle. Bison had once numbered around 30,000,000 and ranged across much of North America, but by the end of the 19th Century, only about 1,000 remained. The slaughter of bison was a deliberate strategy to subjugate warring tribes as well as meet market demands driven by the sale of hides in the eastern U.S.

In 1870, there were 137,000 cattle in New Mexico. The 1870s had been wet and grass was prolific. By 1880, there were 1,380,000 cattle in New Mexico, but the wet 1870s turned into a decade of severe drought during the 80s. Thus,

Rio Mora © Evan Cantor

came the greatest livestock die-off in western history. Before dying, however, livestock denuded the grasses. This caused arroyo erosion (which we still see today) and started juniper (*Juniperus* spp.) invasion of the grassland. Loss of vegetation allowed exotic plants to invade. Roads, fences, market hunting, and exotic species hastened the decline of wildlife. By 1900, wild ungulates were so reduced in numbers that they bordered on extinction. Game laws helped recover ungulates, except for bison, but persecution of carnivores continues today and that has removed the role of predators in top-down ecological processes.

These are some of the legacy effects we still feel today, and they are a focus of restoration at Rio Mora National Wildlife Refuge. We are fortunate that in this part of northern New Mexico many landowners, agencies, and NGOs are committed to changing those legacy wounds.

[This essay is condensed from a chapter of Brian Miller's upcoming book, Spirit of Nature in Northern New Mexico, *on a landscape he has been carefully rewilding back to health for many decades.* Rewilding Earth *had previously run another pre-publication excerpt from Brian's upcoming Rio Mora phenology, on the wildlands philanthropy story behind the conservation science center at Rio Mora National Wildlife Refuge. Brian's book will be available in our Rewilding Bookstore soon. –* Rewilding Earth *editors]*

Embers from the Campfire

By Uncle Dave Foreman, TRI Founder

When Republicans Loved Endangered Species

Dave with Major John Bowen (ret.) at a New Mexico Wilderness Study Committee retreat in the 1970s. © Dave Forman

Once upon a time, conservation was bipartisan, with leadership from both Republicans and Democrats at various stages, from the administration of Teddy Roosevelt to that of Richard Nixon and a bit beyond. In the early days of the New Mexico Wilderness Study Committee in the 1970s, many of its leaders, even yours truly, were Republicans. We worked closely with New Mexico's Republican members of Congress—Sen. Pete Domenici and Rep. Manuel Lujan, Jr.—on new Wilderness Areas, including a pocketful of areas stoutly opposed by the Forest Service, such as the Sandia Mountains and Chama Canyon Wilderness Areas. When I strode the marble hallways of the Congressional office buildings on my trips to Washington, D.C. for The Wilderness Society and NMWSC, I always had appointments with the Republican staff of the House Interior Committee to palaver over strategy.

In 1973, one of the great conservation bills was passed with the strong support of Republican members of Congress. The Eastern Wilderness Areas Act was fought by the Forest Service as though it would usher in Armageddon. And yet, its lead sponsor in the Senate was Republican James Buckley (brother of William F. Buckley) and in the House by Republican John Saylor, who had been the lead House sponsor of the 1964 Wilderness Act.

But what of the great bugbear of today's congressional Republicans (better called Trumpicans)—the 1973 Endangered Species Act?

Today the Endangered Species Act is under threat as never before by Republicans and the Trump administration. But on July 24, 1973, the Senate unanimously approved the Act, followed on September 18 by a House vote of 390-12. It was gladly signed by President Gerald Ford, also a Republican.

In debate on the bill, Senator Ted Stevens (R-AK), speaking in favor, quoted former Senator Spong who had said that "Extinction is quite literally a fate worse than death." Stevens added, "I agree." Senator Marlow Cook (R-KY) recommended the legislation include "a provision which would prohibit the destruction or modification of the critical habitat of such [endangered] species." Senator Bill Roth (R-DE) said in support that the Act was a "long overdue piece of legislation," and Senator Pete Domenici (R-NM) added, "It is a fact that man has been the culprit in bringing certain species to the point of extinction: it would be a double indictment against humanity to ignore the present situation and allow the destruction of our resource of wildlife to continue." Senator Charles Percy (R-IL) called for the Senate to act promptly and "hopefully unanimously" on the bill, and it was so.

As Mary Hopkin sang around that time, "Those were the days, my friend…." Yep, and we believed they would never end. Land sakes alive! (The strongest oath my Republican grandmother ever uttered.) How, how, how has the Republican Party fallen so low?

Now is the time to restore bipartisan support for conservation! We old geezers for conservation are counting on you, young conservative folk.

—*In the Sandia Wilderness, listening to the uplifting song of my chickadee friends*

Cow-Bombing the World's Largest Organism

By Andy Kerr

The slightest breeze will make quaking aspen leaves dance. The leaves' bright green upper surfaces contrast sharply with their dull green undersides against the backdrop of their white bark and a blue sky. Viewing golden quaking aspens on a crisp and clear autumn day is a powerful reminder that all is not wrong in the world.

The largest organism on Earth is one quaking aspen clone with more than forty-seven thousand stems (trees). This organism is being cow-bombed and otherwise abused. The cow-bombing, if not stopped, might well eventually result in the demise of the organism. As goes this singularly large quaking aspen clone, so may go the rest of the quakies in the American West.

A Wide-Ranging Tree and a Keystone Species

The quaking aspen (*Populus tremuloides*) is the most widely distributed tree in North America. The species ranges from Alaska to Newfoundland and from Virginia to northern Mexico. It is found at sea level in the northern end of its range and at 1,500 feet elevation in the southern end. In Oregon, the brilliant spring green and magnificent golden fall foliage of quaking aspens can be seen in the Cascades, the East Cascades Slopes and Foothills, and the Blue Mountains ecoregions. Only a few aspen stands

Aspens © John Miles. The quaking aspen (Populus tremuloides) *is the most widely distributed tree in North America, ranging from Alaska to Newfoundland and from Virginia to northern Mexico, found at sea level in the northern end of its range and at 1,500 feet elevation in the southern end.*

occur in the Coast Range and the Klamath Mountains. More can be found in the high ranges of the Oregon desert such as Steens Mountain and Hart Mountain.

Aspen forests are biologically rich and provide cover as well as nesting and feeding habitat for a wide range of birds. Rabbits eat the bark, and grouse feed on aspen's winter buds. Deer and elk heavily graze aspen twigs and foliage, as they do the associated understory. A quaking aspen grove may have 3,000 pounds of understory growth per acre, compared to 200 pounds per acre in a conifer forest. Humans like to carve their initials and ideograms in the bark. Those carved by lonely late-nineteenth- and early-twentieth-century sheepherders can still be found and are often sexual in nature.

Aspens grow in wet areas and are a favorite of beavers. Both quaking aspen and beaver are keystone species, meaning their existence makes an outsized contribution to a diversity of habitats and therefore to a diverse array of species that depend on such habitats. For example, many woodpecker species generally love aspen stands. A stand of aspen trees adjacent to a pond full of beavers is a wonderfully biologically diverse condition.

While individual trees (which are actually stems of a much larger, underground organism) are relatively short lived, a stand of aspens is not. Aspen trees typically grow twenty to seventy feet tall and live seventy to ninety years. However, an aspen grove can survive indefinitely even if it burns occasionally. Burning can be beneficial in knocking back invading conifers. Within six weeks of a burn, aspen shoots will rise through the forest floor from the clonal rootstock below and have a distinct advantage over any conifer seeds from cones.

If you see several clumps of aspen trees, each with a distinctive color, know that each chromatic cluster is a clone (genetically identical) from the same original tree that sprouted from a seed thousands of years before.

Cow-Bombing of Aspen Groves

In the American West, the original 9.6 million acres of quaking aspen is down to just 3.9 million acres. The decline of quaking aspen in the American West has been severe and is mostly

Natural Communities © Sheri Amsel

attributable to the onslaught of domestic livestock. Any amount of grazing by domestic livestock is harmful to aspens, as the bovines trash the understory and nip off all the replacement shoots from the root system.

Some examples:
- In Oregon's Malheur National Forest, aspens have been reduced by 80 percent from historic levels by livestock grazing.
- In Utah's Fishlake National Forest, aspen cover has declined 60 percent from historical levels.
- Many aspen stands in northern Nevada have not regenerated in more than a century and are dying out.
- In the late 1880s, with the arrival of livestock, the rate of new individuals being added to aspen groves (also called recruitment rates) in what would become the Hart Mountain National Wildlife Refuge in Oregon plummeted. After livestock were banned from the refuge in 1990, recruitment rates increased by an order of magnitude.

Like domestic ungulates such as cattle and sheep, native ungulates such as deer and elk can have deleterious effects on quaking aspen reproduction. However, there are some important differences:
- Quaking aspen co-evolved with native ungulates and is not evolutionarily equipped to address an onslaught of alien livestock.
- The individual intensity of grazing pressure from native ungulates is far less than from domestic ungulates.
- The collective intensity of grazing pressure from native ungulates is not only far less overall but also spread out over the year.
- Wolves and other large predators keep native ungulates within ecological bounds, while wolf presence near domestic livestock can be a capital offense.

Range conservationists [sic] and range scientists [sic]—professions generally populated by those who don't have the means to be ranchers themselves but nonetheless love to wear hats, boots, and buckles—tell us (see extension.usu.edu/rangelands/ou-files/Determine_Stocking_rate.pdf) that one cow and calf consume as much forage as about five deer, pronghorn antelope, or bighorn sheep, or as much as about two elk. These figures assume a standardized cow of 1,000 pounds. Today, the average cow is 1,384 pounds, a 40 percent increase. Native ungulates have not increased in size, so the discrepancies are actually far greater.

Fire Suppression and Aspen Groves

While domestic livestock are unquestionably a large part of the problem, another culprit is Smokey Bear. Aspens sprout profusely after a fire. The first year after a burn may see 150,000 sprouts per acre. A few years later, the aspens will be a few feet tall with a density of 40,000 to 50,000 sprouts per acre.

The decline of quaking aspen in the American West has been severe and is mostly attributable to the onslaught of domestic livestock.

The suppression of fire throughout most of the West due to federal policies allows shade-tolerant conifers to slowly invade aspen stands. The conifers then outcompete new aspen shoots by using the aspens' biology against them. Live and healthy adult aspens send a growth-inhibiting hormone down their trunks and into their roots to discourage excessive shoot production, thereby inhibiting the growth of young aspens. When adult aspens die, this hormonal impediment to new shoots ceases. If conifers have overtaken the forest floor by the time adult aspens die out, new aspen shoots cannot get established, and the aspen stand may eventually be replaced by conifers.

The Pando Problem, a Case in Point

It is the nature of quaking aspen trees to reproduce most often from shoots that arise from the roots of existing trees. DNA analysis has shown that a particular cluster of aspens in the Fishlake National Forest in Utah is actually one big-ass (a scientific term) clone. It's one single organism of ~106 acres in extent with an estimated weight of more than 6,600 tons, manifesting with ~47,000 "ramets" (stems, commonly understood to be trees). The organism is called Pando, Latin for "I spread out."

The age of Pando (a.k.a. The Pando or the Pando Clone; I like to think we're on a first-name basis though we've yet to meet) is in scientific dispute, with estimates ranging from 8,000 to 10,000 years up to 80,000 years. Pando did not spontaneously arise in the 1880s, as speculated by someone with an increment borer and a forester mentality who thought he was coring a few trees rather than a few ramets of a much larger single organism.

While ramets age out and die and fall over, under normal conditions such ramets are replaced. For Pando to survive in the long run, the number of new ramets must be at least equal to the number of old ramets. But alas, the world's largest organism is slowly dying from repeated intense livestock grazing. Even though the aspen is the state tree, Utah has not been kind to the quaking aspen (of course, neither has Oregon been kind to the Douglas-fir).

Given the grazing problem and that it is the world's largest organism, the Forest Service has facilitated some experimental fencing designed to exclude all ungulates or just large (code for cows) ungulates. The scientific evidence is pretty clear that domestic livestock are the overwhelming cause of inadequate recruitment of new ramets (commonly known as shoots or suckers). While native deer also play a role, it is minor and would not be an issue if not for being compounded by cows.

Pando has not only suffered the simultaneously chronic and intense indignity of being cow-bombed for going on 1.5 centuries but is also bisected by a highway and defiled by recreational development. Finally, its ramets can be affected by the sooty bark canker.

Petroglyph © Karen Boeger

A Damning Report on a Damnable Situation

The Western Watersheds Project has produced an excellent report entitled "What's Eating the Pando Clone?" (see westernwatersheds.org/wp-content/uploads/2019/06/Whats-eating-the-Pando-Clone-opt.pdf). The subtitle of the June 2019 report says it all: "Two Weeks of Cattle Grazing Decimates the Understory of Pando and Adjacent Aspen Groves." The report's four authors—Jonathan Ratner, Erik Molvar, Tristin Meek, and John Carter—are to be commended.

The report not only examines the literature on the effects of ungulates on aspen groves but also includes images from four time-lapse cameras set up by the researchers (see edited sequences here: westernwatersheds.org/pando-clone-time-lapse/) to gather evidence on just which ungulates are eating up all the forage (including new aspen shoots).

What to Do

1. Fence off the world's largest organism from domestic livestock.
2. Reintroduce wolves for natural regulation of deer numbers.

Of course, such would be equally appropriate for the world's second largest organism, as well as the third, not to mention the fourth . . .

May I suggest that you also make a donation to Western Watersheds Project (westernwatersheds.org) so they may continue their fine work. Because of their work at the leading edge of public lands conservation by seeking to end abusive livestock grazing, Western Watersheds has received relatively little foundation support. It's up to us.

[Andy Kerr originally published this article as his Public Lands Blog #139, on 26 July 2019. Images and charts to document Pando's decline in this original version were provided by the Western Watershed Project and may be seen in Rewilding Earth *online and on Andy's blog at andykerr.net/kerr-public-lands-blog/category/Federal+Lands. Andy drew some of the text for his blog from his book* Oregon Wild: Endangered Forest Wilderness *(Timber Press, 2004; see andykerr.net/oregon-wild-the-book).* —Rewilding Earth *editors]*

Cow-battered wetlands in the Upper Green River Valley, a grazing allotment that lies between the Gros Ventre Range and Wind River Range on the Bridger-Teton National Forest, Wyoming. © George Wuerthner

Wildlife Versus Livestock in the Upper Green

By George Wuerthner

The Upper Green River grazing allotment on the Bridger Teton National Forest (BTNF) lies between the Gros Ventre Range and Wind River Range. The allotment is one of the most important wildlife habitats outside of Yellowstone National Park. Indeed, the Upper Green's wildlife habitat quality has been compared to Yellowstone's famous Lamar Valley.

Among the endangered or at-risk species known to inhabit the allotment are Colorado River cutthroat trout, various amphibians, sage grouse, and grizzly bear. It is also home to significant populations of elk, moose, pronghorn, and mule deer.

That is one reason why the BTNF Forest Plan has categorized 93% of the area as DFC 10 and 12 status where protecting wildlife values is the primary goal. Yet the Forest Service manages it as more or less a feedlot for a few local ranchers.

According to the Forest Service's own analysis, the range condition of most of the allotment is between poor and fair. Don't let the word "fair" fool you: fair is technically 26-50%

of potential, so most of the allotment has lost at least half of its original vegetative potential. In range parlance, this means that much of the Upper Green allotment is "cow burnt."

In the BTNF's Final Environmental Impact Statement, the No Grazing alternative had the most benefits and least impacts on dozens of resource values. In every instance, the No Grazing allotment would bring about more rapid improvement, more positive benefits, and better ecological outcomes than any of the other grazing options. Indeed, the only negative impact reported would be on "traditional uses," which is a euphemism for livestock grazing.

Since 1995, at least 42 grizzly bears have been killed or "removed" from the Upper Green River allotment, including 8 bears this past summer. The US Fish and Wildlife Service in a biological opinion estimates that another 72 grizzlies are likely to be killed or removed from the Upper Green Allotment in the next ten years.

Grizzly bears are still protected under the Endangered Species Act, and even if they were not, they are still public wildlife that many love to see and know exist, as well as being vital members of healthy natural communities. This raises the inevitable question of why private businesses, namely Wyoming welfare ranchers, are permitted to graze our public lands when their presence is so detrimental to rare and special wildlife like grizzly bears, not to mention negative impacts on sage grouse, boreal frogs, elk, and Colorado cutthroat trout.

It is clear from the Forest Service's own analysis that

> *Where there is a conflict between private livestock and OUR public wildlife, it is the private livestock that should be removed, not native animals.*

continued livestock grazing on the Upper Green allotment has significant negative impacts on public wildlife and ecosystems. The BTNF says the Upper Green is supposed to be managed primarily for wildlife, yet it's clear from the above that our wildlife is being sacrificed for the financial benefit of a few ranchers.

When I queried the BTNF why they allow our public resources to be damaged for private gain, I was given the same old excuse that "we are a multiple use agency and livestock grazing is a permitted use." But whenever you hear that line, remind the Forest Service that they are working for the American people, not welfare ranchers, and they have an obligation to protect our wildlife and our resources from abuse.

Where there is a conflict between private livestock and OUR public wildlife, it is the private livestock that should be removed, not native animals. At this point, BTNF managers appear to favor private interests over the public interest, and everything from grizzly bears to Colorado River cutthroat trout are suffering.

What You Can Do

Write or call Bridger Teton National Forest managers and ask them to close the Upper Green livestock grazing allotment due to conflicts with endangered species. Remind them that their own Forest Plan calls for putting the health of wildlife populations and habitat first.

Bridger Teton National Forest, POB 1888, Jackson, WY 83001; (307) 739-5500

Pica © KIT West Designs

New Mexico's Wildlife Corridors Act: A Path Toward Success

By Michael Dax, Defenders of Wildlife

Whether it's pronghorn on the eastern plains, elk in the upper Rio Grande, or bighorn sheep in the Red River Gorge, New Mexico's wildlife, both big and small, requires large tracts of intact habitat. Species need the ability to move, whether that means seeking out lower elevation areas during winter, moving throughout river systems to avoid localized threats, or migrating to cooler environments as climate change makes certain areas inhospitable.

In the twentieth century, conservation efforts focused on protecting important wildlife strongholds like national parks and wildlife refuges. However, a growing body of science has recently helped elucidate the importance of daily and seasonal migration routes that can span hundreds of miles with little respect for political boundaries. Over the last decade, the U.S. Forest Service designated the first wildlife corridor in Wyoming, the Western Governors Association launched an initiative designed to further understand and protect connectivity, the Department of the Interior issued a Secretarial Order encouraging western states to increase research efforts, and congressional leaders introduced legislation to identify and designate wildlife corridors throughout the country.

Now, even states are getting involved. Wyoming has proposed designating two additional corridors; and in April 2019, New Mexico became the first state to pass legislation intended to comprehensively identify and maintain the habitat areas that wildlife depend on the most.

Wyoming has proposed designating two additional corridors; and in April 2019, New Mexico became the first state to pass legislation intended to comprehensively identify and maintain the habitat areas that wildlife depend on the most.

While precedent-setting, this was not the first legislation that New Mexico passed related to corridor conservation. In 2003, State Senator Mimi Stewart (D-Albuquerque) sponsored a memorial encouraging New Mexico Department of Transportation (DOT) and New Mexico Department of Game and Fish to share information about wildlife crossings. In 2011, she passed another memorial directing the agencies to develop a pilot traffic safety project that helped produce successful work in Tijeras Canyon, east of Albuquerque, along I-40. Then, in 2013, she passed a third memorial to further identify high collision areas and educate the public on how to avoid them.

Building off those successes, Senator Stewart prepared to run a bill during the 2019 legislative session. Late during the summer of 2018, we sat down with staff from DOT and Game and Fish, including Jim Hirsch and Mark Watson, both of whom had been integral to the Tijeras Canyon project.

While we had our own ideas of what a corridors bill might look like, we started by learning about what connectivity related work the two agencies had been doing and what they saw as their major needs.

As they explained, their work up to that point had been sporadic and piecemeal. When road construction was planned, they would look for potential conflicts with wildlife and build safe passage infrastructure into the existing projects. Over the previous decade they had been able to plan and build a number of structures that made New Mexico's roads safer for people and wildlife, but as they recognized, this opportunistic approach failed to capture

Rocky Mountain Elk migrate between the Sangre de Cristo Mountains, Taos Plateau sky islands, and San Juan Mountains. © John Miles

any larger picture. What they needed was the direction and authority to plan based on the needs of wildlife, not the construction priorities of road managers.

Over the following months, we worked with colleagues at Wildlands Network to draft what eventually became SB 228, the Wildlife Corridors Act. The bill directed the two agencies to work with one another to develop a Wildlife Corridors Action Plan (WCAP), modeled on State Wildlife Action Plans that identify sensitive species and habitats. Included in this plan would be information about existing highway crossings and about roads and other human barriers that negatively impact wildlife migration, projections of anticipated effects from climate change, and science on how increased movement of species could benefit highly impacted habitats like riparian areas. It also encouraged the agencies to collaborate with stakeholders and required consultation with tribal governments.

In this way, the WCAP would serve as a clearinghouse for information and research related to how wildlife moves throughout the state; but beyond that, it was also important that the bill help produce on-the-ground projects. To this end, the WCAP would include a list of priority safe passage projects. With projects already identified through an objective review process, the agencies would then be able to proceed with construction as funds became available and would not need to wait for other planned road construction.

With the bill's language starting to come together and the legislative session quickly approaching, we began to reach out to partner organizations to secure support. Unlike any other bill I have worked on, endorsements came pouring in. From traditional environmental and humane-focused groups like Sierra Club, Animal Protection New Mexico, and Audubon to more sportsmen-oriented groups like New Mexico Wildlife Federation and HECHO (Hispanics Enjoying Camping, Hunting and the Outdoors), enthusiasm for the bill was unbelievable. The Pueblo of Santa Ana, which has completed significant on-the-ground work to improve wildlife connectivity, also endorsed the bill, as did the conservation-minded landowner group, Western Landowners Alliance. During committee hearings, we even enjoyed favorable testimony from Allstate Insurance, which also wants to reduce wildlife-vehicle collisions. For a brief period, one of my biggest challenges was figuring out how to squeeze everyone's logos on our fact sheet!

With so much support leading into the session, I couldn't help but be optimistic about the bill's prospects. Governor Michelle Lujan-Grisham, who was sworn into office just before the session, had already indicated support for other conservation initiatives, and the State House had gained a conservation majority during the mid-term elections.

Despite this positive energy, the committee process proved more difficult than we expected. In speaking about the bill, we stressed its dual purpose—wildlife conservation and public safety. We explained that wildlife-vehicle collisions were becoming more common. In 2013, DOT reported 1,228 such accidents, but by 2016, that number had jumped 33% to 1,637 collisions. According to DOT, this amounted to an annual cost of nearly $20 million between insurance claims, medical bills, lost time at work, and other subsequent expenses.

But the good news, we explained, was that safe passage infrastructure works. We cited examples from Arizona and Banff, Canada, where such projects were able to reduce elk collisions by 90% and all wildlife collisions by 80%, respectively.

In our first committee hearing, at least one senator, who had hit a deer a few years earlier, understood the importance and potential good that could come from the bill. Unfortunately, another senator raised a concern about the possibility of conflict with ranchers and private property rights, which would prove to be the bill's most significant point of contention.

Arroyo, Diablo Canyon © Janice St. Marie

In fact, though, the bill did not contain any regulatory mechanism that could force participation. Its focus was on identifying places where wildlife was *already* moving and aiding those migrations, not arbitrarily "building a corridor" and forcing wildlife into new areas, as certain skeptics believed. Some people also feared facilitating wildlife passage would lead to more livestock being struck by cars on roadways. Buoyed by support from agricultural interests, this concern came up again and again, even after a Senate floor amendment ensured that any participation of private landowners would be voluntary.

Funding for the bill also became a point of contention; and as the bill made its way through the Senate and into the House, the funding mechanism seesawed at each committee hearing. The introduced bill appropriated $500K from the state's general fund, but after hearing from the chairman of Senate Finance that would untenable, we worked with Game and Fish to leverage funds from their budget. At that point, the Department was only willing to commit $100,000 with the idea that $300,000 could be matched through a Pittman-Robertson grant.

However, after a separate attempt to transfer funds from Game and Fish to another state agency created political backlash, the new DOT secretary committed the original $500,00 from their budget.

Despite these lingering issues, the bill moved through the process relatively smoothly. After passing Senate Conservation 7-1, it squeaked through Senate Finance 5-4, thanks to a Republican Senator from Farmington who had experienced the benefits of wildlife fencing designed to protect wildlife migrating out of Colorado to winter range in New Mexico. The debate on the Senate floor lasted more than an hour, but the bill passed 24-18.

In the House, it faired much better, passing 7-5 in the Energy, Environment, and Natural Resources committee, and 7-0 in State Government, Elections, and Indian Affairs committee, chaired by our House sponsor, Rep. Georgene Louis (D-Abq). On the House floor, it sailed through with a resounding 51-12 vote. Two weeks later, Governor Lujan-Grisham signed the bill into law, making it the first of its kind anywhere in the country!

Since SB 228 was signed into law, national attention on corridor conservation has continued to grow. US Senator Tom Udall (D-NM) and Rep. Don Beyer (D-VA) reintroduced their Wildlife Conservation Corridors Act, which would create a national system of wildlife corridors and provide $50 million in grants to help states protect these migration routes. The Bureau of Land Management (BLM) has distributed additional funds to western states, including New Mexico, to conduct GPS collaring studies to better understand how wildlife are using the landscape.

Meanwhile, DOT and Game and Fish have been taking the first steps toward fulfilling the vision of SB 228. We will continue our work with them to make sure that the plan is as robust and detailed as possible, so that New Mexico will prove to be the model we know it can be.

We will help advise the state on what projects should make the priority list. Among our recommendations are infrastructure on I-25 to reconnect the Jemez Mountains with the Sandia Mountains via the Pueblo of Santa Ana, on US-550 between Cuba and Farmington—a notoriously high collision area, and across I-10 in southwestern New Mexico where the highway bisects desert bighorn habitat in the Peloncillo Mountains. Of course, we also hope for the state's first overpass and can't help but think that Tijeras Canyon—the first major corridor project—would be the perfect place to bring this effort full circle!

As much work as it was for this bill to become law, the real work has barely begun if we are to make this vision of connected wildlands a reality on the ground. With support at all levels of government and across a broad range of stakeholders, I know New Mexico is ready to be the leader our wildlife needs.

What You Can Do
- Write and call your US senators and representative in support of the federal Wildlife Corridors Conservation Act.
- Study examples from New Mexico, Oregon (which just passed a similar bill), New Hampshire, and California, and speak with your state representatives about advancing similar legislation in your state.
- If you live in one of the states that recently passed a corridors bill, pay attention to where you're seeing roadkill and animals close to roads and engage in the development of your state's corridors action plan.
- Support the connectivity work of Defenders of Wildlife, Wildlands Network, Center for Large Landscape Conservation, and other groups working for safe wildlife crossings.

Embers from the Campfire

By Uncle Dave Foreman, TRI Founder

Quitobaquito Springs

One of my most treasured places in Organ Pipe Cactus National Monument is Quitobaquito Springs, pictured below at dusk. This exquisite oasis is now threatened, along with two dozen other archaeological sites in arizona.

They are in the path of Trump's proposed border wall, the goal of which is to completely wall off the entire Monument from north-south migration. As I write this, large machinery is trashing essential habitat, and if finished, the wall would essentially split one of the finest Sonoran ecosystems in half. Organ Pipe Cactus National Monument and adjacent protected areas in Mexico are home to threatened and endangered species. Trump's politically motivated, unnecessary wall would prevent all terrestrial species from migrating across the border and also prevent the Tohono O'odham from moving through their historical homelands, among other atrocities.

Quitobaquito is an oasis, the primary source of water for birds and other animals in the region. DHS is drilling wells every five miles in an area where drawdown of ground water is already a serious threat. If completed, the wall would require an estimated 28 million gallons of water to build concrete footers to support 30-foot panels, leaving a monstrous obstruction, destroyed habitat, and little or no water.

If my health were better, I would be there today protesting this ill-conceived, terrible, and illegal destruction. We must find some way to stop this crime against nature and our public lands.

Quitobaquito Pond and Fremont Cottonwood at Dusk. © Dave Foreman

Puma © Larry Master, MasterImages.org. Changing dedicated wildlife funding is a long haul; but until we broaden the base of financial support for wildlife conservation, our efforts to restore puma and wolf and other top carnivores will be uphill struggles.

Tapping the Third-Rail: Wildlife Watching and State Wildlife Funding Reform

By Chris Spatz

In their October 2018 *Rewilding Earth* article "Wildlife Governance Reform: Where to Begin," Kirk Robinson and Dave Parsons note that funding deficits for state wildlife programs from a decline in hunting and fishing revenues—these programs' primary funding source—have been met with retrenchment. Rather than creating funding from the much larger constituency of non-consumptive wildlife interests, state wildlife agencies are trying to create new opportunities for hunting and fishing recruitment. The agencies continue to deny those wildlife interests a voice in state wildlife management. It's a scenario that has played out largely unchanged for decades, as hunting and fishing popularity has been cyclical, while few substantive supplemental, non-game funding sources have been created even when the hand-wringing over wildlife funding deficits resumes.

Since the Outdoor Recreation Industry lobby (Patagonia, Black Diamond, REI, et al.), successfully fought off the "backpack tax" of 2000, non-consumptive wildlife interests have reached a virtual nadir in creating alternative funding sources. The backpack tax—an excise tax on outdoor gear to fund 12,000 at-risk species through the newly created federal Teaming With Wildlife program (TWW)—was similar to the federal Pittman-Robertson/Dingell-Johnson Acts (PRDJ) on hunting and fishing gear which provides one-third of all U.S. dedicated wildlife funding. The other two-thirds comes from hunting/fishing license sales. The most successful alternatives have been tiny, 1/8-3/8 of 1% general sales taxes in Missouri and Arkansas which spread the burden and give all citizens an equal say—theoretically—in how wildlife is managed, while dedicating critical funding for non-game species. State gear excise taxes, wildlife license plates and wildlife stamps, tax return check-offs, cigarette taxes, real estate transfer fees, percentages from state lotteries, and fees from resource extraction dedicated to wildlife have also met with some success. Fifteen of these state funding initiatives have been analyzed in an extensive University of Michigan study (see seas.umich.edu/ecomgt/pubs/finalReport.pdf). The Michigan study found just one attempt—a failed effort in Alaska to create a wildlife watching tourism pass—to tap the more lucrative, third branch of wildlife recreation revenue: wildlife watching.

Every five years, the US Fish & Wildlife Service (USFWS) produces the National Survey on Fishing, Hunting, and Wildlife-Related Recreation. The most recent survey, from 2016, found that 86 million US citizens pursued some form of wildlife watching annually, generating $75.9 billion in spending. This compares favorably to 35.8 million anglers and 11.5 million hunters, generating $46.1 for fishing and $25.6 billion for hunting. Though hunting-related expenditures dropped from $36 billion in 2011 to $25.6 billion in 2016, fishing expenditures increased from $45 billion to $46.1 billion. What those numbers don't tell is that handgun and handgun ammo sales—merchandise unrelated to consumptive recreation taxed for wildlife funding—accounted for half of total gun sales during the Obama years (the "Obama Bump"), offsetting hunting-related deficits. Consequently, PRDJ funding went unchanged from 2014-2017 at $1.1 billion annually. If the backpack tax had been instituted in 2000, it would have generated $6.4 billion in 2014 for those 12,000 at-risk species and their habitats, dwarfing the PRDJ funding. Teaming With Wildlife currently receives about $63 million annually in appropriated funding.

In 2016, TWW controversially created a Blue Ribbon Panel of sportsmen, businessmen, academics, and executives from Toyota, Shell, and Hess to develop a supplemental wildlife funding source. Non-consumptive wildlife interests were not represented on the panel. The panel recommended a bill to tap oil/gas drilling on federal lands similar to one proposed and defeated on off-shore drilling in 2000 after the backpack tax went down. HR 4647, The Recovering America's Wildlife Act, would redirect existing hydrofracking royalties and fees of $1.3 billion annually for TWW. Introduced in December of 2017 with 116 cosponsors, the bill has not moved beyond hearings by the House Natural Resources Subcommittee on Federal Lands.

In the spirit of tapping existing revenues, biologist Dr. John Laundré and I, as executives of the Cougar Rewilding Foundation (easterncougar.org), in 2014 created an option from state wildlife watching expenditures to fund non-game and at-risk species. Our idea was to reward wildlife for the work wildlife watching does in the economy. Using state revenue numbers from the 2011 USFWS Wildlife Recreation Survey (which are not included in the 2016 survey), we found that our home state of New York had the highest wildlife watching numbers in the nation: $10.6 billion, $4.1 billion of it in-state, producing $328 million in state taxes, or $3.2% of New York State's $10.9 billion sales tax for 2011. By piggy-backing on the New York State Department of Environmental Conservation's NY Watchable Wildlife program, our goal was to market wildlife watching spending as the incentive to boost wildlife re-investment. Utterly lost on the Outdoor Recreation lobby, marketing wildlife re-investment is a highly successful tactic well established in "sportsmen pay for wildlife" promotion to increase "game" management revenues.

Our formula, which I am modifying for the purposes of this article, takes a percentage of existing state taxes on wildlife watching revenues to reinvest them into non-game and at-risk species. New York State currently receives about $12 million annually for wildlife from all sources, including PRDJ. To create a $12 million match, New York would take 3.6% of its $328 million in state wildlife watching tax revenues, or about 4 cents from every $100 spent on wildlife-related sightseeing in New York State.

Under this scenario, just as Pittman-Robertson first redirected its gear excise tax from the U.S. Treasury to the Department of the Interior, there is no new tax to collect; the wildlife watching sales percentage is simply gleaned and dedicated from the total state sales tax. And according to the New York League of Conservation Voters, each $1 invested in wildlife and wildlife habitat returns $7 in jobs and business to the state's economy. An Association of Wildlife Agencies economic study of PRDJ's excise taxes produced an $11-$21 return for every $1 spent—an *1100% return on investment*. Based on these studies, that $12 million in wildlife reinvestment would return $84-$252 million in revenues, or $6-$20 million in additional state sales tax: good for retailers, good for Discover NY's Nature attractions, and good for state coffers.

Our original formula also included taking a percentage of state hunting and fishing revenues. Point being that reinvesting some percentage of the revenues produced by wildlife watching and also fishing and hunting for a dedicated state wildlife fund is viable for every state with a sales tax wishing to supplement non-game and at-risk wildlife. Two experts long in the wildlife funding trenches, Mark Humphries from TWW and John Organ from the USFWS, gave our formula—and its novel proposal to target state wildlife watching expenditures—the thumbs up.

Critics of state wildlife agency management, especially for non-game and predator management, have long argued against giving the agencies any more money, lest they siphon it to game programs. The answer to this valid concern is legislation dedicating the wildlife watching funds to non-game and at-risk species: the funds would be earmarked by law, protecting them from use for hunting and fishing programs.

In the final meeting of the advisory committee for the 2015 New York State Wildlife Action Plan—the TWW program that every decade assesses the status of those 12,000 at-risk species, creating intervention plans on their behalf—John and I pitched our funding formula. In the room were DEC wildlife biologists and administrators, state Audubon chapter representatives, Wildlife Conservation Society reps, hunting, fishing and trapping reps, and land conservation advocates. In a nutshell, TWW's 6,400 partner organizations are the very broad-based coalition non-consumptive wildlife advocates have long dreamed of, providing Cougar Rewilding Foundation exceptional access to state wildlife agencies, colleagues, and their constituents over a nearly three-year process. As the discussion came around to creating funding sources, John and I presented our wildlife watching funding formula, including the revenues and taxes it could generate for funding the state wildlife action plans (SWAPs); and we offered to lead a campaign with the assembled to create legislation for this funding source. The response: crickets.

Our formula ... takes a percentage of existing state taxes on wildlife watching revenues to reinvest them into non-game and at-risk species.

I often wonder if our proposal would have received more traction had reps from Audubon or Ducks Unlimited made the funding pitch, rather than the guys who drafted the controversial wolf and puma action plans. Wolf and puma are extirpated species that qualified for listing but were kept off the final NY State Wildlife Action Plan list. Nevertheless, a presentation I made last April at the Northeast State Fish and Wildlife Agencies conference was well received; and we continue trying to gain publicity among agencies and state legislators for funding wildlife re-investment from wildlife watching.

For wildlife advocates seeking access to state agencies to effect change, Cougar Rewilding Foundation recommends joining your state's 2025 Wildlife Action Plan committee. Changing dedicated wildlife funding is a long haul, but until we broaden the base of financial support for wildlife conservation, our efforts to restore puma and wolf and other top carnivores will be uphill struggles.

Planting for Bees and Butterflies

By Gary Lawless

the air was here
before us
the water, the rock,
the unnamed insect
the wandering tribes of
earth and sky
every day I
bless the aster
bless the milkweed
bless the goldenrod
sing to the bees
the monarchs the
rising song of the birds
every day an elegy
a death song
the heart cries out for
love and loss
grief and joy
the birds flying through
the heart, rising.

Butterfly & Sunflower © John Miles

Wilderness in the Anthropocene: What Future for its Untrammeled Wildness?

By Roger Kaye

My aim in addressing this question is three-fold: First to stimulate your thinking about the future of Wilderness in the next century of the *Anthropocene*. Second, to alert you to the "dilemma of wilderness stewardship" that confronts us. Third to convince you that we should take steps, now, to protect the most essential and most threatened quality of Wilderness—its untrammeled wildness.

Let's begin with the *Anthropocene*. Atmospheric chemist and Nobel laureate Paul Crutzen co-coined the term and has done the most to promote it. He and other Earth-system scientists proposed the Anthropocene to describe a new epoch wherein "Human activities have become so pervasive and profound that they rival the great forces of Nature and are pushing the Earth into planetary terra incognita." In this emerging epoch of Earth history, human activities have become a dominant, disturbing, and destabilizing force upon the entire Earth system.

Every year more of the Earth's surface is modified to serve human purposes. More of the chemical, biological, and thermal properties of its atmosphere, hydrosphere, lithosphere, and ecosphere are being pushed outside their historic range. Many Earth system scientists believe the rate of environmental and technological change is accelerating exponentially.

The Anthropocene was intended to both describe this emerging Earth state and prescribe a stewardship approach to it. While it is scientific term offering a name for the totality of human-Earth interactions, the Anthropocene also challenges us to rethink our current conservation paradigm, our role in the biosphere, and our long-standing, but increasingly problematic notion of nature.

Already in the Early Anthropocene, we are part of a post-natural world in which anthropogenic and "natural" effects on the Earth system are ever more intertwined and inseparable, evolving ever more synergistically with humans. A post-natural world? It's hard to accept. But our footprint is everywhere and expanding. There is no longer any nature separate from us. On this increasingly hybrid planet, the venerable distinction between what's natural and what's human becomes less and less viable.

Then try to imagine the future of "nature" in the next century of the Anthropocene, 2100. Imagine our continuing ecological effects coalescing with designer ecosystems, assisted evolution, synthetic biology, geoengineering, and who-knows-what. What will be the "new natural" on this ever-more altered, manipulated, and managed planet?

The Arctic National Wildlife Refuge first confronted me with the Anthropocene and this troublesome issue of naturalness. I first visited this landscape on a hunting trip 41 years ago and have worked on it for the last 33 years as a U.S Fish and Wildlife Service planner, pilot, and wilderness specialist. Renowned as the Last Great Wilderness, the Refuge is widely regarded as the nation's archetypal natural area. Since the Refuge was first established in 1960, it has been the agency's mission, and it became my mission, to keep it this way. Keep out developments and harmful uses and it will always be natural—so we had long thought.

However, five years ago, as the Refuge's scientists began to summarize observed and predicted changes for a conservation plan for the Refuge's future, reality took hold. They documented the many impacts of human-caused global-scale change, ranging from glaciers melting away to shrinking coastal ice and polar bear habitat. More alarming were the projected changes: thawing permafrost, eroding shorelines, shifts in the range and composition of both plant and animal communities, decline in wetlands and soil moisture, changes in water temperature, chemistry and alkalinity, increased fire frequency and intensity, more likelihood of invasives and pathogens—the list goes on.

This is the best science and the most likely future I had to accept for the Arctic Refuge.

This iconic landscape now confronts us with previously unimaginable Anthropocene questions. Questions like, how long will we be able to consider this preeminent wilderness "natural" by the common meaning of natural—that is, not shaped by or substantially changed by human activities?

The Anthropocene fact is this: All wilderness areas will continue to become less and less natural. (Though because global scale effects are amplified in the Arctic, change is coming faster to the Refuge.) This loss of naturalness has led to what is now recognized as "the dilemma of wilderness stewardship." Should we intervene in wilderness to try to maintain or restore natural historic conditions? Or should we just allow wilderness ecosystems to adapt and evolve as they will? If the latter, we would need to accept, as one example, that some of our preferred species may be extirpated and eventually replaced by others more suited to the changing conditions.

Interventions and restoration efforts include manipulating vegetation, suppressing or managing wildfires, removing or introducing wildlife, and modifying the flow or chemistry of water. A recent study of US Wilderness Areas showed that already, 37% of Wilderness units

By artist Lindsay Carron, in the public domain. The Anthropocene concept speaks to the deepening intertwining of natural and human systems and challenges us to rethink long-standing notions of naturalness and wildness.

engaged in such management interventions in response to global-scale change. On the horizon are proposals for assisted migration and genetic engineering of plant and wildlife to enable them to persist in their changing environments. Who knows what will follow? But when considering such actions intended to perpetuate or restore "natural" conditions, we must remember that every intervention, however important the resources or uses it seeks to protect, diminishes an area's wildness.

What then is wildness? It's a state wherein the landscape remains free from the human intent to alter, control, or manipulate its components and ecological and evolutionary processes. But it's not the absence of all human effect: Wildness persists in environments influenced by human factors such as climate change—as long as we refrain from interfering with the ecological system's autonomous response. So while interventions and restoration actions are intended to maintain "natural" conditions, that is, the products of evolutionary creativity at one point in time, maintaining wildness is about perpetuating the very process itself. In short, wildness is unfettered evolution.

There were two great milestones in establishing this process as a landscape entity of intrinsic value. One was the campaign to enshrine the wilderness idea in federal law, resulting in the Wilderness Act. The other was to establish a Last Great Wilderness in northern Alaska, resulting in the Arctic National Wildlife Refuge. These concurrent and controversial efforts sought to perpetuate wildlife, ecological, scenic, recreational, and spiritual values in the face of the 1950s post-war march of progress.

They were a response to the era's accelerating loss of natural areas, to destructive logging, mining, and agricultural practices, to pollution and pesticides, and to the awful power and fallout of the Bomb. Ultimately, they were a reaction against what is called the Dominant Western Worldview—the belief in human separateness from and right to dominate nature, a confidence that consumption, growth, and progress can continue as it has, and the assumption that science and technology can solve any environmental problems incidental to progress.

Should we intervene in wilderness to try to maintain or restore natural historic conditions? Or should we just allow wilderness ecosystems to adapt and evolve as they will?

Howard Zahniser and Olaus Murie, co-directors of The Wilderness Society and leaders of both campaigns, were among those beginning to question whether future generations would even inherit the same Earth. They argued that a new ethic was needed to guide human-Earth relations for the changing world.

Foreshadowing Anthropocene thinking, Zahniser and Murie's writings often placed their advocacy in the larger context of the globe, the planet, the world, and the Earth. In fact, at the height of the Arctic Refuge campaign, Murie summarized the controversy over the area's future as emblematic of "the real problem . . . of what the human species is to do with this earth."

They were concerned about how we relate to—and know ourselves in relation to—the larger world. This explains why Zahniser, who became the principal author of the Wilderness Act, chose *untrammeled* as the key word of the Act's **Definition of Wilderness**." It states "A wilderness is . . . an area where the earth and its community of life are *untrammeled* by man . . ."

Untrammeled became the main descriptor of designated Wilderness because Zahniser's intent for the designation went beyond maintaining an area's natural condition. More important was to respect and perpetuate the freedom of its ecological and evolutionary processes, its wildness. But beyond that, Zahniser hoped that designating some areas for this purpose would serve as a step toward expanding thinking about our role within, as the Wilderness Act says, "the earth and its community of life."

Untrammeled adds a transcendent dimension to Wilderness because it describes areas that are wild because we have consciously chosen to restrain ourselves and our will to subdue and dominate. At heart, untrammeled is the inter-relational dimension of Wilderness. More than what is kept alive in wild places is also something of ourselves—a way of relating to the larger world and its other inhabitants and a way of being when we find it within ourselves to allow some of it this freedom from our willfulness.

Untrammeled wildness is a manifestation of respect for the autonomous creativity of unwilled processes and a relationship to those timeless forces that formed and shaped—and connect—our species, all species, all the Earth. It's a relationship of deference to an area's non-anthropocentric reason for being, a recognition of its intrinsic value. It's a measure of that better part of us that still holds reverence for something outside human utility and desires.

Thus, the deeper purpose of wilderness, as historian Roderick Nash summarizes it, was to serve as "an important symbol of a revolutionary new way of thinking about man's relationship to the earth." And today, the Anthropocene has become a symbol of revolutionary thinking, reminding us that, as the Earth system scientist Paul Crutzen emphasizes, "We must change the way we perceive ourselves and our role in the world." These insights from the past and of the future speak to the need to question the assumptions underlying the human hubris and willfulness of the Dominant Western Worldview now enveloping the planet as thoroughly as its changing atmosphere.

Perhaps perpetuating some areas of untrammeled wilderness as the far end of the spectrum of human-Earth relations will be part of the legacy we leave. If so, we need to address that dilemma of wilderness stewardship.

I have reluctantly, grudgingly, come to the conclusion that in the disconcerting non-analogue future we face, the trend toward more intervention in Wilderness—and loss of wildness—will continue. As more resources within and near the boundary of Wilderness are threatened by change, there will be more calls to take action. I wish it weren't so, but the entire Wilderness system is not and cannot be practicably maintained in the untrammeled state Zahniser and the other wilderness movement leaders intended. They were visionaries, certainly, but couldn't have foreseen today's growing tension between perpetuating wildness and "natural" conditions.

So what should we do? We need to develop a process to identify some Wilderness Areas where limited and temporary interventions may be permissible to maintain desired historic conditions or high-value species. But some areas should be dedicated to untrammeled wildness, designated as strictly hands-off, non-intervention areas. Within them, our role would be as humble guardians, to watch and learn as wilderness systems transition as they will, not according to our will.

Which Wilderness Areas should remain as true hands-off wild areas? Hard decisions and tough tradeoffs will need to be made. They'll need to be informed by science but made through public process and in consideration of many factors, including probable effects on adjacent lands and the presence of high-value resources or vulnerable species. This approach may be the only viable means to ensure that the multiple values of the untrammeled wild condition are perpetuated in some Wilderness Areas.

But first, if we are to maintain this ineffable, invisible, and immeasurable quality of wilderness, then the reasons for perpetuating untrammeled wildness need to be fairly considered along with the more tangible reasons for intervening and controlling. We must better understand and articulate the functions and values of untrammeled wild areas. For one, untrammeled wild areas can serve the future, as Aldo Leopold espoused, as a scientific laboratory for understanding how ecological systems function, transition, and respond to anthropogenic change when left alone. Thus one of the reasons Murie argued that the Arctic Refuge should be preserved as "a little portion of our planet left alone" was that it would enable us to "see how Nature proceeds with evolutionary processes."

Might not the heirs of this Brave New World appreciate inheriting some refugia of wildness? Might they not benefit from some areas whose freedom from human agency provide the ultimate contrast to the dominant value-and-manage-everything-for-us paradigm?

But as our descendants move further into the terra incognita of the Anthropocene, the potential of untrammeled wild areas to serve as an anchor point may prove even more important. As humanity reshapes its world, it will also reshape itself.

So consider also today's trends and projections for future humans, now that we are directing our own evolution. Think beyond to when genetic engineering, computer-brain interfaces, artificial super-Intelligence, synthetic neural algorithms, and-who-knows-what will have changed our minds and bodies. Might not the heirs of this Brave

New World appreciate inheriting some refugia of wildness? Might they not benefit from some areas whose freedom from human agency provide the ultimate contrast to the dominant value-and-manage-everything-for-us paradigm? Might they not value a few authentic remnants of this Earth? Might they not cherish these areas whose authenticity is not based on some historic or desired condition but rather grounded in their unbroken connection to the autonomous creativity of their genesis and unfolding?

Areas of untrammeled wildness could become evolutionary heritage sites. Such areas could be like places that, across cultures and throughout history, have been set apart as sacred groves, shrines, monuments, and memorials. They could serve as places to remember and reflect. They could serve to keep in memory conditions and ways of the past that provide insight into our species's origin, its nature, and how it became as it is. They could serve as an archive and reminder of their co-evolutionary kinship with all lifeforms.

For those who visit, the main values of the "Wilderness Experience" within these monuments to untrammeled wildness may lie in the nowhere-else opportunity they provide for an atavistic, experiential glimpse of the world in which their evolutionary journey began and to feel the sheer otherness of a place that is there for itself.

As places set apart from human willfulness and hubris, their otherness can serve Zahniser's hope for enhancing understanding of how these traits have distanced humankind from its sense of dependence on and interdependence with the rest of life. No, we cannot know what ethics or perhaps algorithms might guide our descendants. But untrammeled wild areas will be there—if we are willing—for perspective as they decide what of their culture, genome, and world will be passed on.

And untrammeled wild areas can be there as an encouraging demonstration of our capacity for restraint. They can stand as symbols of the willingness to think outside our utility and beyond our time that is needed to further the emergence of a new planetary sensibility. It is what Zahniser hoped might open us to "a sense of ourselves as a responsible part of a continuing community of life." It is what he and Murie knew is the essential precondition for entering into a sustainable relationship with this finite and conflicted Earth system we share.

Train #7, North Dakota

By Susie O'Keeffe

An old man and his dog
are watching
our train
liquefy in the early light.
We slip by, a dissolving dream.

One fox,
two deer,
one fawn.

The crops are growing fallow
and pass like murky water.
The white church stands alone
one temple on the ruins of another.

Further on
men lay open
the land,
thrust down the black headed shadow
of our thirsts
      and pump.

In pools dark as old blood
the sun is a vacant iris.

An abandoned hole flares.

Three lambs on a dirt mound
One young buck,
      running.

Combat Overpopulation Denial

By Richard Grossman, M.D.

"Most economic fallacies derive from the tendency to assume that there is a fixed pie, that one party can gain only at the expense of another."
—Milton Friedman

I first met people who denied the population problem in 1994 at the International Conference on Population and Development. They supported their claim that there was no population problem with the statement that all the world's people could fit into Texas.

Well, they are correct, however there are problems with this contention. If everybody crowded into Texas we would each have almost a thousand square feet! That's plenty of room, wouldn't you say?

What about food? Where would food come from, and how would it get distributed to all those people? What about drinking water? How would we stay warm in the winter? And what would happen to all the waste? Clearly people require more than just a thousand square feet.

How much land does each person currently use? The best way of calculating this seems to be the Ecological Footprint. The EF has been calculated for people in many countries, and it combines the land needed to live on, grow our food on, the area needed to develop natural resources, and also the land to dispose of our waste. It is a comprehensive method of evaluating a person's impact on Earth, although it does leave out one factor. More about that factor below.

The area of land in square feet, and the world population, are both very large numbers, of course. The EF only includes what is called "bioproductive" land—leaving out mountains and deserts. It turns out that an average citizen of the world is using about 291,000 square feet of land, or about 6 2/3 acres. This is more than 290 times the area allotted if we all squeezed into Texas! The people who deny overpopulation use an argument that is based on drastic misinformation.

Indeed, not only could we all not fit into Texas for any period of time, but we also don't really fit into Earth. To be sustainable, with our current population and level of consumption, we would need 1.7 times the land area available to us. We have overdrawn on our global savings account in order to enjoy our consumptive lifestyle.

We can already see the effects of overpopulation and overconsumption. Perhaps most evident is climate change. Land is eroding, fisheries are depleted, and toxic chemicals are ubiquitous. Furthermore, we are killing off other species at terrifying rates—at least 1,000 times normal. Although the Ecological Footprint is an excellent tool for comparing what people are using with what is available, it has a major limitation. It does not leave any resources for other species.

I haven't read the book *Empty Planet: The Shock of Global Population Decline*, but I've read reviews. The authors, neither of whom is a demographer, maintain that the world is not overpopulated and, indeed, needs more people. They are concerned that the birth rate is falling more rapidly than the UN and other demographers realize. I wish they were correct, but I disagree!

The Wall Street Journal review of the book uses the term "global population collapse"—but there is little reason to believe that this will happen this century; we're still adding 80 million people to the planet each year. The review is concerned that the growth of the economy will slow. Only a madman or an economist can believe that perpetual economic growth is possible.

What is wrong with this book? There seem to be many errors. The authors don't focus on sub-Saharan Africa, where the average woman still has almost 5 children, and parents want large families. The authors seem to ignore demographic momentum, which causes growth to continue for several decades even after a country reaches replacement family size.

COMBAT OVERPOPULATION DENIAL

OVERPOPULATION

Number 6789

Earth © Jerry Thomas

The major problem with *Empty Planet* is that nowhere (in reviews I've read) do the authors compare the resources we humans are using with what is available. The Ecological Footprint does that, and the result is not pretty. Unfortunately that book is not alone in not considering the finiteness of our planet. Even though Milton Friedman won a Nobel Prize for economics, he was not thinking globally when he wrote the quote at the beginning of this column. Our global "pie" is fixed in size. We in rich countries are endangering people in other countries with our growing population and extravagant lifestyle. We are also endangering our progeny.

[This essay was originally published in the Durango (Colorado) Herald. *—Rewilding Earth editors]*

Ecotone

By David Crews

It's such a wilderness

It surrounds us
    she says

go through it, pull yourself to the center
open your heart to what the mind remembers
which too is a forgetting
Don't you feel it
begin outside the body
    once a voice
that speaks the language of all things
touched, caressed
held too close
that yearns for the words of a thousand mysteries
small hurts that come from loss
    (she touches her arm)
how to live in such bewilderment?

~

There is a place I go to remember
when I forget there are
    and have been
good souls who love me
It is simple really, she says
you give when you have and when you get
you get too much
    May I touch
the lamb's ear?
    Is it true
hummingbirds come to beebalm?
Will the honeybees
    return?
It hurts to love this hard
I have a tired heart

~

How far back must I travel
to see him
to hold him with my arms and say
what right do you have to my body?
I sense the loss
of all things—sunlight in grass
tiny bees that once I did not know were bees
gentle pollinators
    giving, getting—
how the little birds would sing
and the other ones
scratching through undergrowth

~

How far back must I go
to love my body?   When the memory
of stone still speaks
Once, they called it the backlands
a hinterland of wilderness—
I have a body
    she says
and no voice, the wilderness a voice
and no body
Is there no way to save it?
    All streams flow
        to the sea
how far back must I go
to love another's body?

~

There is a loneliness, she says
and it leaves little room
to remember
    Count me—
among the animals, their small
committed

Petroglyph © Karen Boeger

        I heard
souls
          Calls, she says
            (puts a hand to her face)
The forest receives exiles
solo natives
some call it the healing woods
too much longing
for a body to contain
I want to shatter every reflection I see
want my body to be free
of its weight
        in water
I forgive you
you are loved

~

Void, voice, violence
solace in everything but the body
I want to ask for a departure
lone trek to the edge of things—
deep conifer forest
ground soft and cold, needles
tossed by prints of mustelids, foxes
the burrowings of sparrows
crisp fresh breath, air
and lung, quiet release
        Here, I forget
          In a dream
I see endless forest—
        dark, damp
a far field at center
water dammed and slowed near the source
(The woods
were once filled with them)

I must believe
a voice outlives the body—
no sound, buzz
        (she looks into the tree)
           To love
she says
        comes from the body
you give yourself first
you may not believe it
        To hurt
in tenderness
love to violence I'm sorry
you will never inhabit my body
        so love it
as it were your own

~

It is such a wilderness
        this body
the body is a wilderness
bewilderment of the body
what is wild
in its being—to bewilder, to be
        wild, willing
vulnerable to element
I cannot bring you safety
        but believe
I will never cause you harm
It is such a wilderness, they say

italicized lines from Jennifer S. Cheng, Lao Tzu, and Jane Mead

written for INTONATION, a project with ARTS By The People

Petroglyph © Karen Boeger

The Cliff Edge: Generating Political Will for the Required Level of Change

By Randy Hayes

Randy is Executive Director of Foundation Earth, a new organization fostering the big rethink to help protect the planet's life support systems. © Randy Hayes

In the high desert near the Grand Canyon is one of the oldest tribes in the Western Hemisphere, the Hopi. The old people there say that we newcomers need to get our industrial foot off the throat of nature and allow their people to live.

Some of us, from many walks of life, get the urgency of the impending ecological collapse. We know as well that major change must happen now and that we must build a new way of living on this planet. We also know that there isn't the political will in society to do what needs to be done.

How do we generate greater political will? We start by sharing our message with many. Demand attention to this on all fronts. Provide a comprehensive plan to get people started.

In the 1970s, I lived off and on with the Hopi and worked to support the elders. These eighty, ninety, and over a hundred-year-old women and men talked to us newcomers about their ways. Much of their daily lives, their economies, came from their own biologically diverse regions. They knew their neighboring tribes well. They traveled and traded far and wide. The stories were fascinating; but as a newcomer I kept coming back to two key lessons from these native elders: Get the industrial society foot off the throat of nature. Whether natives or newcomers, we must all live the natural way.

Where do we begin? How do we get BIG with footstep removal? To many, it is foolish to talk of shifting to a continental network of bioregional economies with green infrastructure servicing all. Suggestions of low impact living, using much less energy, and giving up high consumption high tech economies go nowhere with

Cottonwood © John Miles

most business leaders and political "servants." The sad truth remains: the required level of change in humanity's damaging industrial operating systems is far greater than most are willing to face. Yet, without quick massive change to societal operating systems, our damaging economy will lead to greater breakdowns. Think of the 2008 economic spasm only worse. Think of a six-year drought lasting twenty.

Business as usual is oriented to short-term profit. Vested interests, particularly in commerce, will keep fighting major change. Remember the saying that power concedes nothing without a fight. It never did and it never will.

However, with the next set of economic down-steps, more minds will open. Telling the story of the ecological truth of these times may help garner the much-needed political will for decisive action. So, get out there and make noise in every sector of society. Sound the alarm with these points:

The Reality of Our Situation is Dire and Urgent

Industrial technologies, modern chemistry, and billions of over-consuming wasteful people are destroying Earth's life support systems. Weather pattern deterioration and extinction of pollinators are just two major examples. Synthetic chemicals poison food and our body tissues. We must stop shredding the interconnected unity of the biosphere, if humanity is to survive, because natural systems sustain all life on earth.

Call Out to Advance Major Changes

These points are offered to provide a sample holistic approach for the transition (Foundation Earth's seven-point new green deal has greater details on this action agenda).

1. Promote a *True Cost Economy*. This is a steady state circular economy that structurally eliminates pollution externalities. We must replace the current polluting model.
2. Quickly achieve 100% renewable energy, while using less and wasting none. Quid pro quo, shut down a gigawatt of fossil energy with every gigawatt of renewable energy.
3. Quickly achieve 100% ecological farming. Remove fossil fertilizers and other toxics. Shift to a plant-based diet.
4. Halt the extinction crisis. Protect and restore damaged natural systems. Remove the funding for ecologically damaging infrastructure projects. Honor biological diversity everywhere.
5. Shift to low-impact lifestyles. Along with how we live, we need smaller numbers and a population educated about the ways of the biosphere, our life-support system. Remove the foot of ignorance and unthinking lifestyles.
6. Ensure appropriate technology policy. Study unintended consequences. Remove technologies causing more problems than they solve.
7. Other! This list can't account for all that is important and needed. We trust you will help cover other vital issues, solutions, and foot removals.

Every sector of society must engage. All must speak out for high-level action. The hour is late, and we only have time for big steps in the right direction. What "leaders" can you write a letter to today? Such acts make you a kindhearted revolutionary in the love letter army.

Teach compassion to combat anger and fear. We need broad empathy for our world to change and survive. We don't need to follow the path of strongman leaders and fascism. Cooperative community survival is the key to individual survival.

Bring your awareness into a bioregional community and take collective action. Fortify disaster response safety nets, especially first responders. Stockpile some food for yourself and some neighbors.

Develop a deep understanding of and respect for nature's ways. Protected and restored natural systems locally, continentally, and globally are key to our medium-term survival and the long-term survival of the web of life. Get to know your bioregional neighbors.

A transition is coming—which may include catastrophic disruptions and then having to rebuild. Some neighbors are already working for continental networks of bioregional economies and the green infrastructure for a better world.

Foster compassion as did the Hopi elders. At some point the unobservant and the denial types will realize that the "alarmists" were right. We should then welcome their newly offered support.

Every sector of society must engage. All must speak out for high-level action. The hour is late, and we only have time for big steps in the right direction.

To conclude, in most places globally, there were the natives and now there are the newcomers. The current migrants into Europe are yet another such wave. No matter one's ancestral origin, we must all learn to live a deeply natural way. It is the path to authentic hope.

[A longer version of this essay ran in the MAHB Blog, *a venture of the Millennium Alliance for Humanity and the Biosphere. For information on MAHB, contact joan@mahbonline.org. Randy Hayes drafted this on behalf of Foundation Earth (FDNearth. org; whose motto is* Rethinking society from the ground up!). *Foundation Earth is a generous sponsor of this* Rewilding Earth *anthology.* —Rewilding Earth *editors]*

From No Sense of Wild to a Need to Rewild North America

By John Miles

Ever since I read a book in college in the mid-1960s titled *A Wilderness Bill of Rights* by William O. Douglas, I have pondered, enjoyed, and advocated for wilderness. Growing up in New Hampshire I was unaware of the idea of wilderness though I knew wild woodlands, swamps, and meadows where I found wildlife and youthful adventure. Douglas introduced me to the idea of legislated Wilderness and the Wilderness Act of 1964. Since then I have believed in the idea of wilderness and have buttressed that belief with much experience of designated Wilderness and de facto wild lands.

The wilderness idea has been attacked over the decades by interests who sought to exploit the resources "locked up" there, and by intellectuals who have made various arguments against it. One such argument is that there is no wild, that indigenous people had no sense of wild and wilderness, that it is only an idea introduced by Europeans. As I've studied the idea over decades and seen Native Americans paraded out to claim they had no sense of wilderness, that it is only a cultural construction of Euro-Americans, I have been troubled. Many tribal people today do embrace the idea of wilderness. Euro-Americans did give that state of nature a name, bringing the concept with them from Old World roots, but colonists of the New World did not invent places where the works of humans were absent or nearly so. I have in the field experienced wildness, so I know it as a physical reality, not just as an idea or cultural construction.

In this essay I would like to review the history of the idea because now I am dedicated to rewilding parts of North America where wildness has been lost. Some have argued that the idea that there is wilderness erases history. I disagree and argue that history confirms, as does experience, that there is indeed wildness and wilderness and there always has been.

Much of what follows will be familiar to veteran wilderness advocates and rewilders. Parts of the story have been told in great detail, as in Roderick Nash's classic *Wilderness and the American Mind*, but it seems important to review the path to a perceived need to rewild parts of North America and elsewhere in the late 20th century. We need to understand the historical context of rewilding. Hopefully this essay will inform young wilderness advocates and rewilders of the deep roots of what is happening in this field today.

The Skagit River in northwest Washington drains part of the very rugged North Cascades in Washington and British Columbia. The river drains into the Salish Sea, and the upper reaches of the river were home to indigenous people since time immemorial. When archaeologists sought to learn of the prehistory of these people, they looked in the river valley and dismissed the likelihood that they would find anything of archaeological value in the mountains. Why would people blessed with the riches of the salmon runs on the Skagit, their thinking went, spend much time in the glaciated, steep, often snow-covered high country? Archaeologists initially did not even look up there.

Bob Mierendorf, who became the archaeologist for North Cascades National Park in the 1980s, thought that perhaps indigenous people had ventured into the mountains, that at least he should look there for signs of their presence. He found considerable evidence that ancient ones had indeed used the high country. These early human inhabitants had found and quarried and traded chert,

Pueblo Peak (12,305') known also as Taos Mountain, sacred land of the Taos Pueblo. © John Miles

hunted deer and mountain goats, picked for winter hair that goats shed annually in predictable places, and gathered abundant huckleberries and other native fruits. Much of the year the mountains were bathed in deep snow and people lived in the valleys, but in summer they ventured into the high country.

Today much of the North Cascades range is part of the National Wilderness Preservation System, protected—with both National Park and Wilderness designation—as much as any landscape in America can be. I studied and explored this region for many years, examining and writing about the way this land had been perceived and used by the people who lived on and around it. Though indigenous people had been up there, I found it wild and wilderness. As I became an advocate of Wilderness, I celebrated its designation anywhere but especially in the North Cascades. I read and thought deeply about wildness and its values to us today, and this ultimately led me to rewilding, to a recognition that we must reverse the loss of wild places upon which many of our fellow Earth Travelers depend for their existence.

All of this has led me to ponder conceptions of wildness and wilderness in America, which began with indigenous people considering the nature around them as home, lacking any concept of "wildness" or "wilderness." Europeans arrived who perceived the New World as "wild and savage," a condition to be corrected. Their missions were colonization and settlement of what they saw potentially as home but also as a resource bank to be harvested and marketed. Some of the colonizers gradually came to believe that wild land was necessary for survival and "conservation" emerged, a movement to protect wildness in Wilderness and to sustain "natural resources." Then, late in the 20th century, intellectuals critiqued a "received wilderness" idea and at the same time the idea of rewilding appeared. All of these stages of thought about the "wild" have been analyzed and described, but as an advocate of rewilding, I will briefly examine each stage as a way to understand how we have arrived at the idea of rewilding.

Stage One: No Sense of Wild

Before European colonization there were many indigenous cultures in North America and no single view of nature or way to interact with it. Some were hunter-gatherers who moved across the land with minimal impact upon it, while others were sedentary, practiced agriculture, and significantly modified the land. Interactions with the land were governed by geography and ecology. The Upper Skagit Indians, for instance, could establish relatively permanent villages along the river up which salmon would run each year. They could anticipate a reliable food supply swimming up to them, and their presence in surrounding mountains was seasonal. People living on the Great Plains, on the other hand, had to move with the bison herds upon which they depended. Woodland dwellers in the East modified the forested landscape to practice some agriculture, hunted and gathered on the surrounding landscape, and used the tool of fire to assure habitat for ungulates they hunted, especially deer.

One commonality of belief about nature held by these people was that the natural world was home; they lived within nature and were part of it. The natural world held spiritual qualities and values for them, which required them to respect nature. They were also at the mercy of this world, which required humility and often myth and ritual to demonstrate their respect and give them some sense of control over their fate. They used nature and manipulated it when they could. Human populations rose and fell over time, with greater or lesser impact on the nature they used. In the Southwest over millennia, for instance, lifestyles grew from pit houses to the great houses of Chaco Canyon, then drought and conflict depleted and redistributed populations to cliff dwellings of Mesa Verde and other sites. Ancient Puebloans rebuilt their communities in new places and new ways. Through a vast time and space, change was constant, but indications are that indigenous people had no concept of wilderness or a "wild" separate from them. Nature was home.

Stage Two: Wild is Bad, Conquest of Wilderness a Duty

Roderick Nash, in *Wilderness and the American Mind*, explains at length how Europeans brought to America a dualistic sense of separation from nature and the idea that wilderness was "the earthly realm of the powers of evil." Early colonists adhered to the scriptural admonition in Genesis to "Increase & replenish the earth & subdue it." Their mission was to transform a "cursed and chaotic wasteland" into civilization. Nash points out that colonists and settlers faced real dangers as they established civilization in the New World—Indians who resented their incursions and sometimes attacked them, wild animals who could harm them, and harsh environmental conditions that could kill them. Their attitudes toward wilderness, argues Nash, were primarily the product of Old World ideas about nature, but the conditions they faced added to their antipathy for the wild.

European colonization of the New World was a battle from the beginning for the Spanish in the Southwest and other European settlers to the east, a battle against "savages" and wilderness. Some came to make a home, to enjoy freedom and independence denied them in Europe, and some came for riches to boost powers of conquest. None of them came with a sense of nature as "home" in the way the indigenous people already living there saw themselves. Whereas native people exploited nature for sustenance and survival and considered themselves a part of the natural world, many of the newcomers saw nature as a source of riches, a provider of "natural resources." The newcomers subscribed to the belief that land was property, could be owned, and all of nature was a commodity. Conquering the wild and the "savages" would create a civilization based on withdrawing commodities from the resource "bank" that God had made for them. They would be doing God's work and reaping the benefits in this world and the next.

> *Through a vast time and space, change was constant, but indications are that indigenous people had no concept of wilderness or a "wild" separate from them. Nature was home.*

As Nash explains, these ideas prevailed from the 16th to the 19th centuries and to the present. They evolved into the idea of Manifest Destiny and of subjugating the wilderness as "progress." Indigenous people were simply pushed out of the way by a genocidal wave of settlers pursuing their God-given destiny and expanding Western civilization, a familiar and sad story. Europeans saw the New World as a resource bank from which they could and should make withdrawals, the Spanish literally taking gold from the bank, or trying to, and the French and English withdrawing fur, which they could exchange for gold back in the Old World. Again, a familiar story—the modus operandi was to "subdue" the wild and take from it what they could. To be fair, many colonists sought only to make a living as small farmers. Thomas Jefferson thought the future of America should be a nation of small, self-sufficient farmers, but Alexander Hamilton had other ideas. As the country grew and the wilderness receded, the commodification of nature progressed with often devastating effects.

Stage Three: Wild and Wilderness are Good

In the late 18th and early 19th centuries, a countercurrent to all of this stirred. A romantic conception of nature emerged in Europe and was exported to the United States. Nash writes that "Enthusiasm for wilderness based on Romanticism, deism, and the sense of the sublime developed among sophisticated Europeans surrounded by cities and books. So too in America the beginnings of appreciation are found among writers, artists, scientists, vacationers, gentlemen—people, in short, who did not face wilderness from the pioneer perspective." Among such people were early naturalists John and William Bartram, artists Thomas Cole and John James Audubon, and Henry David Thoreau. Thoreau pronounced "We need the tonic of wildness" and "In wildness is the preservation of the world." He was a lyrical spokesman for a new concept of wild and wilderness, quite the opposite of ideas of most of his mid-18th century contemporaries, but his ideas would grow, as Nash says, in "the American mind."

Most of Thoreau's fellows held a strictly utilitarian view of nature; they saw it of primarily, if not exclusively, instrumental value. What could they make from it, do with it, gain from it? Along with his more utilitarian mentor and friend Ralph Waldo Emerson, Thoreau emphasized instead the spiritual and intrinsic value of nature. These were radical ideas in the middle of the 19th century and remained so for decades until, late in the century, values of the wild and wilderness were discovered by many Americans. This discovery was fueled by a growing separation from nature as people moved from farms to cities, and by the realization that subduing and commodifying the natural world was leading to undesirable consequences such as extinction of some species like passenger pigeons and near extinction of others.

Stage 4: Conservation

Americans pursuing their Manifest Destiny assumed that the bounty of nature was endless until they began running out. Some didn't care, of course, but others started to worry. Hunters like Theodore Roosevelt and George Bird Grinnell worried that game animals they preyed upon, but which they also loved, faced extinction—"The Great Slaughter" of bison in the 1800s a case in point. Bird lovers began to see more birds on hats than in the wild and decided something had to be done to stop the slaughter. Diminished pineries and severe wildfires in the Upper Midwest raised concerns about the future of timber supply. Painters and photographers portrayed remarkably beautiful places in the West, and a scramble to protect these places from privatization and exploitation resulted.

All of this led to conservation, which in the beginning was a movement with many faces. Forester, advisor to Theodore Roosevelt, and first Chief of the Forest Service, Gifford Pinchot, said conservation "stands for development" and "The first duty of the human race is to control the earth it lives on." His goal was efficient management of natural resources, his mantra "wise use," and his philosophy anthropocentric and utilitarian. Roosevelt mostly agreed with him. Progressive conservationists like Pinchot sought to manage natural resources—forests, water, wildlife—so there would be a sustainable timber supply, wildlife in perpetuity for hunters, and water to make the deserts bloom. A wilder face of the movement was John Muir, more an acolyte of Thoreau, who extolled the spiritual values of wild nature and advocated protection of "Nature's sublime wonderlands, the admiration and joy of the world" as Nash summarized Muir's contribution to conservation. Many others in the movement focused their energies on conserving wildlife (George Bird Grinnell, Frank Chapman, Willian T. Hornaday), water (WJ McGee), soil (Hugh Hammond Bennett), and scenery (Robert Underwood Johnson, J. Horace MacFarland). The goal of all of them was to assure future generations would enjoy the values of these resources whether the value be aesthetic, economic, or even intrinsic.

Stage 5: Preservation and Wilderness

Muir wrote and spoke often of wilderness. He wrote in his 1901 book *Our National Parks*, "The tendency nowadays to wander in wilderness is delightful to see. Thousands of tired, nerve-shaken, over-civilized people are beginning to find out that going to the mountains is going home; that wildness is a necessity; and that mountain parks and reservations are useful not only as fountains of timber and irrigating rivers, but as fountains of life." This wilderness was fast disappearing to the saws of loggers, to dam builders, and to other forms of development. Pinchot-style conservation, rather than slowing loss of wilderness, was increasing it by encouraging "wise use" and development. A resource not wisely used was wasted. Surprisingly, given their agency's Pinchot-inspired mission, Forest Service leaders led advocacy for preservation of wilderness. Arthur Carhart, the first Forest Service landscape architect, was ordered to survey summer home sites around Colorado's Trappers Lake, but concluded the place was too wild and beautiful to be developed. Carhart then shared his views on wilderness with another Forest Service leader, Aldo Leopold, who advanced them and successfully advocated for the first national forest wilderness in the Gila National Forest of New Mexico. Then, in the 1930s, Bob Marshall, also of the Forest Service, nudged the agency toward expansion of its wilderness areas, and outside the agency, he funded and founded The Wilderness Society. A preservationist wing of the conservation movement, initiated by Muir with a focus on national parks, took up the cause of preserving wilderness as an ever scarcer "resource." The Wilderness Society and Muir's Sierra Club would soon lead the push for wilderness protection.

After a pause for World War II, work for wilderness preservation increased as did logging and other development in national forests. Demand for timber, suppressed by the Great Depression and the War, increased post-war road building and logging, which rapidly reduced wilderness. On another front conservationists successfully confronted dam-builders on several western rivers, the Green River foremost. As conservationists gained confidence and energy, they launched a campaign to create a national wilderness preservation system. They succeeded in passing the Wilderness Act of 1964, and over the ensuing fifty years managed to build a National Wilderness Preservation System of 109 million acres and protect rivers like the iconic Colorado in the Grand Canyon.

This successful effort of 120 years and continuing, was driven principally by anthropocentric values, as John Muir expressed them in the passage quoted above. Wilderness preservation was sold primarily as assurance of a future for wilderness recreation. Shortly after the Wilderness Act was approved, the Endangered Species Act became law in 1973. This legislation recognized that many species were being pushed to extinction, and with its passage, another value of wilderness was more widely recognized—its value for wildlife conservation in general and endangered species protection in particular. Conservation biology emerged when many scientists documented that biological diversity was declining worldwide. This mission-focused biology cultivated understanding of the consequences of habitat fragmentation, the need for functional connectivity between habitats, the need to focus conservation on large landscapes and predators, and much more. The value of wilderness areas as reserves and assets for conservation of biodiversity joined recreation as a principal goal of wilderness preservation.

The value of wilderness areas as reserves and assets for conservation of biodiversity joined recreation as a principal goal of wilderness preservation.

Stage 6: Critiques of Wilderness

The acreage in the National Wilderness Preservation System seems large yet is a bit less than 5% of the land base of the United States, including Alaska. This small portion of the nation is too much for some, and reactionaries began to publish critiques of wilderness and deconstructions of the wilderness idea in the 1990s. Surprisingly, they were not the forces that had always opposed wilderness in the United States as a "lockup" of resources—players with an economic interest in exploiting the land that would become part of the National Wilderness Preservation System. They were mostly academics, historians, and philosophers like William Cronon and J. Baird Callicott. They argued that designation of wilderness meant "release" of land not so designated for development and abuse; that designation of wilderness was unjust, depriving people of resources they needed; that there was no such thing as wilderness anyway because much of what, in the Euro-centric view was wild and pristine, had in fact been inhabited by indigenous people; that the idea of wilderness was flawed because it sought to freeze-frame states of nature which are always changing; that the idea of wilderness implies separation of humans from nature, worsening a dangerous dualism.

Such critiques launched a *Great New Wilderness Debate* as it was cast in the 1998 book of that name edited by Callicott and Michael P. Nelson, which presented criticism and defense of the wilderness idea. Critiques and refutations continue in the early 21st century as wilderness advocates and opponents fight over the last remnants of roadless and wild land in the American public domain. While the debate in academic circles was engaged, discussion and insight into the roles wild lands play in protecting endangered species and restoring biological diversity continued to grow in the scientific and conservation communities. Despite the critiques, more wilderness was added to the National Wilderness Preservation System with passage by Congress of the Omnibus Public Lands Management Act of 2009, which added 2,050,964 acres, and the John D. Dingell Jr. Conservation, Management, and Recreation Act of 2019, which added 1.3 million. Smaller areas have also been added and more are being sought.

These significant additions to legislated wilderness would seem to suggest that the critiques and deconstructions of the wilderness idea have not had much effect on wilderness protection, but that remains to be seen. As population and demand for resources continues to grow, the power of the wilderness idea will continue to be challenged while the need for it will grow. Some critics argue that there is no wilderness, but this "no wilderness" is not a return to the "no wild" perception of the natural world held by indigenous people. Rather, it advocates that all nature should be accessible and usable by human populations, an anthropocentric, utilitarian, and supremacist view of nature which writer Eileen Crist calls "techno-managerialism." She writes, "A diverse world infinite in beauty, mystery, interdependencies, sheer being, past heritage, and future evolution . . . is redefined and dissipated into just-being-for-using."

Stage 7: Need to Rewild

The idea of rewilding began to gain traction at the same time the deconstruction of the wilderness idea was launched. Conservation leader Dave Foreman came up with the term "rewild" in the late 1980s and it began to appear in print in the early 1990s. In 1997, the Yellowstone to Yukon Conservation Initiative, or Y2Y, was established for the benefit of wide-ranging animals like wolves and grizzlies. Conservation biologists Michael Soulé and Reed Noss contributed an article to *Wild Earth* in 1998 focusing their approach to rewilding on the 3 Cs—"Cores, Corridors, and Carnivores." Protected areas like wilderness and hotspots of biological diversity, they argued, should be connected in ecological networks restoring the functioning of natural processes on a significant scale. In 2003, Dave Foreman published *Rewilding North America: A Vision for Conservation in the 21st Century*. His vision for returning the "wild" where possible in North America would be based on six areas of ecological research: extinction dynamics, island biogeography, metapopulation theory, nature disturbance ecology, top-down regulation by large carnivores, and landscape-scale ecological restoration. Such research would guide protected area design.

Soulé, Noss, Foreman, and their colleagues were describing the ecological value of protected areas like wilderness. They were not focused on human costs or benefits of wild lands, as were the critics of the wilderness idea, but rather on the benefits to ecological systems and the organisms of which they are comprised, many of which were on the way to extinction if something was not done to slow and stop their decline. While scientists dug into how this might be accomplished, the conservation movement responded as David Johns has described:

> *As grassroots conservation groups joined together and sought to delineate a common vision for regional systems of protected cores and landscape connectivity, deciding which species to take into account became a very practical concern. A variety of approaches were taken, some relying on 20-30 focal species representing a wide range of life needs and processes and including keystone, umbrella, indicator, and iconic species. Other approaches focused on healing wounds to the land (e.g. fragmentation), recovering regionally extirpated species, and restoring natural disturbance regimes.*

All of this came to be called "rewilding."

The first stage of the evolution of the concept I have tracked here described indigenous Americans as understanding themselves as part of nature, considering it home, with no thought of separation from the wild world around them. Indigenous language had no word for "wild" or "wilderness," no conception of it. Over the centuries, Euro-Americans embraced a mission of subduing the "wild," and as they succeeded, it became scarce and morphed into "wilderness," which was where creatures were not under human control, where life was "self-willed." Out of this conception came a social movement to save this diminishing quality of the natural world. Ultimately a law was passed in the United States that defined wilderness "in contrast with those areas where man and his own works dominate the landscape, is hereby recognized as an area where the earth and its community of life are untrammeled by man, where man himself is a visitor who does not remain." As human populations and their resource consumption grew, self-willed creatures went into serious decline, and conservation evolved to embrace a less anthropocentric "resourcist" focus. Wilderness became a "protected area," and such areas became "core areas" essential to maintenance and restoration of functioning ecosystems and species communities. The goal was to bring "wild" back into enough land to allow this to happen. In 2016, the eminent biologist E.O. Wilson argued that this would require protecting half of the total area of terrestrial and aquatic ecosystems on Earth.

One current criticism of rewilding is that it embraces an unrealistic goal of "going back" to a pristine nature, to turning large areas into wilderness like those established under the Wilderness Act in the United States. The goal of protecting areas where the works of humans have not degraded ecological processes and extirpated species continues, and is part of the rewilding effort, and to that extent it embraces wilderness, but the main goal is not to "go back" to some imagined pristine past. As David Johns has noted, a thorny issue for rewilding is what in fact is the state of nature that would be considered adequately wild. And if rewilding has restored functioning ecosystems and species communities, what then?

The concept of rewilding has achieved enough recognition to appear in dictionaries. In the *Oxford Dictionary* it is defined as "restore (an area of land) to its natural uncultivated state (used especially with reference to the reintroduction of species of wild animals that have been driven out or exterminated.") *Merriam Webster Dictionary* defines it as "the planned reintroduction of a plant or animal species and especially a keystone species or apex predator (such as the gray wolf or lynx) into a habitat from which it has disappeared (as from hunting or habitat destruction) in an effort to increase biodiversity and restore the health of an ecosystem." Rewilding Europe defines it as "letting nature take care of itself, enabling natural processes to shape land and sea, repair damaged ecosystems, and restore degraded landscapes." This Rewilding Europe definition raises the question of what the active role of humans, if any, should be in rewilding and that is a controversial topic for another essay, but it reveals how far we have to go in figuring out what the verb 'rewild' means and how we should do it.

There is no doubt that the human population will continue to grow, and pressure on the wild will increase, while we debate what to do and how to do it. At this point in the story of wild, we understand that rewilding is emerging as an effective approach to conservation, but that there are many questions about it to be asked and answered. The Rewilding Institute states that "Rewilding, in essence, is giving the land back to the wildlife and the wildlife back to the land." A worthy and noble cause in these daunting times.

Howling Coyotes © Dave Parsons, Carnivore Conservation Biologist, The Rewilding Institute and Project Coyote.
After a long nap in the sun, these coyotes are tuning up for a night of hunting.

Appendix

About the Cover Artist

Steven Kellogg is one of the Champlain-Adirondack Biosphere Reserve's most cherished friends, artists, and advocates. A wildly successful illustrator and author of scores of children's books, Steven is also an extraordinarily generous supporter of conservation groups, animal shelters, and civic organizations.

Steven grew up in Connecticut, visiting the Adirondack Coast each summer and hoping he could become a wildlife illustrator for *National Geographic*. Fortuitously, he did even better. After graduating from the Rhode Island School of Design, Steven began illustrating children's books (often with editor David Reuther, another *Rewilding Earth* supporter), and he quickly won widespread acclaim. He married esteemed art historian Helen Hill (who passed away last year, sadly), and they eventually made a home in Essex, New York, eastern edge of Adirondack Park. Steven has passed on his love of wildlife to his whole family. His grandson Zack Porter is now Lake Champlain Keeper for the Conservation Law Foundation.

Steven has told stories and shown children how to draw wild creatures in hundreds of classrooms across the country. Books he has illustrated and/or written include *Frogs Jump: A Counting Book*, *Is Your Mama a Llama?*, *Engelbert the Elephant*, *The Invisible Moose*, *Best Friends*, and *The Mysterious Tadpole*, and most recently *The Word PIRATES*. Steven has served on many charitable boards of directors, including the National Children's Book and Literacy Alliance. He is a co-founder of Champlain Area Trails (CATS), a key partner in Split Rock Wildway (one of The Rewilding Institute's focal projects).

Steven's cheering style sets him above daily tribulations. As cognizant as anyone of the extinction and climate crises, Steven still finds the will to paint wild hope and happiness, as with this *Rewilding Earth* cover illustration. Steven adapted this painting from a book he illustrated fifteen years ago, *If You Decide to Go to the Moon*, keeping the general uplifting, natural feel but adding the Puma, Wolf, and Landlocked Atlantic Salmon, to suggest the successful return of our missing wild neighbors.

The scene here is a future rewilded view from the west shore of Lake Champlain in New York's great Adirondack Park looking across to Vermont's Green Mountains, including the most distinct in profile, Camel's Hump. The creatures depicted either are or were gravely diminished from the region. Bald Eagle and Black Bear have enjoyed remarkable recoveries—are rewilding success stories. The fish shown survive in reduced numbers, but need removal of more dams on tributaries of Lake Champlain to regain healthy numbers. Puma and Wolf, the Northeast's top carnivores, are still missing, and we are overdue to welcome them home.

Artists and storytellers like Steven Kellogg are critical to building the public support needed to knit back together an Atlantic/Appalachian/Adirondack Wildway and restore its missing species—our wild neighbors. The whole *Rewilding Earth* team thanks Steven warmly for his many decades of helping kids keep their sense of wonder about other life forms, and we look forward to sharing more of his inspiring art with our followers.

About the Contributors

Bill Amadon, Stewardship Coordinator, Champlain Area Trails, has a BA degree in Fine Arts and is an accomplished artist and photographer, and past-president of the Adirondack Art Association. He was born and raised in New York's Adirondack Park and knows the local landscape and the people who live here and has great knowledge of natural science and environmental issues. He is a founding member of Champlain Area Trails and has served as a board member. For many years prior to being hired as a staff member in 2015, Bill worked as a CATS volunteer, creating and maintaining trails.

Sheri Amsel has written and illustrated more than 25 children's books and field guides. In 2009, she was awarded the Elizabeth Abernathy Hull Award for *Outstanding Contributions to the Environmental Education of Youths* by the Garden Club of America. Her work has moved online with exploringnature.org, a comprehensive illustrated science resource website for students, educators, and homeschool families. Sheri works out of her home studio in the Adirondacks.

Mark Anderson is director of conservation science for The Nature Conservancy's Eastern U.S. Region. He provides science leadership, ecological analysis, and landscape assessments for conservation efforts across twenty-two eastern states. He holds a doctorate in ecology from University of New Hampshire and has published widely on climate change resilience, large landscape conservation, biodiversity, and forest dynamics. In 2016, Mark won The Nature Conservancy's Conservation Achievement award. Mark also serves on the board of directors of Northeast Wilderness Trust.

Karen Boeger is a retired schoolteacher, Nevada "Desert Rat," and has been a conservation activist for over 40 years. She loves to hike, ski, canoe, and forage. Karen feels fortunate to have grown up at a time when much of the West was still wild and the dominant recreational uses were traditional human-powered ones. Within her generation, those opportunities have vastly diminished. She works to ensure that future generations will continue to have the same wilderness opportunities and traditional outback experiences that she has been fortunate to enjoy.

Evan Cantor is a long-time Colorado wilderness artist. His works are impressionistic windows into the wilderness places he loves and hopes to protect, images that capture the sacredness of the earth through landscape. These images are informed not only by his own experiences back-of-beyond, but by transcendental philosophies ranging from Thoreau and Whitman to Aldo Leopold and Edward Abbey. Conservationists may recall Evan's scratchboard drawings in *Wild Earth* and Wildflower magazines. His images have also appeared in several of John Fielder's books, and works of several University presses, the Rocky Mountain Land Library, Southern Rockies Wildlands Network, and the Northwest Earth Institute. He is a member of the Temagami 22, an invitational group of North American artists concerned with environmental preservation, and was the Rocky Mountain Land Library's 2005 artist-in-residence. In 2006 he was honored with an award from the Southern Rockies Conservation Alliance for his "outstanding contribution" of both art and music to the wilderness preservation effort in Colorado. He took up oil painting at Ghost Ranch in October 2016 and has been going strong ever since. Evan is also the lead singer of the classic-rock outfit The CBDs, playing the guitar and blues harp.

David Crews is author of *Wander-Thrush: Lyric Essays of the Adirondacks* (Ra Press, 2018) and *High Peaks* (Ra Press, 2015)—a poetry collection that catalogs his hiking of the "Adirondack 46ers" in northern New York. He holds an MFA from Drew University where he studied with poets Ross Gay, Aracelis Girmay, Ira Sadoff, and Judith Vollmer. Crews serves as artist-in-residence with ARTS By The People, where he edits poetry and lyrical prose for *Platform Review* and the *Platform Chapbook Series*, and contributes as writing coordinator for *Moving Words*—a project that makes possible international collaboration among artists of prose, poetry, voice acting, and animation. His poem "Ecotone" will be featured this year in the ABTP project *Intonation*—a collaboration between American poets and composers from the Jerusalem Academy of Music and Dance.

Eileen Crist received her Bachelor's from Haverford College in sociology in 1982 and her doctoral degree from Boston University in 1994, also in sociology, with a specialization in life sciences and society. Between 1989 and 1991 she lived in Amherst, MA where she studied environmental evolution (Gaia theory) with Lynn Margulis. Following two post docs after graduation from Boston University (at University of California San Diego and Cornell), she accepted a position at Virginia Tech in the Department of Science and Technology in Society where she has been teaching since 1997. She is author of *Images of Animals: Anthropomorphism and Animal Mind* and *Abundant Earth: Toward an Ecological Civilization*. She is also coeditor of a number of books, including *Gaia in Turmoil: Climate Change, Biodepletion, and Earth Ethics in an Age of Crisis*; *Life on the Brink: Environmentalists Confront Overpopulation*; and *Keeping the Wild: Against the Domestication of Earth*. Eileen was a contributor to the late journal *Wild Earth*, and now serves on the Rewilding Leadership Council. She lives in Blacksburg, Virginia, with her husband Rob Patzig where they also teach yoga together.

John Davis is executive director of The Rewilding Institute and editor of *Rewilding Earth*. He rounds out his living with conservation field work, particularly within New York's Adirondack Park, where he lives. John serves on boards of RESTORE: The North Woods, Eddy Foundation, Champlain Area Trails, Cougar Rewilding Foundation, and Algonquin to Adirondack (A2A) Conservation Collaborative. In 2011, John completed TrekEast, a 7600-mile muscle-powered exploration of wilder parts of the eastern United States and southeastern Canada—sponsored by Wildlands Network and following lines suggested in Dave Foreman's book *Rewilding North America*—to promote restoration and protection of an Eastern Wildway. His book about that adventure, *Big, Wild, and Connected: Scouting an Eastern Wildway from Florida to Quebec*, was published by Island Press. In 2013, John trekked from Sonora, Mexico, north along the Spine of the Continent as far as southern British Columbia, Canada, again ground-truthing *Rewilding North America* and promoting habitat connections, big wild cores, and apex predators. This second continental wildways trek is the subject of the film *Born to Rewild*.

Michael Dax is the New Mexico Representative for Defenders of Wildlife, based in Santa Fe. Before moving to New Mexico, Michael worked in Grand Canyon and Yellowstone National Parks as a trail groomer and tour guide. Michael earned a master's degree in environmental history from the University of Montana where he began work on his book, *Grizzly West*, which focuses on the attempt to reintroduce grizzly bears to the Selway-Bitterroot Wilderness in Montana and Idaho.

Kenyon Fields, former western strategic director of Wildlands Network, now co-manages Mountain Island Ranch with his wife Mary Conover. Kenyon and Mary both serve on the board of directors of Western Landowners Alliance, which they co-founded (and where they met!).

Mark Fisher is the author of *Self-willed Land*, an advocacy website for wild land and nature (self-willed-land.org.uk). He is an honorary member of the Wildland Research Institute at the University of Leeds, the aim of which is to determine the requirements, strategies, and policies for a transition to a greater presence of wild land in Britain and Europe. Mark recently became a member of the IUCN Commission for Ecosystem Management. Along with his critique of the nature development interpretation of rewilding included in this book, Mark has written a carefully researched history of rewilding thought and work, which is available on his website: *NATURAL SCIENCE AND SPATIAL APPROACH OF REWILDING –evolution in meaning of rewilding in Wild Earth and The Wildlands Project*. Mark also is in our Rewilding Earth podcast series, episode number 17.

Dave Foreman is a legendary conservation leader and wilderness strategist. His half-century career in conservation has changed, and bettered, the course of the wilderness movement.

Dave's professional work in conservation has included serving as Southwest regional representative for The Wilderness Society (1973-1980), co-founder of Earth First! (1980), publisher of *Wild Earth* magazine (1990-2005), co-founder of The Wildlands Project (1991), co-founder of the New Mexico Wilderness Alliance (1997), and founder of The Rewilding Institute (2003). In these capacities, Dave has coined the phrases and articulated the concepts behind Earth First!, No Compromise in Defense of Mother Earth, Rewilding, and Born to Rewild. He has officiated the marriage between wildlands advocacy and conservation biology. He has empowered the conservation community to think BIG, to strive to protect and restore the whole biotic community, not settle for preserving a few remaining scraps.

Among Dave Foreman's many outstanding conservation accomplishments are getting big additions to the Gila and other Wilderness Areas, blocking numerous timber sales in National Forests, blockading logging roads into various old-growth forests, forcing the Forest Service to re-do its inadequate Roadless Area Review and Evaluation, serving as lead author on several wildlands network designs, co-founding *Wild Earth* magazine, and getting rewilding adopted as a fundamental goal in conservation. Dave received the 1996 Paul Petzoldt Award for Excellence in Wilderness Education and was recognized by Audubon Magazine in 1998 as one of the 20th century's most important conservation leaders.

Dave has shared his visionary ideas on big connected wild places complete with top carnivores through hellfire & brimstone public sermons and through his books. Dave's books include such landmarks as *The Big Outside* (the first roadless areas inventory since Bob Marshall's a half century earlier), *Confessions of an Eco-Warrior, Rewilding North America, Man Swarm,* and *The Great Conservation Divide* (all available through rewilding.org).

Dr. Richard Grossman has been concerned about human overpopulation growth since 1960, and practiced OB-GYN in Durango, CO, for 40 years. Dr. Grossman writes a monthly column "Population Matters!", which long ran in the *Durango Herald* and is now often run in *Rewilding Earth*. If you would like to receive these regularly, you can contact him at: subscribe@population-matters.org (the hyphen is obligatory!).

Randy Hayes has been described in the *Wall Street Journal* as "an environmental pit bull." He is Executive Director of Foundation Earth, an organization fostering the big rethink from the ground up to help protect the planet's life support systems. Hayes, a former filmmaker, then founder of Rainforest Action Network, is a veteran of many high-visibility corporate accountability campaigns and has advocated for biocentric worldviews and Indigenous peoples throughout the world.

Jerry Jenkins is a biologist, writer, and photographer who directs the Northern Forest Atlas Project. He is a former staff scientist with the Wildlife Conservation Society Adirondack Program. He was trained in physics and philosophy, and has fifty years of field experience as a botanist and ecologist in the Northern Forest. He is the author of *The Adirondack Atlas, Acid Rain in the Adirondacks, Protecting Biodiversity on Conservation Easements,* and *Climate Change in the Adirondacks*. He has received, among others, the Harold K. Hochschild award from the Adirondack Museum and the W.S. Cooper award from the Ecological Society of America.

Roger Kaye came to Alaska in the mid-1970s, where he spent the summer working at Camp Denali, a wilderness, eco-tourism lodge located 90 miles inside Denali National Park. He went on to attend the University of Alaska Fairbanks, and he eventually earned a Ph.D. there in 2009. Roger has spent more than 30 years serving the public lands in Alaska. He spent a year with the Alaska Department of Fish and Game, following that with work at the US Fish and Wildlife Service as a Wilderness Specialist and pilot. Currently, he is a Wilderness Specialist and pilot for the Arctic National Wildlife Refuge, stationed in Fairbanks, Alaska. Roger played a significant role in shaping the Wilderness Stewardship Policy of the USFWS, has contributed to countless management plans, and is the author of *Last Great Wilderness: The Campaign to Establish the Arctic National Wildlife Refuge*. Roger also has taught wilderness management and environmental psychology at the University of Alaska Fairbanks, and conducted numerous oral history interviews that are housed with the US Fish and Wildlife Service and at the Alaska and Polar Regions Collections and Archives at Elmer E. Rasmsuon Library, University of Alaska Fairbanks.

Steven Kellogg (See "About the Cover Artist")

Andy Kerr is the Czar of The Larch Company and consults on environmental and conservation issues. The Larch Company is a for-profit non-membership conservation organization that represents the interests of humans yet born and species that cannot talk. He is best known for his two decades with Oregon Wild (then Oregon Natural Resources Council), the organization that brought you the northern spotted owl. Kerr began his conservation career during the Ford Administration. At last count, Kerr had been closely involved in with the establishment or expansion of 46 Wilderness Areas and 47 Wild and Scenic Rivers, 13 congressionally legislated special management areas, 15 Oregon Scenic Waterways, and one proclaimed national monument (later expanded). He has testified multiple times before congressional committees.

Gary Lawless is a poet, bioregional advocate, and co-founder of Gulf of Maine Books, in Brunswick, Maine. He and his wife Beth Leonard care-take the old farm of Henry Beston & Elizabeth Coatsworth (both acclaimed authors of the mid-20th century), near Damariscotta Lake. Gary's score of poetry collections includes *Poems for the Wild Earth* and *Caribou Planet*. His new book of poems is *How the Stones Came to Venice*, and his poetry blog is mygrations.blogspot.com. Gary was one of the poetry editors for the late great journal *Wild Earth*.

Jon Leibowitz is Executive Director of Northeast Wilderness Trust—the only land trust in the northeastern United States focused exclusively on protecting forever-wild landscapes. He has worked in the private land conservation field since graduating from Vermont Law School in 2011 with a Juris Doctor and Masters in Environmental Law and Policy. Before joining Northeast Wilderness Trust, Jon was the Executive Director of Montezuma Land Conservancy, where he worked to conserve farms, ranches, and landscapes of pinion and juniper, ponderosa, and sage right on the edge of the Colorado Plateau, in Cortez, Colorado. Jon serves on the Board of Vermont Parks Forever in addition to being part of the Rewilding Leadership Counsel. He lives on the outskirts of Montpelier, Vermont, with his family.

Rob Leverett, son of the East's preeminent old-growth sleuth Bob Leverett, carries on the family tradition of finding and protecting big old trees. Rob is rooted in Native American traditions, and he teaches flint-napping as well as exploring and sketching old-growth forests. Rob lives and rambles in New York's Adirondack Park, where old-growth forest still comprises much of the landscape.

Paula MacKay is a freelance writer, researcher, and field biologist who has studied wild predators for the past two decades. Paula served as managing editor for *Noninvasive Survey Methods for Carnivores* (Island Press, 2008) and earned an MFA in creative writing from Pacific Lutheran University in 2015. She has written for numerous conservation groups, books, and magazines. Paula was on the editorial team of the predecessor to *Rewilding Earth*, *Wild Earth* magazine. She lives with her biologist husband Robert Long and their dog Alder on Bainbridge Island, Washington. Visit Paula's website at paulamackay.com.

Angela Manno has been a professional artist for the past 40 years. Her virtuosity in a number of painstaking art forms both east and west, ancient and contemporary, put her in a class by herself. Her media include encaustic, batik, plein air pastel landscapes and traditional and contemporary icons in egg tempera and gold leaf on wood. Her mixed media work including photography, fiber and acrylic, is a synthesis of diverse cultural sensibilities symbolizing unity in diversity—an urgent message for our time. Angela Manno's art has been featured in 20 solo and over 80 group exhibitions in distinguished venues in North America and Europe. In 1988, Manno was commissioned by NASA to commemorate the U.S. return to space flight with the launch of *Discovery*, the first after the *Challenger* accident. In 2000, her one-woman traveling art exhibition *Conscious Evolution: The World At One* became part of the permanent fine art collection of the Smithsonian

Institution's National Air & Space Museum. Manno has taught and lectured widely on her work through university and museum programs including Parsons School of Design in New York. Her artwork has been noted in numerous publications.

Larry Master is a conservation biologist, a zoologist, and, in his retirement, a conservation photographer. He has been photographing wildlife and natural history subjects for more than 60 years. After doctoral and post-doctoral studies at the University of Michigan, Larry spent 20 years with The Nature Conservancy (TNC) and 6 years with NatureServe, most of that time as their Chief Zoologist. NatureServe is an offshoot of the Conservancy and is the umbrella organization for the network of natural heritage programs and conservation data centers in every U.S. state and Canadian province as well as in many Latin American countries. Larry started several of these programs (e.g., MI, NH, VT) and also oversaw the development of TNC's and NatureServe's central zoological databases and revisions to the Network's Conservation Status Assessment methodology. Larry co-authored *Rivers of Life: Critical Watersheds for Protecting Freshwater Biodiversity*. He has also authored numerous other publications and chapters in several books (e.g., *Precious Heritage, Our Living Resources*). In his retirement he serves on boards of the Adirondack Explorer, the Ausable River Association, and the Northern Forest Atlas Foundation, as well as on the Center for Ecostudies Science Advisory Council, The Biodiversity Conservancy's Advisory Board, NatureServe's Strategic Advisors Council, and the American Society of Mammalogists' Mammal Images Library. Larry resides in Keene, NY and West Cornwall, CT.

Tim McNulty is a poet, essayist, and nature writer based on Washington's Olympic Peninsula. He is the author of ten poetry books and eleven books of natural history. Tim has received the Washington State Book Award and the National Outdoor Book Award, among other honors.

Tim's newest book of poems, *Ascendance*, is published by Pleasure Boat Studio. His natural history books include *Olympic National Park: A Natural History*, and *Washington's Mount Rainier National Park*. His work has been translated into German, Chinese, and Japanese. Tim lives with his wife in the foothills of the Olympic Mountains.

Brad Meiklejohn served until his recent semi-retirement as Alaska State Director for The Conservation Fund, where he has worked since 1994. Brad has directed conservation projects protecting over 300,000 acres of wild land in Alaska, New Hampshire, and Nevada. Brad is also a co-founder of the American Packrafting Association, with over 2,000 members in 30 countries. Brad is a conservationist, birder, and wilderness explorer and has completed packraft expeditions on 6 continents. Brad served as Associate Director for the Utah Avalanche Center during the 1980s, and later as President of the Patagonia Land Trust. Brad is a past board director of The Murie Center and the Alaska Avalanche School.

Patty Meriam grew up in Nyack, NY and received a BA from Boston College in Art History/PreMed where she concentrated on Dutch 17th Century art and studied composition, style, theory, and cultural influence. She received an MS in Historic Preservation from Columbia University's College of Architecture, Planning, and Preservation with a concentration in materials conservation. Patty has been accepted into such artist societies as the Allied Artists of America, Oil Painters of America, Northern Vermont Artist Association, and the Catherine Lorillard Wolfe Art Club in Manhattan, The Vermont Academy of Arts and Science, Bryan Memorial Gallery, The National Art League, and the National Association of Women Artists. She now lives in Barre, Vermont, where she is board chairperson of the Vermont Granite Museum and Stone Arts School and past chair of the Barre Opera House. Patty's medium is oil paint and her website is PLMeriam.com, "Celebrating the strength of art to bring attention to nature's beauty and fragility."

John Miles grew up in New Hampshire and graduated from Dartmouth College with a degree in anthropology. He earned an MA at the University of Oregon in Recreation and Park Management and a PhD in Environmental Studies and Education at the Union Institute. While at Dartmouth, John attended a talk by David Brower, then Executive Director of the Sierra Club, who spoke about the threat of dams to Grand Canyon National Park. Inspired by Brower's talk and books, such as Stewart Udall's *The Quiet Crisis*, John was hooked.

ABOUT THE CONTRIBUTORS

After grad school he landed in Bellingham, Washington, where he became involved in his first conservation issue, the establishment of North Cascades National Park. At Western Washington University, John was in on the founding of Huxley College of Environmental Studies, where he taught environmental education, history, ethics, and literature, and ultimately served as dean of the College. He taught at Huxley for 44 years, climbing and hiking all over the West, especially in the North Cascades, for research and recreation. Author and editor of several books, including *Guardians of the Parks, Koma Kulshan*, and *Wilderness in National Parks*, John served on the board of the National Parks Conservation Association and the Washington Forest Practices Board, and he helped found and build the North Cascades Institute.

Retired now and living with his wife Susan near Taos, New Mexico, he continues to work on national parks, wilderness, and rewilding the earth, and he hikes, bikes, and skis whenever possible. He contributes to the nationalparkstraveler.org, as well as *Rewilding Earth*, and is writing a history of the North Cascades Institute.

Anabella Miller is a twenty-one year-old student in ecology at New Mexico Highlands University. She is studying conservation with an interest in herps, particularly boreal toads. She runs cross-country, indoor distance, and outdoor steeplechase at NMHU.

Brian J. Miller received a PhD from the University of Wyoming in behavioral ecology and conservation of black-footed ferrets and was then awarded a Smithsonian Institution Fellowship at their Conservation and Research Center. Brian worked on black-footed ferret conservation for a decade, then lived in Mexico for five years beginning an ongoing research project on jaguars and pumas in the dry tropical forest of Jalisco, Mexico. After seven years as a Coordinator of Conservation and Research at the Denver Zoological Foundation, Brian accepted a position to develop conservation and education programs at the Wind River Foundation. His main research interest concerns the role of highly interactive species (keystones) in regulating ecosystem processes and how to improve protection for those species when designing reserves. He has published 100 scientific articles, seven books, and has been on the board of five conservation organizations. He has helped start two protected areas, one of which is Rio Mora NWR. In 2009 he was given the Denver Zoo's Annual Conservation Award.

Susan Morgan studied Southwest archaeology and holds degrees in English and environmental studies. In 1967 she began as Director of Education for The Wilderness Society where she worked for over ten years and has subsequently worked in education and outreach positions with wilderness, wildlands, and public lands conservation organizations. She is currently president of The Rewilding Institute and senior editor of *Rewilding Earth*.

David Moskowitz works as a biologist, photographer, and outdoor educator. He is the author of two books, *Wildlife of the Pacific Northwest* and *Wolves in the Land of Salmon*. He has contributed to a wide variety of wildlife studies in western North America, focusing on using tracking and other non-invasive methods to study wildlife ecology and promote conservation. David's extensive experience includes training mountaineering instructors for Outward Bound, leading wilderness expeditions throughout the western United States and in Alaska, teaching natural history seminars, and as the lead instructor for wildlife programs at Wilderness Awareness School. He lives in Winthrop, Washington.

Susie O'Keeffe lives at the headwaters of the Sheepscot River in Montville, Maine. She is an independent writer and teacher and a Research Associate at the College of the Atlantic. Susie holds a Master's of Science with distinction in Environmental Management from Oxford University, England. Her writing has appeared in *Spring: A Journal of Archetype and Culture, Biological Conservation, Phylogeny*, the *Spoon River Poetry Review*, and *The Maine Review*. In addition to writing poetry and teaching, Susie is an organic gardener, and a member of our Rewilding Leadership Counsel. She is on the board of the Northeast Wilderness Trust and Upstream Watch.

David R. Parsons, MS, received his Bachelor of Science degree in Fisheries and Wildlife Biology from Iowa State University and his Master of Science degree in Wildlife

Ecology from Oregon State University. Dave is retired from the U.S. Fish and Wildlife Service where from 1990-1999 he led the USFWS's effort to reintroduce the endangered Mexican gray wolf to the American Southwest.

Dave's interests include the ecology and conservation of large carnivores, protection and conservation of biodiversity, and wildlands conservation at scales that fully support ecological and evolutionary processes. He is the Carnivore Conservation Biologist for The Rewilding Institute, a member of the Science Advisory Board of Project Coyote, a former member and chairman of the Board of Directors of the New Mexico Wilderness Alliance, and a former graduate advisor in the Environmental Studies master's degree program at Prescott College. Dave serves as a science and policy advisor for organizations and coalitions advocating for wolf recovery and landscape-scale conservation in the Southwest.

In 2001, Dave received the New Mexico Chapter of The Wildlife Society's annual "Professional Award." In 2007 at the North American Wolf Conference, Dave received the "Alpha Award" for his "outstanding professional achievement and leadership toward the recovery of Mexican wolves." In 2008 Dave received the "Outstanding Conservation Leadership Award" from the Wilburforce Foundation and the "Mike Seidman Memorial Award" from the Sky Island Alliance for his conservation achievements.

Dave enjoys wildlife viewing, wilderness adventures, and dancing. He lives in Albuquerque, NM, with his wife, Noralyn.

Shelby Perry, Stewardship Director for Northeast Wilderness Trust, received her master's degree from the University of Vermont's field naturalist program, and holds a bachelors in environmental engineering from Rensselaer Polytechnic Institute. A Vermont native, she has also lived in the Adirondacks, California, the Caribbean, Wyoming, and West Africa, where she served a term in the US Peace Corps. In her free time Shelby enjoys hiking far away from trails, swimming in mountain streams, and identifying mysterious plants, fungi, and slime molds.

Stuart Pimm holds the Doris Duke Chair of Conservation at the Nicholas School of the Environment, Duke University. He is also the President of Saving Nature, a non-profit that raises money for partners in biodiverse-rich countries to reforest degraded habitats and restore connections between isolated forest fragments.

Robert Michael Pyle is a lepidopterist and a professional writer who has published twelve books and hundreds of papers, essays, stories and poems. His acclaimed 1987 book *Wintergreen* describing the devastation caused by unrestrained logging in Washington's Willapa Hills near his adopted home was the winner of the 1987 John Burroughs Medal for Distinguished Nature Writing. His recent books include *Where Bigfoot Walks: Crossing the Dark Divide*, *Wintergreen: Rambles in a Ravaged Land*, and *Sky Time in Gray's River: Living for Keeps in a Forgotten Place*. He won the 2007 National Outdoor Book Award. In 2011, he won the Washington State Book Award in the biography/memoir category for his most recent work *The Mariposa Road: The First Butterfly Big Year*.

David T. Schwartz is the Mary Frances Williams Professor of Humanities, and Professor of Philosophy, at Randolph College in Lynchburg, VA. His scholarly research is in the field of "public philosophy," which applies philosophical methods to the understanding of significant public issues. Before focusing on rewilding, Schwartz wrote books on the ethics of consumer choice (*Consuming Choices: Ethics in a Global Consumer Age*) and government support for the arts (*Art, Education, and the Democratic Commitment*). At Randolph College, his courses include Ethics and Public Life, Bioethics, Environmental Philosophy, and Philosophy of Art. In 2017, Schwartz held the Garrey Carruthers Endowed Chair in Honors at the University of New Mexico, where he taught a course on rewilding.

Chris Spatz, inspired by Dave Foreman announcing the birth of Earth First! on *The Today Show* in the early '80s, procured a copy of *Eco Defense* and began his peripatetic pursuits as an eco-gadfly. Yanking surveying stakes, canvassing for Greenpeace in Boston, performing with Trenton, NJ's Klark Kent eco-street theater troupe, directing the Gunks' Climbers Coalition, and advocating for puma recovery as president of the Cougar Rewilding Foundation were some of his ventures. He lives and writes from the Shawangunks in southern New York State.

About the Contributors

Janice St. Marie paints and draws representational landscapes. She is based in Santa Fe, New Mexico and in addition to being an acclaimed artist, has a successful career in graphic design She lives in the woods with her husband, Joe, Bella the dog, and Chica the cat.

"The drama of sky and earth, light and shadow entrances me. Living in New Mexico has provided me with an abundance of beautiful destinations for landscape painting. Returning to the same location allows me to explore the many variations of form and rhythms that the scene has to offer. I combine my love of travel with my love of art and have been fortunate to paint in Spain, Italy, Ireland, and Sri Lanka, among other places. I paint *en plein air* as well as in the studio, with pen and ink, watercolor, pencil, and acrylic, but I have always loved pastels and they are my primary medium."

Janice is a member of the Pastel Society of America, the Plein Air Painters of New Mexico, and a Signature Member of the Pastel Society of New Mexico. She is represented in the Abiquiu Inn, Abiquiu, and Cerrillos Station, Cerrillos, New Mexico.

Andrew Thoms grew up in rural upstate New York State. After studying Environmental Sciences at SUNY Plattsburgh, he worked for ten years in Latin America as an environmental specialist in international development projects. Most of his projects focused on the interface between the sustainable use of natural resources and the conservation of tropical biodiversity. One of his favorite jobs was developing and integrating new techniques for cultivating coffee in an environmentally sustainable way on a Guatemalan coffee farm that he managed for a few years. Andrew received a Master's degree in Conservation Biology and Sustainable Development at the University of Wisconsin where he concentrated his studies on conservation and economics. Andrew enjoys being outdoors hunting, birdwatching, fishing, and exploring.

Katie Tozier, of KIT West Designs, grew up north of Yosemite National Park in California, where her parents taught her to canoe, camp, and explore the outdoors. Throughout her youth, Katie's family visited National Parks in the Western US and Canada, motivating her to pursue her Bachelor's of Science in Environmental Science and Management from UC Davis. During her summers home from college, Katie worked for the US Forest Service on the Stanislaus National Forest. Afterward, she went on to earn her Master's in Education focused on Environmental Education from Western Washington University and the North Cascades Institute. Her time in the northwest taught her to slow down and appreciate our intricate and personal connections to the natural world. Katie has fond memories of working seasonally in North Cascades and Mesa Verde National Parks as an Interpreter. Since 2013 she has enjoyed working in Grand Teton National Park as an Educator, Interpreter, and now Secretary to the Superintendent's Office. Despite the overwhelming challenges posed by global climate change, Katie finds hope in the power of environmental education and intends to help foster positive environmental stewardship and responsible resource use in the years to come. Currently, Katie enjoys watercoloring, watching good movies, and living in Wilson, WY with her partner, Colby.

Sophi Veltrop is the Outreach Coordinator for the Northeast Wilderness Trust. She comes to NWT with a background in land conservation, communications, and outdoor and environmental education. She received her B.S. in Environmental Science in 2013, and has since worked at the Vermont Land Trust, Yestermorrow Design/Build School, and Earthwalk Vermont, where she now serves on the Board of Directors. Sophi is committed to helping create a world where all species have the chance to survive, thrive, and evolve. Outside of the work week, she can be found roaming forests and rivers, tending an ever-expanding garden, and cultivating community and creative practice.

Kevin Webb is currently pursuing a master's degree in Sustainability Science at Columbia University in New York City. A recent transplant, Kevin grew up in the San Francisco Bay Area, where he worked as an early-stage software investor for the better part of a decade. Kevin's interests include natural history, biology, comedy, making things, and spending as much time as possible with his dog Chewie.

ABOUT THE CONTRIBUTORS

Saul Weisberg is executive director and co-founder of North Cascades Institute. Saul is an ecologist, naturalist, and writer who has explored the mountains and rivers of the Pacific Northwest for more than 30 years. Saul worked throughout the Northwest as a field biologist, fire lookout, commercial fisherman and National Park Service climbing ranger before starting the Institute in 1986. He authored *From the Mountains to the Sea, North Cascades: The Story behind the Scenery, Teaching for Wilderness,* and *Living with Mountains*. Saul serves on the boards of directors of the Association of Nature Center Administrators, the Natural History Network, and the Environmental Education Association of Washington. He is adjunct faculty at Huxley College of the Environment at Western Washington University. Saul and his family live near the shores of the Salish Sea in Bellingham, Washington.

Christopher R. Wilson is a conservation scientist, wildlife ecologist, and president of Conservation Ecology LLC. Since the late 1990s, Chris has led biological inventories and conservation planning efforts for private and corporate landowners, land conservancies, and philanthropists around the country, and has participated in hundreds of conservation easement land protection projects. Before founding Conservation Ecology LLC, Chris served as the first Conservation Biologist for North American Land Trust, Director of Stewardship and Science for Sweet Water Trust (a wildlands grant-making philanthropy working in northern New England), Director of Conservation Science for the Santa Lucia Conservancy (Carmel, CA), and Director of Conservation Science for wildlands philanthropist Tim Sweeney. Chris holds a B.A.&Sc in Conservation Biology and Wildlife Ecology from Evergreen State College and an M.Sc in Biology from Appalachian State University. He is author of the book *Documenting and Protecting Biodiversity on Land Trust Projects: an introduction and practical guide*, published by the Land Trust Alliance.

Brendan Wiltse is a conservation and nature photographer based in New York's Adirondack Park. His work focuses on connecting people to wild places with the intention of building enthusiasm for supporting wildlands conservation. Brendan is also the Vice President of The Waterman Fund which is dedicated to preserving the spirit of wildness in the Northeast. He holds a Ph.D. in biology from Queen's University and is the Science & Stewardship Director for the Ausable River Association. Brendan's academic focus is on understanding the effects of road salt and climate change on Adirondack lakes and conserving wild brook trout populations.

George Wuerthner is an ecologist, former river ranger for the Alaska BLM and backcountry ranger in the Gates of the Arctic NP in Alaska. He has visited more than 400 designated Wilderness Areas and approximately 200 National Park units. A prolific author, he has published 38 books including such titles as *California Wilderness Areas, Alaska Mountain Ranges, Nevada Mountain Ranges, Montana's Magnificent Wilderness, Forever Wild: The Adirondacks, Welfare Ranching-the subsidized destruction of the American West, Yellowstone: A Visitor's Companion, Protecting the Wild: Parks and Wilderness–Foundation for Conservation,* and *Wildfire; A Century of Failed Forest Policy*.

About The Rewilding Institute and *Rewilding Earth*

The Rewilding Institute (TRI) is a wild bunch of fiercely dedicated conservation activists and scientists who promote and employ strategies to protect, restore, and reconnect wild places and creatures at all scales, across North America and beyond. *Rewilding Earth* is our online publication, and our annual print anthology is comprised of many of its best articles and art.

Rewilding Earth is quickly growing into the publication of record for rewilding projects far and wide, and will soon include a Rewilding Directory, briefly describing and giving contact information for hundreds of projects around the world. We are volunteer-led and reader-supported, so cannot pay for articles or art, but we welcome contributions, literary, artistic, and financial. We especially want to share species recovery and wildways protection success stories and lessons therefrom.

Along with our publications, The Rewilding Institute has several focal on-ground campaigns. These initiatives we help lead (as outlined in parts of this book), even while lending our expertise—soon largely through our nascent Rewilding Leadership Council—to Continental Wildways and species recovery efforts farther afield.

Lobo Recovery – Our Carnivore Conservation Biologist Dave Parsons oversaw the original reintroduction of Mexican wolves into the wilds of southern New Mexico and Arizona as a biologist with the US Fish & Wildlife Service. Dave now leads TRI's advocacy and education work on behalf of Mexican wolves, in partnership with other members of the Mexican Wolf Coalition. Dave Parsons also serves as advisor to Project Coyote; and we assist that small but mighty group in its efforts to end persecution of predators and ban wildlife-killing contests. We also join efforts with Western Wildlife Conservancy and other good groups to reform state wildlife governance.

Mogollon Wildway – Critical to the long-term prosperity of Lobos and other wide-ranging animals of the Southwest is better protection of the wildlife corridor linking the Gila wildlands complex in southwest New Mexico with the Grand Canyon wildlands complex in northern Arizona. We advocate for the Mogollon Wildway in part by scouting and working with conservation and trail partners to chart a Lobo National Scenic Trail, to popularize the wildlife corridor. Together with groups like New Mexico Wilderness Coalition, Wildlands Network, and Wild Arizona, we push for stronger protections of National Forests and other public lands in Mogollon Wildway.

Puma Recovery for Eastern Wildways – Using ecological, ethical, health, and aesthetic arguments, we promote restoration of the missing top carnivores of the East, including puma and gray and red wolves. Currently, we focus on the puma, or cougar, in concert with Cougar Rewilding Foundation and other carnivore advocacy groups, because its absence means unnaturally high deer numbers and widespread over-browsing of eastern deciduous forests and its reintroduction ought to be achievable in the near term. Many relatively wild parts of the Southeast Coastal Plain, Appalachians, and Adirondacks have good habitat and abundant prey for pumas, but many biologists think it unlikely that pumas will recolonize the East in functional numbers any time soon and that active reintroduction needs to be considered. As with wolves in the West, puma recovery in the East will depend upon building strong public support and reforming state wildlife governance.

Adirondack Wildways – TRI is part of the Eastern Wildway Network formed by Wildlands Network (and informed by Dave Foreman's book *Rewilding North America* and John Davis's book *Big, Wild, and Connected: Scouting an Eastern Wildway from Florida to Quebec*). We pay extra attention to areas we've explored extensively, particularly within New York's great Adirondack Park and habitat connections to surrounding wildlands. Most especially, we work with Northeast Wilderness Trust, Champlain Area Trails, Adirondack Land Trust, Eddy Foundation, and other partners to protect Split Rock Wildway, linking Lake Champlain and its valley with the Adirondack High Peaks. In Split Rock Wildway, we will soon explore with The American Chestnut Foundation the potential for planting disease-resistant American Chestnuts in old fields, as well as native oaks and hickories and other food-rich species that may thrive in a warming climate and may help keep forests resilient in a century of climate chaos. We also work for the Algonquin Park (Ontario) to Adirondack Park wildway, with the A2A collaborative. For the larger Eastern Wildways effort, part of our contribution will be promoting efforts to restore American eel and other diadromous fish populations.

Population – Society cannot avert the overarching crisis of our time—extinction—or the related climate crisis without addressing the fundamental driver of biodiversity loss and greenhouse gas accumulation: too many people consuming too many resources. TRI acknowledges that we humans are billions too many already; and we support compassionate, fair, and effective means of achieving population reduction to ecologically sustainable numbers. We believe that supporting small families, education and empowerment of girls and women, and providing universal access to safe family planning methods, ought to be high priorities for all conservation, environmental, social justice, and peace groups.

Needless to say, we welcome your support for this work of restoring a wild Earth.

Donations can be made online (**www.rewilding.org**) or checks mailed to:

The Rewilding Institute
P.O. Box 13768
Albuquerque, NM 87192

If you'd like to write an article, please contact John Davis at **hemlockrockconservation@gmail.com** or Susan Morgan at **susancoyote@icloud.com**. If you'd like to do a podcast with us, please contact Jack Humphrey at **jdh358@gmail.com**.

Rewilding Earth Website Post Index

Below is an index showing all articles that were published on the Rewilding Earth website through 2019. Articles are listed by the article title and are within website category/plate sections in order of date published. Interested readers will be able to access any articles here by entering either the author's name or the article name in SEARCH near the top right of the main website page at rewilding.org.

Around the Campfire

Around the Campfire, #80, "Wild Things for their own Sake," by Dave Foreman, adapted from his chapter "Five Feathers for the Cannot Club" in Peter H. Kahn, Jr., and Patricia H. Hasbach, eds., *The Rediscovery of the Wild* (MIT Press, Cambridge, MA, 2013), in which he discusses origins of the word "wildlife" and how *H. Sapiens* has not historically been a good neighbor. (11.5.19), Plate: Around the Campfire.

Around the Campfire, Part II, #79, "Whence the Antiquities Act," by Dave Foreman, who discusses how and why Civil War battlefields, National Parks, Forest Reserves (later National Forests), and the Casa Grande Ruin Reservation were set up. He then summarizes the visionary 1900 Lacey Antiquities Act and the campaign to get it passed. (5.29.19), Plate: Around the Campfire.

Around the Campfire, Part 1, #78, "Whence the Antiquities Act," by Dave Foreman, where he describes how "The Antiquities Act and the National Monuments created under its authority came out of the backwater territory of New Mexico in 1900." He summarizes the end of the Frontier, the rise of archaeology, and the rise of conservation leaders and who they are, wrapping up the first part of this history with a description of the General Land Office. (3.22.19), Plate: Around the Campfire.

Stoking the Campfire, by John Davis, sending an inspiring note to take heart in these dark times, that our brilliant but sometimes curmudgeonly leader is convalescing, and that the Campfire is burning again. John also included a word about *Rewilding Earth* and the core team of rewilding editors and activists. (1.23.19), Plate: Around the Campfire.

Embers from the Campfire

Embers #1, Quitobaquito, by Dave Foreman writing about his love of Quitobaquito and Organ Pipe Cactus NM and the threats they now face from the Trump wall, which would split the Monument in half and prevent north-south migration. (9.19.19), Plate: Around the Campfire, Embers.

Images with Captions (posted in "Around the Campfire")

Tuning up for a night of hunting, © Dave Parsons, "After a long nap in the sun, these coyotes are tuning up for a night of hunting. They're relatively safe here in the in the Bosque del Apache National Wildlife Refuge in New Mexico, one of the states where Project Coyote has succeeded in passing legislation to ban unscientific and unethical wildlife killing contests. © Dave Parsons, The Rewilding Institute and Project Coyote." (12.15.19), Link: Wildlife Defense.

Wildway Rambles

Adirondack Wildways Update, by John Davis, who writes that "Connectivity work continues in New York's Adirondack Park and beyond. Priority areas and species include Split Rock Wildway, the Algonquin to Adirondack axis (A2A), Puma reintroduction, dam removal for native fish, and American Chestnut replanting." (5.20.19), Plate: Wildway Rambles.

Action Center

Tongass National Forest Sample Letter, by Kim Crumbo, to accompany the Tongass N.F. alert. (12.14.19), Plate: Action Center.

World Scientist Warning of a Climate Emergency, by William J. Ripple, Christopher Wolf, Thomas M. Newsome, Phoebe Barnard, and William R. Moomaw. Their paper is now in *BioScience* magazine. They write that "In this paper, we present a suite of graphical vital signs of climate change over the last 40 years. Results show greenhouse gas emissions are still rising, with increasingly damaging effects. With few exceptions, we are largely failing to address this predicament. The climate crisis has arrived and is accelerating faster than many scientists expected." (12.11,19), Plate: Action Center.

Support the Tongass National Forest, Action Alert from Sitka Conservation Society, calls for comments to support the Alaska Roadless Rule before midnight, December 17. (12.4.19), Plate: Action Center.

Tongass National Forest Targeted!, Action Alert from Great Old Broads for Wilderness, calling for comments by December 16, 2019, urging the USFS to take the "No Action Alternative" on the proposed Alaska Roadless Rule to keep Roadless Rule protections intact for the Tongass National Forest. (11.27.19), Plate: Action Center.

***Sea of Shadows* has been nominated for Four Critics' Choice Awards**, an announcement from Sea Shepherd. (10.18.19), Plate: Action Center & Greenfire Bulletins.

Today is the Youth Climate Strike!, by Rewilding Earth, calling attention to the bold action taken by young people to address climate change and support the Green New Deal. (9.20.19), Plate: Action Center.

Tongass National Forest Alert, by Andrew Thoms, executive director of the Sitka Conservation Society, who writes that long the target of logging companies, the Tongass National Forest occupies almost the entire Southeast Alaska Panhandle. The Tongass, one of the few temperate rainforests left on Earth that has not been lost because of human actions, is the largest National Forest is the country. It is comprised of 176 million acres of rugged mountains, glaciers, ice-fields, wetlands and estuaries, lakes and rivers, and beautiful moss-laden forests with Sitka Spruce, Western Hemlock, and Red and Yellow Cedar trees. (9.14.19), Plate: Action Center.

Interior Finalizes Trump Extinction Plan, a repost from the Endangered Species Coalition, Author: Corry Westbrook, Senior Grassroots and Policy Advisor. Westbrook writes the Trump Administration and former Secretary of the Department of Interior, Ryan Zinke, are corrupt, riddled with conflicts-of-interest and under multiple-investigations. This Administration has just published final Endangered Species Act regulations that will undermine protections for our most imperiled wildlife. They will weaken biodiversity for decades and may drive species to extinction. (8.19.19), Plate: Action Center.

Will you join us in defending the Arctic Refuge?, by Brad Meiklejohn, who writes an inspiring account of his meeting in Washington, DC, with Alaska adventurers, Luc Mehl, and Roman Dial to tell Congress why they care so deeply about the Refuge and ask for support for HR 1146, the Arctic Cultural and Coastal Plain Protection Act. (5.23.19), Action Center.

Wildlife Corridors Conservation Act of 2019 to be released today, alert from Susan Holmes, Wildlands Network, announcing May 16 release in the House and Senate with multiple sponsors and asking readers to take action. Also included is a media kit from Gabby Saunders. Plate: Action Center, (5.16.19), Plate: Action Center.

Northern Rockies Ecosystem Protection Act is introduced into Congress, by George Wuerthner, who writes that NREPA would protect all the remaining roadless lands in the Northern Rockies by designation under the 1964 Wilderness Act, the "Gold Standard" for land protection, and that readers should express their support to their legislators. (4.4.19), Plate: Action Center.

Rio Grande National Forest Again Sides with Developer in Wolf Creek Access Issue, from Rocky Mountain Wild alerting readers that RGNF Supervisor Dan

Dallas signed a Final Record of Decision that could result in an easement to facilitate construction of the massive "Village" at Wolf Creek, circumventing a federal court ruling that invalidated prior approvals to this controversial real estate development by a Texas billionaire. (3.3.19), Plate: Action Center.

Sea Shepherd Ship's Windows Smashed and Hull Set on Fire by Poachers, alert and video from Sea Shepherd about the second attack on one of their boats in the Refuge, this time on January 31st, when the *M/V Farley Mowat* was violently attacked by over 50 assailants on board 20 high-speed boats while conducting maritime conservation patrols inside the Vaquita Refuge in the Upper Gulf of California. (2.4.19), Plate: Action Center.

Wildlife vs. Livestock in the Upper Green, by George Wuerthner, writing to alert readers of widespread damage to the landscape in the Upper Green River Grazing Allotment in the Bridger Teton National Forest, between the Gros Ventre Range and Wind River Range, one of the most important wildlife habitats outside of Yellowstone National Park. (2.3.19), Plate: Action Alert.

Support Wilderness Protection for Montana's Gallatin Range, by George Wuerthner, frequent contributor, who advocates for wilderness designation for 230,000 acres in the Gallatin, specifically the Buffalo Horn Porcupine and West Pine Creek, South Cottonwood Creek. (1.3.19), Plate: Action Alert.

Greenfire Bulletins
Sea of Shadows, an announcement by Sea Shepherd that their winner of the Sundance Audience Award for World Cinema Documentary is now in theaters. (7.13.19), Plate: Greenfire Bulletins, Rewilding Waters.

Announcing the 11th World Wilderness Congress: Advancing Nature Based Solutions for Climate and Human Livlihoods. The Congress will be held March 19-26, 2020. Wilderness Foundation Global and the WILD Foundation, in partnership with the Sanctuary Nature Foundation and the Government of Rajasthan, India, announced today a new opportunity for the public to influence and take part in a growing international movement to defend Earth's remaining wilderness. (5.29.19), Greenfire Bulletins, and added to Randy Hayes, The Cliff Edge.

Ecosulis Rewilding Tech Challenge, an opportunity from Ecosulis to enter the challenge, which has "always invested in technology"…" to provide innovative solutions to today's conservation challenges." (1.30.19), Plate: Greenfire Bulletins.

Killing Games, Wildlife in the Crosshairs, film by Project Coyote, showing in Albuquerque. (1.7.19), Plate: Greenfire Bulletins.

Population
Draft Position Statement on Overpopulation, An Invitation to Endorse, by Kim Crumbo, Rewilding Leadership Council, A complementary population position statement to accompany The Rewilding Institute Position on Population. Kim writes: "Human overpopulation presents an existential threat to the diversity of life. Wildlands conservation groups exist to protect habitats so that life in all its diversity can thrive." He offers suggestions that conservationists can do to contribute to a permanent resolution of the problem and also lead to a brief position statement for wildlands conservation groups to consider adapting and endorsing for their own groups. (12.22.19), Plate: Population.

8 Billion Angels, the trailer on Vimeo for his forthcoming film, by Terry Spahr, who features the overpopulation crisis. (6.5.19), Population.

The cover of a book that made a big difference: *Respect The Population Bomb*, by George Grossman, MD, discusses that *The Bomb* made a big difference in the 1960s and 1970s, then the US drifted back into complacency, but global climate change is making us realize the cost of that complacency. (5.31.19), Population.

The Cliff Edge: Generating Political Will for the Required Level of Change, by Randy Hayes, writes that "some of us, from many walks of life, get the urgency of the impending ecological collapse. We know as well that major change must happen now and that we must build a new way of living on this planet. We also know that there isn't the political will in society to do what needs to be done." In order to "generate greater political will we start by sharing our message with many. Demand attention to this on all fronts. Provide a comprehensive plan to get people started." (5.8.19), Plate: Population.

Envisioning Protected Area Networks & Local Economies in the Bioregional Web of Life, by Randy Hayes, who writes, "In this late stage of capitalism, it is critical to achieve ecologically sustainable economic systems. Such a shift will require more local, regional, and continental self-reliance. Most food and energy you use should come from your part of the planet – and they can! Now is the time for a new era of low-impact lifestyles, smaller numbers, and a new economic model characterized by zero waste, closed-loop, sustainable production and consumption systems." (4.18.19), Plate: Population.

Combat Overpopulation Denial, by Dick Grossman. This originally appeared in his blog, where Dr. Grossman writes of *Population Matters, Empty Planet: The Shock of Global Population Decline* that our "global pie is fixed in size and that "nowhere do authors compare the resources we humans are using with what is available. (4.2.19), Plate: Population.

Rewilding Bookstore
The Wisdom of Bears and the Perfidy of Bureaucracy, by Barrie Gilbert, Reviewed by Stephen Stringham. He writes that one of the first cognitive ethologists to study bears was Barrie Gilbert, as detailed in his 2019 memoir *One of Us: A Biologist's Walk Among Bears*. It recounts his experiences researching black and grizzly bears in Yosemite, Yellowstone and Katmai National Parks, beginning in the 1970's when a grizzly tore off half his face. (12.7.19), Plate: Rewilding Bookstore.

Re-Bisoning the West: Restoring an American Icon to the Landscape, by Kurt Repanshek, reviewed by John Miles. Kurt has written a book that should encourage and give hope to all who are interested in rewilding North America. He offers his reasons for optimism and that of experts. He reviews paleontological evidence of early bison, how they survived the late Pleistocene, early human idolization and reliance, the Great Slaughter, and how *Bison bison* were unexpectedly able to survive as a species. (10.23.19), Plate: Rewilding Bookstore

To Think Like a Mountain: Environmental Challenges in the American West, by Niels Sparre Nokkentved, book review by John Miles. Nokkentved who has covered environmental issues in the west for over four decades, has documented the history of an environmental issue, explore how and why we will be better served by Leopold's metaphorical "thinking like a mountain," explain the issues' complexities and clashing values of the parties involved, and where it stood when he concluded his coverage. (10.7.19), Plate: Rewilding Bookstore.

About Submissions, by Rewilding Editors, republishing *Wild Earth* style guidelines, for nostalgia and guidance to newer contributors. (10.5.19), Plate: Rewilding Bookstore

CATRUNNERS, Chapter 3, by Ken Swift. (8.17.19), Plate: Eco-Fiction

CATRUNNERS, Chapter 2, by Ken Swift. (2.24.19), Plate: Eco-Fiction.

The Northern Forest Atlas Project, by RE editors, who have presented this profile drawn from the NFAP website, northernforestatlas.org. Field guides, plant charts, blogs, and photos from NFAP are all state-of-the-art works of biological wonder and important tools for helping build support for protecting the Northern Forest. ~ editors. (8.11.19), Plate: Rewilding Bookstore.

This Land: How Cowboys, Capitalism, and Corruption Are Ruining the American West, by Christopher Ketcham, review by John Miles. "Ketcham is an investigative journalist who digs deep into the situation of western public lands, finds a mess, and spares no one in his attribution of responsibility – mythological cowboys, cowboy culture, public land ranchers, cows; lawless anti-public land activists, especially the Mormon family of Cliven Bundy, the Church of Jesus Christ of Latter Day Saints, and Utah politicians; federal land managers, especially the BLM and Wildlife Services; collaborative environmentalists, such as The Nature Conservancy and Wilderness Society." (7.23.19), Plate: Rewilding Bookstore.

Abundant Earth: Toward an Ecological Civilization, by Eileen Crist, review by John Miles. Crist writes that what ultimately is needed is rejection of consumerism and restraint in all actions that affect the environment. She recognizes that many dimensions of the global ecological crisis are outside the consciousness of most of the world's people, ignored by media and politicians, and asks why this is so. Crist essentially speaks for a revolution of civilization. (7.10.19). Rewilding Bookstore.

Conservation Politics, The Last Anti-Colonial Battle, an Excerpt, by David Johns, writing to address a longstanding crisis, the human destruction of life on Earth, all the while recorded by scientists and others that included a 52% loss of vertebrates over the last forty years and ocean dead zones. (6.24.19), Rewilding Bookstore.

Down River: Into the Future of Water in the West, Book Review by John Miles. John reviews Heather Hansman's story as, "obsessed with the river, she decided to run its entire length to try and understand "the complexity of the ways rivers are used." Over the months of her trip and many interviews with river users, a deeper complexity than she had imagined emerged." (6.9.19), Rewilding Bookstore.

Rewilding: A Walk on the Academic Side of Rewilding, by Vance Russell, of Ecosulis, who reviews this collection of essays written by leaders in the field in Europe about rewilding in the UK and Europe. (5.17.19), Plate: Rewilding Bookstore.

Guardians of the Forest: Returning Wolves and Pumas to the East, adapted from the Preface of John Laundré's upcoming book. John writes that "During the previous millions of years of history of what is now the Eastern United States, the ecosystems there existed, like all ecosystems have, with the presence of large mammalian prey and large mammalian predators, top predators. Now they're gone. …In the East, the howl of the wolf is still silent. The stealthy pawprint o the puma can only be found in the southern tip of Florida." (5.16.19), Plate: Rewilding Bookstore.

Celebrate Earth Day the Rewilding Way, by Rewilding editors, who are launching the 2018 anthology of *Rewilding Earth Unplugged*, in spring of 2019. From over 100 articles published online in our first year, we have selected about 30 to enjoy, and to motivate readers to donate to *Rewilding Earth* on Go Fund Me. (4.22.19), Plate: Rewilding Bookstore.

In Defense of Public Lands, The Case Against Privatization and Transfer, by Steven Davis, book review by John Miles. Davis writes that "In today's fraught political environment, scant attention is paid nationally to public land issues even as campaigns are mounted to exploit and even divest the American people of this part of their legacy." (4.8.19), Plate: Rewilding Bookstore.

Citizen Science, Searching for Heroes and Hope in an Era of Extinction, by Mary Ellen Hannibal, also author of *Spine of the Continent*. She describes the importance and role of citizen volunteers working with a credentialed scientist to study and protect areas and species from further extinction, (2.4.19), Plate: Rewilding Bookstore.

Wildlife Migrations, Atlas of Wyoming's Ungulates, by Matthew J. Kauffman, James Meacham, Hall Sawyer, Alethea Y. Steingisser, William J. Rudd, and Emilene Ostlind. Review by John Miles who writes that, "Migration is a well-known phenomenon, but only recently have researchers been able to precisely track migration corridors, and just in time." Recognizing this, researchers today are using technology to trace migratory routes in hopes of protecting them and thus conserving migratory species. Such research is especially important to rewilding work, which seeks to protect and restore connectivity on the landscape necessary for conservation of biological diversity." (1.27.19), Plate: Rewilding Bookstore.

Path of the Puma, The Remarkable Resilience of the Mountain Lion, by Jim Williams, reviewed by John Miles, who writes that Williams has presented a memoir, a primer in puma ecology, and an accessible introduction to core principles of conservation biology as they pertain to large carnivores. (1.2.19), Plate: Rewilding Bookstore.

Rewilding Initiatives

European Experiments in Rewilding: Elbe River Biosphere Reserve, by David Schwartz, who writes that UNESCO's Man and the Biosphere program, Flusslandschaft Elbe Reserve covers 340,000 hectares of ecologically diverse habitat along the Elbe River in northern Germany. The Elbe-Brandenburg section of reserve encompasses 53,000 hectares of sensitive flood plain along a section of the Elbe that once served as the border between East and West Germany. (12.31.19), Plate: Rewilding Initiatives.

Wild Carbon, A Synthesis of Recent Findings, by Mark Anderson, reposted from the Northeast Wilderness Trust, WILD WORKS VOLUME 1, by Jon Leibowitz. Mark summarizes studies published in top science journals during the last decade supporting findings that trees accumulate carbon over their entire lifespan, old growth forests accumulate and contain vast quantities of it, old forests accumulate carbon in soils, forests share carbon between and among tree species, and forest carbon can help slow climate change. (10.22.19), Plate: Rewilding Initiatives.

Rewilding Scotland, by Kenyon Fields, who writes that "while true that Scots have denuded nearly every hectare of native forest and extinguished nearly every native creature larger than your rubber boot, the simple fact remains that much of Scotland still simply feels wild. It's for good reason that rewilding is not a foreign term there. Fields goes on to identify areas where ancient forests exist and to describe initiatives in Scottish rewilding. (8.27.19), Plate: Rewilding Initiatives.

European Experiments in Rewilding: Oostvaardersplassen, by David Schwartz, who writes about one of the most intriguing yet controversial restoration projects in the world today is the Oostvaardersplassen nature preserve in the Netherlands. (8.22.19), Plate: Rewilding Initiatives.

New Mexico's Wildlife Corridors Act: A path toward success, by Michael Dax, Defenders of Wildlife, who tells the story of wildlife corridors in New Mexico, culminating with the passage of SB 228, the Wildlife Corridors Act, a bill that directed the NM Department of Transportation and NM Game & Fish to work together to develop a Wildlife Corridors Action Plan (WCAP), modeled on other State Wildlife Action Plans that identify sensitive species and habitats. (6.15.19), Plate: Rewilding Initiatives.

Drifting from Rewilding, by Mark Fisher, of Self-willed Land, who points out that The Dutch concept of Nature Development – *Natuurontwikkeling* was started as a means of maintaining conservation reliant species by livestock grazing, but has been turned by Rewilding Europe and private foundations in the Netherlands into an ideology with a bizarre hatred of native structural vegetation. The undermining in Europe of the principles of rewilding is helped by media that give little acknowledgement to its original meaning, nor any evidence of the sound ecological understanding from which it was derived. (3.29.19), Plate: Rewilding Initiatives.

Rio Mora Conservation Science Center at Rio Mora National Wildlife Center, by Brian Miller, longtime conservation biologist and founding science director, now retired, at Rio Mora. Here he tells the story of Rio Mora's establishment and development and what about the work they continue to do. (3.18.19), Plate: Rewilding Initiatives.

A National Corridors Campaign for Restoring America the Beautiful, by Michael Soulé, who writes that many conservation biologists would define success as *the protection of inter-connected lands and waters that provide sufficient habitat and security for vigorous and well-distributed populations of all native species and the restoration of ecological functions provided by them.* (2.16.19), Plate: Rewilding Initiatives.

Mogollon Wildway Ramble, by John Davis and Kelly Burke, Grand Canyon Wildlands Council cofounder and map lover. They write that "Mexican Wolves are trying to return to the Grand Canyon via the Mogollon Wildway. Despite obstacles, lone, intrepid lobos have made the journey toward *home*, setting down four swift paws along the forest pathways out from the heart of their recovery area, in America's Southwest. (1.19.19), Plate: Rewilding Initiatives.

Following Alice the Moose, Notes from an A2A Reconnaissance Hike, by John Davis, who relates his hike along the Adirondack to Algonquin Wildway, tracking Alice's route through moose country help guide our exploration and advocacy work for 2019 and beyond. (1.16.19), Plate: Rewilding Initiatives.

Rewilding Players
Introducing the Santa Fe-Based Cactus Rescue Project, Rescuing an Endangered Cactus: Restoring the Santa Fe Cholla, by Nancy Lehrhaupt with the Cactus Rescue Project, who describes the citizen science effort initiated by Santa Fe "cactusphyles" to locate the cactus in Santa Fe County and replant in protected areas before redistributing them to museums, schools, and gardens. (2.2.19), Plate: Rewilding Players.

Rewilding Waters
Sea Shepherd Crew to Assist the Republic of Senegal's Patrols Against Illegal, Unreported and Unregulated Fishing, report from Sea Shepherd's website, stating Sea Shepherd Global, providing a ship, fuel and crew, will spend the next several months conducting law enforcement patrols in Senegalese waters under the direction of the Government of Senegal to assist the Ministry of Fisheries. (9.17.19), Plate: Rewilding Waters.

Something Wicked This Way Comes: The Menace of Deep-Sea Mining, by Eileen Crist, who describes the threats and existing destruction of the "next gold rush," mining the ocean floor and its ecological costs. She discusses what is happening now, the primary targets, how the commons are being destroyed by large mining companies, and how we should respond. (8.3.19), Plate: Rewilding Waters.

Friends of Merrymeeting Bay Address Altered Flows, by Ed Friedman, of (FOMB), tells about this membership nonprofit grassroots organization in mid-coastal Maine that uses research, advocacy, education and land conservation to protect, preserve and enhance the unique ecosystems of Merrymeeting Bay and Gulf of Maine. (6.5.19), Plate: Rewilding Waters.

Wild Ideas
A Necessary Quiet, by Sophi Veltrop, writing that every wildland protected by the Northeast Wilderness Trust is visited annually and this was her her first visit to Hershey Mountain. Stunned by its beauty, she writes "I'm not sure this feeling has a name, and I'm not sure it needs one. But if you have felt it, this mad love of the wild, then you know that nameless force well." (12.17.19), Plate: Wild Ideas.

From No Sense of Wild to a Need for Wild, by John Miles, who writes this essay for new readers to trace how "wild" has been perceived throughout history leading up to our present work in rewilding. (12.15.19), Plate: Wild Ideas.

Integrity Stew, Integrity Intensive, by Stu Brody who has shared his inaugural interviews of a new video series featuring people with provocative insights about it, or the lack of it, in our culture. His first two interviews are with John Davis and Richard Robbins. (11.2.19), Link: https://rewilding.org/integrity-stew/

How to Bring the Bison Home, by Susie O'Keeffe, a beautiful poem accompanied by a recording of Susie reading it. (10.16.19), Plate: Wild Ideas.

Wilderness in the Anthropocene: What Future for its Untrammeled Future?, by Roger Kaye, who writes that his aim in addressing this question is three-fold: First to stimulate thinking about the future of Wilderness in the next century of the Anthropocene. Second, to alert readers to the "dilemma of wilderness stewardship" that confronts us. Third to convince readers that we should take steps, now, to protect the most essential and most threatened quality of Wilderness—its untrammeled wildness. (10.2.19), Plate: Wild Ideas.

A Buddhist View of Conservation, by Brad Meiklejohn, who begins with the Bodhisatva Vow, "Beings are numberless. I vow to save them all" and writes about

Buddhism affects his conservation work and his ability to preserve. (9.29.19), Plate: Wild Ideas.

Benedictio, by Ed Abbey, Earth Apples, 1994, with permission from Clarke Abbey. (6.12.19), Plate: Rewilding Poetry.

Wildlands Defense
Diverse team of ecologists help save the Box Creek Wilderness: a Southern Appalachian biological hotspot, by Christopher Wilson, who tells the story of 20,000 acres in the South Mountains of the Blue Ridge Mountains and another 10,000 acres in the Piedmont. Many of these lands are now actively managed for biodiversity and have been placed under the North Carolina Natural Heritage Program's Registered Heritage Areas program, a voluntary agreement to protect outstanding examples of natural diversity in the state. (11.15.19), Plate: Wildlands Conservation.

Caifornia Mountain Lions - Migration, Distributed by U.C. Davis' Karen C. Drayer Wildlife Health Center, Episode 5 of a mini-series on Mountain Lions in California. "Migration plays a significant role in mountain lions survival as it helps mix genetics throughout California, making the species stronger as a whole." "As top predators, they are huge contributors to a stable ecosystem. But also, they are the spirits of the west, mysteries in the forest, and legends of California." (9.13.19), Plate: Coexistence.

Days of Fire, by Stuart Pimm, who writes about the horrifying Amazonian fires, his visits there, politics surrounding the burning, and what readers can do to help. "No other journey tells me what wonderful places we still have of our planet—and how we might lose them in a generation." (9.3.19), Plate Wildlands Defense.

Cow-bombing the World's Largest Organism, Repost of Andy Kerr's Public Lands Blog #139. He writes that the largest organism on Earth is one quaking aspen clone with more than forty-seven thousand stems (trees). This organism is being cow-bombed and otherwise abused. The cow-bombing, if not stopped, might well eventually result in the demise of the organism. As goes this singularly large quaking aspen clone, so may go the rest of the "quakies" in the American West. Andy points to the Pando Clone and the work being done by the Western Watersheds Project. (8.3.19), Defending our Public Lands.

Collaboration Traps, by George Wuerthner, who writes about the disadvantages of working in collaboration groups to solve conservation issues because most participants in collaboratives in the West are people who generally believe in exploiting natural landscapes for human benefit. (7.15.19), Plate: Wildlands Defense.

The Other Anti-Public-Lands Constituency: Left-Wind Extremists, Repost of Andy Kerr's Public Lands Blog #132. He writes that "the public lands conservation community has long been wary of the existential threat posed by a fringe of right-wing crazies" but that we must also "contend with the existential threat to the nation's public lands posed by fringe groups of *left*-wing crazies who seek to tribalize public lands." (5.1.19), Plate: Wildlands Conservation & Wildlands Defense.

Telling the Scientific Truth about Coyotes, by Mary Katherine Ray and Dave Parsons, which originally appeared in the *Santa Fe New Mexican* and was in response to a previous op-ed "replete with errors." Two bills are advancing in the New Mexico legislature as of February 2019 one to ban coyote killing contests and the other to ban trapping, snaring, and poisoning of wildlife on all NM public lands. (2.19.19), Plate: Coexistence and Action Alert.

Trump Signs DeFazio-Walden-Wyden-Merkley Bill Giving Away 50 Square Miles of Federal Public Land in Oregon, Repost of Andy Kerr's Public Lands Blog regarding what was lost to public ownership and how conservationists either supported this transfer or were uninvolved. He also covers the conquest of Native Tribes in Oregon and the beginning of reparations before concluding with a better way to compensate tribes. (1.11.19), Plate: Wildlife Defense.

Wildlands Philanthropy
Rio Mora Seasons, by Brian Miller, presenting the Introduction and Chapter 2 of his book, which is a phrenology, the study of patterns in nature that repeat themselves periodically through seasons. The base area for this book

is the Rio Mora National Wildlife Refuge, although it also reflects the sequence of events elsewhere on the high plains of northeastern New Mexico. (1.16.20), Plate: Wildlands Philanthropy.

Eagle Mountain Success – A century-old tradition continues in New York's Adirondack Park to solve the ecological crises of today and give us hope. By Jon Leibowitz, who writes that in the 21st century, conserving recovered woodlands of the Northern Forest as forever-wild is the most cost effective, scalable, and efficient tool in our arsenal to combat the interconnected crises of climate change and biodiversity loss. Such a *new wilderness* builds on the foundational ideas of the wilderness movement. (11.13.19), Plate: Rewilding Philanthropy.

Rewilding Patagonia, Jason Mark for Sierra Club, tells the story of about final preparations to officially hand over vast swaths of lands, held by Tompkins Conservation, to the Chilean government to create new national parks and protect the incredible biodiversity of Patagonia.
(9.10.19), Plate: Rewilding Philanthropy.

Iberá Rewilding Update, by Luli Masera, Conservation Land Trust, in which she tells readers which animals have been brought into Ibera' National Park and provides pictures of their introduction and care. (3.4.19), Plate: Wildlands Philanthropy.

Filling the Arc of Appalachia: Restoring Wildness to Southern Ohio, by Nancy Stranahan, Director, Arc of Appalachia, who tells the story of how she, her husband, and a dedicated group of volunteers created the Arc of Appalachia Preserve System, which is comprised of 22 preserves in over 7000 acres, representing 17 million in acquisition dollars, and the Highlands Nature Sanctuary that is nearly 3,000 acres, (2.12.19), Plate: Wildlands Philanthropy.

Wildlife Defense

A Philosophical Critique of the North American Model of Wildlife Conservation, by Kirk Robinson. Kirk examines NAM and focuses on three of the seven principles: #1. Wildlife is a public trust resource. #4. Wildlife may be killed only for a legitimate purpose. #6. Science is the proper tool for discharging wildlife policy. (1.26.20), Plate: Wildlife Defense.

Caribou Rainforest: From Heartbreak to Hope, an excerpt from the book by David Moskowitz in which he provides the necessary dose of information, shares stories of travels in search of elusive mountain caribou, and expresses love for this animal and its wild and beautiful home. The excerpt from the book presented here illustrates what a fine writer he is and how effectively he integrates exposition, personal narrative, and heartfelt concern for his subject, a specialist species, that is in such trouble. (11.19.19), Plate: Wildlife Conservation/Defense.

A Tale of Three Weasels, How biologists are trying to ensure that wolverines, fishers, and martens have a future in Washington, by Paula MacKay. Repost from *Earth Island* Journal. She writes that "Regional scientists are now using innovative technologies, diverse partnerships, and hiking boots on the ground to study these little-known mustelids (members of the weasel family) and try to assist them in their recovery. (11.21.19), Plate: Wildlife Conservation/Defense.

Scientists Urge New Approach to Southwest Wolf Conservation through Court-ordered Rewrite of Management Rules, a press release from the Center for Biological Diversity, Project Coyote, Sierra Club, WildEarth Guardians, and Animal Protection of New Mexico announcing the letter to USFW from leading scientists and wolf conservationists. (10.19.19), Plate: Wildlife Defense.

Hunting by Permission Only, Thoughts on killing, from *Rewilding Earth* editor, wildways scout, and land steward John Davis, who writes that private conservation land-owners may have good reasons to open their lands to hunting, but these reasons will be more often social, political, economic, or personal than ecological or ethical. A sound and simple policy for many land trusts regarding hunting on their reserves may be *Hunting By Permission Only* – and that permission should be granted cautiously. An equally sound and simple, but in many places unpopular, position could be: No Hunting. (10.12.19), Plate: Wildlife Conservation.

Scouting Locations for Wildlife Crossings in the Adirondacks, Part Two, by Kevin Webb, who follows up Part One of "Wildlife Crossings" by highlighting some best practices from Banff National Park in Canada, using these to suggest some potential locations for wildlife crossings in the Adirondacks. (9.26.19), Plate: Wildlife Defense.

How Science Watchdogs Can Protect the Gray Wolf, by Dr. Carlos Carroll, who writes that his new peer-reviewed study sheds light on how far we've strayed from what the science says we should do in protecting the wolf, and how the FWS can return to a science-based path to recovery. (9.21.19), Plate: Wildlife Defense.

What Dave Said..., by Susie O'Keefe, who cares deeply about wild nature, and particularly in this story about coyotes and other species who may be affected by Trump's attack on the ESA, which is complicated by the fact that her property is adjacent to a Trump supporting neighbor who is gearing up for night hunting. She quotes excerpts from her recent letter to her community on night hunting and finishes with a conversation with a friend who quotes Dave Foreman. (8.31.19), Plate: Wildlife Defense.

Biological and Sociopolitical Sources of Uncertainty in Population Viability Analysis for Endangered Species Recovery Planning, by Carlos Carroll, Robert C. Lacy, Richard J. Fredrickson, Daniel J. Rohlf, Sarah A. Hendricks, & Michael K. Phillips. This is a published paper exposing the scientific flaws and political motivations embodied in the 2017 Revised Mexican Wolf Recovery Plan. The paper compares analyses conducted by independent scientists appointed to a previous Mexican Wolf Recovery Team to the contrast of revised analyses influenced heavily by state scientists and policy makers. (7.30.19), Plate: Wildlife Defense.

Michigan Attorney General Opposes Delisting of Gray Wolves, by Dave Parsons who introduces AG Dana Nessel's letter to Bernhardt, calling on the US Fish and Wildlife Service to "abandon this flawed attempt to delist the gray wolf" and declared that the flawed proposal to declare the full recovery of gray wolves nationwide is unlawful" under the ESA. (7.26.19). Plate: Wildlife defense.

Celebrating America's Song Dog, by Camilla Fox, founder and executive director of Project Coyote, writes that "perhaps no other wild animal has endured the wrath of humans, while also evoking such genuine heartfelt admiration than the coyote." She also provides myriad benefits to our communities, but that the tides are turning. (7.5.19), Plate: Coexistence, Wildlife Defense.

The Psychology of Wolf Fear and Loathing, by Kirk Robinson, writing to address "why is the wolf, above all other species, including bears and mountain lions so widely hated and feared?" As a psychologist he delves into deeper explanations than simply the use of wolves in fairy tales or why they are feared and hated more than other large carnivores that compete with humans for wild game and occasionally prey on livestock. (6.28.19), Wildlife Defense.

From the website of the Northern Jaguar Project, two videos copied and linked from the NJP website to RE. The primary feature is "Where Jaguars Roam," showing the Jaguar Preserve in the Sonoran Desert, and the second is "Meet the Young Eco-Guardians," featuring several young Mexican students on their first camping trip into the Preserve. (6.19.19), Plate: Wildlife Conservation.

Arizona Game & Fish Commission Adopts Rule to Ban Wildlife Killing Contests, June 21, 2019, Media Release from Project Coyote and Dave Parsons, announcing the unanimous vote to ban WKCs for predatory and furbearing species in Arizona and the commitment of Commissioner Davis to amending the rule if necessary to prevent participants from evading the ban. The coalition of concerned citizens and wildlife conservation organizations will continue to monitor the situation. (6.26.19), Plate Wildlife Defense.

Social Carrying Capacity Politspeak Bamboozle, by David Mattson, a reprint of his blog on Grizzly Times. He writes that public servants "are tasked with implementing legislated policy as honestly and faithfully as possible, and, through that, maximizing benefits for the broader public they serve." He focuses on "public statements by federal and state agencies that manage our wildlife." (5.24.19), Plate: Wildlife Conservation/Defense.

Tapping the Third-Rail: Wildlife Watching and State Wildlife Funding Reform, by Chris Spatz, who writes that rather than creating funding from the much larger constituency of non-consumptive wildlife interests, state wildlife agencies are trying to create new opportunities for hunting and fishing recruitment, a scenario that has played out for decades. Spatz and Laundré propose a percentage of existing state taxes on wildlife watching revenues to reinvest them into non-game and at-risk species. (4.27.19), Plate: Wildlife Defense.

"The Precautionary Principle" in Conservation, by Kirk Robinson, Executive Director, Western Wildlife Conservancy, who writes that the PP to conservationists is what Aldo Leopold is saying when he writes, "to keep every cog and wheel is the first precaution of intelligent tinkering." He believes that "the prudent exercise of caution requires a sufficient epistemic base, supplemented with a morally adequate set of valuations, to warrant a particular action or inaction" and to avoid unintended consequences. (2.8.19), Plate: Wildlife Defense.

About the Rewilding Bookstore

The Rewilding Bookstore features titles by leaders of The Rewilding Institute, important books by friends of the Institute willing to list their titles, and recommended reading by Institute staff and board. The bookstore also offers reviews of important books relevant to rewilding and related topics. We are expanding our booklist to include new and old titles to inspire and inform readers, and we welcome any suggestions you may have.

Readers may order through the *Rewilding Earth* website (rewilding.org) by going to "Bookstore" in the menu. If you have any questions about ordering featured titles, please contact Roxanne Pacheco at **TRI@rewilding.org** or call at 505-288-9231. Thank you very much for supporting our authors and The Rewilding Institute.

Books for Sale

Rewilding North America: A Vision for Conservation in the 21st Century, by Dave Foreman.

Unmatched for its deep, thorough look at extinction and how humans make it happen; and what conservation biology teaches us about wild things and how to keep them wild. Foreman offers a mind-opening vision for rewilding North America grounded in a North American Wildlands Network. Though *Rewilding* is not an academic book, it is being used as a text in many colleges and universities. Island Press, 2004. 295 pages, index, footnotes, maps, tables. Paperback $35, Hardcover $60.

Man Swarm and the Killing of Wildlife, by Dave Foreman with Laura Carroll.

The first edition of *Man Swarm* reached the conservationist community; in this new and updated edition, Dave Foreman and seasoned editor Laura Carroll expand the readership to the masses. This tight second edition: lays out how the overpopulation explosion is still with us, smartly challenges those who don't believe overpopulation is real, shows that overpopulation is solvable, takes an ecological stand on immigration and its reform in the U.S. as part of the solution, and gives tangible ways all people can be part of the solution. 2014, 196 pages. Paperback $20.

Man Swarm and the Killing of Wildlife, by Dave Foreman.

Human overpopulation—man swarm—is the main driver behind the biodiversity crisis—the greatest mass extinction since the dinosaurs' demise, the scalping of hundreds of millions of acres of forest and other key wildlife habitat, and the atmospheric pollution by greenhouse gases leading to "Global Weirding." Only by stabilizing human population worldwide and in the United States can we stop wrecking our home—Earth. Foreman outlines a sweep of practical steps we can take to bring our numbers down to what Earth can support—if we have the daring, boldness, and love of life to do it. First in the *For the Wild Things* series. Raven's Eye Press, 2011. 274 pages, index, appendices, graphs, tables. Paperback $20.

The Lobo Outback Funeral Home: A Novel, by Dave Foreman.

Foreword by Doug Peacock (paperback only). *Lobo* is the only novel that tells the story of conservation from inside the conservation family. Set in southwestern New Mexico, it's the tale of a tough, winsome conservation biologist, the wolves she loves and studies, the man who loves both her and the wolves but who can't find the strength to make a commitment, and the wolf-hating local lowlifes and their rich rancher leader. Sex, violence, wolves, wilderness. 226 pages. Johnson Books, 2004, University Press of Colorado, 2000. First Edition Hardcover $20.

ABOUT THE REWILDING BOOKSTORE

Take Back Conservation, by Dave Foreman.

Aldo Leopold wrote, "There are some who can live without wild things, and some who cannot." Take Back Conservation is for those who cannot live without wild things, who are the heart and soul of the wilderness and wildlife conservation movement. Second in the *For the Wild Things* series. Raven's Eye Press, 2012, 375 pages, index, glossary. Paperback $25.

Confessions of an Eco-Warrior, by Dave Foreman.

Part memoir, part history of Earth First!, and a rousing heartfelt call to save wild things, *Confessions of an Eco-Warrior* is a landmark of conservation writing. "One of the towering figures, the mighty sequoias, of American conservation…."—Bill McKibben. Out of print, few copies left, First Edition (1991) Hardcover for collectors. Harmony, 1991, 229 pages, index. $75.

The Big Outside: A Descriptive Inventory of the Big Wilderness Areas of the U.S. First Edition by Dave Foreman and Howie Wolke. Foreword by Michael Frome.

A legendary, broad study of the big roadless areas in the United States: 100,000 acres and over in the West, 50,000 acres and over in the East (368 areas in all described). Includes Bob Marshall's 1927 and 1936 roadless area inventories. Both the first and second editions of *The Big Outside* have long been out of print. 458 pages, photos, maps, research sources. Ned Ludd Books, 1988, First Edition. Paperback $50.

Split Rock Wildway: Scouting the Adirondack Park's Most Diverse Wildlife Corridor, by John Davis.

A rambling look at some of the charismatic and enigmatic wildlife thriving in the wooded hills and adjacent waterways linking Lake Champlain with the High Peaks. Author John Davis and artist friends illustrate the ecological importance, conservation value, and natural beauty of the wildway and its many creatures. Residents and visitors alike will grow a little closer to their permanent or occasional wild neighbors, from salamanders to sturgeon to raptors to moose, as they stroll through the pages of *Split Rock Wildway*. This book is intended to help better protect the lands and waters of Split Rock Wildway and the larger Adirondack Park. It is generously sponsored by Eddy Foundation, with a portion of sales benefiting Champlain Area Trails, Northeast Wilderness Trust, and other conservation groups. Essex Editions, 2017, 157 pages. Paperback $15.

Big, Wild, and Connected, by John Davis.

In 2011, adventurer and conservationist John Davis walked, cycled, skied, canoed, and kayaked on an epic 10-month, 7,600-mile journey that took him from the Florida Keys to a remote seashore on the Gaspe Peninsula of Quebec. Davis was motivated by a dream: to see a continent-long corridor conserved for wildlife in the eastern United States and Canada, especially for the large carnivores so critical to the health of the land.

In *Big, Wild, and Connected*, we travel the Eastern Wildway with Davis, viscerally experiencing the challenges large carnivores, with their need for vast territories, face in an ongoing search for food, water, shelter, and mates. On his self-propelled journey, Davis explores the wetlands, forests, and peaks that are the last strongholds for wildlife in the East. This includes strategically important segments of disturbed landscapes, from longleaf pine savanna in the Florida Panhandle to road-latticed woods of Pennsylvania. Despite the challenges, Davis argues that creation of an Eastern Wildway is within our reach and would serve as a powerful symbol of our natural and cultural heritage.

Big, Wild, and Connected reveals Eastern landscapes through wild eyes, a reminder that, for the creatures with which we share the land, movement is as essential to life as air, water, and food. Davis' journey shows that a big, wild, and connected network of untamed places is the surest way to ensure wildlife survival through the coming centuries. Island Press, 2015, 212 pages. Paperback $15.

Moral Ground: Ethical Action for a Planet in Peril, edited by Kathleen Dean Moore and Michael P. Nelson, Foreword by Desmond Tutu.

Sweeping in depth, breadth, thought, and feeling, eighty women and men answer whether we have a "moral obligation to protect the future of a planet in peril." Dave Foreman's short essay, "Wild Things for Their Own Sakes," builds on Darwin and Leopold to be a bedrock stand for the inborn good of wild things. Others answer from intrinsic, humanistic, and practical overlooks. Among them are Barack Obama, John Paul II, Dalai Lama, Ursula Le Guin, Barbara Kingsolver, Terry Tempest Williams, E. O. Wilson, Gary Snyder, and others from all over Earth. Trinity University Press, 2010, 478 pages, authors' bios. Hardcover $25.

The Way of Natural History, edited by Thomas Lowe Fleischner.

Once, biology was natural history, done mostly in the field. Now biology is done indoor mostly by "lab rats." In some universities, one can get a biology degree without doing anything outside. This fading of natural history is a harsh threat to our tie to wild things in wildlands and –seas and to our work to keep and bring back the whole Tree of Life. Fleischner, retired from Prescott College, and fellow biologists and conservationists call for coming home to the mindfulness of natural history. Dave Foreman's little essay, "Talking to Wild Things," builds on Leopold and asks us to get out and meet our wild neighbors in wild neighborhoods as a fellow neighbor or a wayfarer. Among the other twenty-one writers are Robert Aitken, Alison Deming, Kathleen Dean Moore, Bob Pyle, and Steve Trombulak. Trinity University Press, 2011, 218 pages, authors' bios. Paperback $17.

Continental Conservation: Scientific Foundations of Regional Reserve Networks, edited by Michael Soulé and John Terborgh.

Scientifically solid and highly readable, *Continental Conservation* is an anthology written by the top conservation biologists in the U.S., Canada, and Mexico explaining why conservation must be done on a continental scale. It covers the need for big predators; the need for big wilderness areas and how to best design them; the importance of wildlife movement linkages, ecological and evolutionary processes of wildlife, flooding, and predation; and much more. Soulé and Terborgh give a warm-hearted, tough-minded call to save wild things and their wilderness homes. Island Press/Wildlands Project, 1999, 227 pages, index, footnotes, some illustrations. Paperback $20.

Sponsors

The generous support of *Rewilding Earth's* donor foundations, corporations, and individuals underpins our growing success in running a vibrant online publication (rewilding.org), and we are again showcasing some of our most notable articles and art in this anthology. We would like to thank this wild bunch of conservation leaders and to briefly single out for praise several sponsors helping to make possible this second print edition of *Rewilding Earth*. We encourage you to support these truly green businesses. Please contact us about becoming a *Rewilding Earth* sponsor via our website or you can send mail to:

The Rewilding Institute
P.O. Box 13768
Albuquerque, NM 87192.

Biohabitats

Increasingly we find ourselves living in an artificial world. A world where ecosystem processes are compromised, and biodiversity is marginalized and commodified. Biohabitats believes that nature, in its wildest form, provides the blueprint for conserving, restoring, and regenerating the full expression of biological diversity and ecosystem functions necessary for survival.

Biohabitats applies the science of ecology to restore ecosystems, conserve habitat, and regenerate the natural systems that sustain all life on Earth. They do this through assessment, research, planning, design, engineering, and construction. Since the firm's early days improving the ecosystems and watershed of the Chesapeake Bay, Biohabitats has grown to serve communities all over the world, helping them to protect wildlife, conserve water, enhance biodiversity, link the natural world with the built environment, and plan for the future in ways that enhance ecology and resilience. Behind their work is the intention to respect Earth's ecological limit, heal ecological processes, and catalyze mutually beneficial relationships among the land and all forms of life.

A purpose-driven company that believes in the power of business to be a force for the greater good, Biohabitats is a certified B Corporation®, member of 1% for the Planet, and recipient of the JUST™ label. Learn more at biohabitats.com and find them on **@Biohabitats** on LinkedIn, Twitter, Facebook, and Instagram.

Essex Editions

Essex Editions is an independent press located on the Adirondack shores of Lake Champlain.

Part artisanal publisher and part transmedia consultancy, Essex Editions collaborates with authors, artists, and activists who believe that storytelling should be innovative, provocative, culturally enriching, and ecologically responsible.

Learn more at **essexeditions.com**.

We are creators.
Mavericks.
Risk-takers.
Adventurers.
Connectors.
Collectors.
Curators.
Catalysts.
Incubators.
We are storytellers.

foundation EARTH
Rethinking society from the ground up!

Foundation Earth is a national, non-profit, public interest advocacy organization founded in 2011. Our focus includes: economic models, technology, biospheric education, and earth jurisprudence. We call for a rethink of society from the ground up. We envision more self-reliant communities embedded in a continental network of bioregional economies. Time is not on our side. A rapid shift from an industrial society that ignores nature's carrying capacity limits and irresponsibly pollutes (cheater economics) to a True Cost Economy will require examining the dimensions of a deeply resilient economy, arguing for it, and providing advisory services to social movements concerning systems change. Our mission is to bring an earth-centered "True Cost Economy" into reality.

Learn more at fdnearth.org and find them **@FoundationEarth** on Facebook and Twitter.

SPONSORS

Gulf of Maine Books
INDEPENDENT BOOKSELLERS
134 MAINE STREET • BRUNSWICK, MAINE

Gulf of Maine Books is an independent bookstore in Brunswick, Maine, founded in 1979 by Beth Leonard and Gary Lawless and still going strong! Considered a downtown staple that brings together book lovers and readers young and old, where people gather to find a good book to read and to connect with friends and community members. They feature publishing parties, book signings, and readings and aspire to be a bookstore that is a part of their literate and engaged community.

Leonard and Lawless know what they like and who their customers are. Regular Gulf of Maine customers are generally interested in literary fiction, sustainable living, wild Nature, organic farming, and poetry. The store has always kept sizable sections devoted to women's studies, environmental topics, Maine books, LGBTQ books, and indigenous literature, while its poetry section is unrivaled in Maine. Lawless is to thank for that; as a poet and publisher himself, he made a commitment early on to carry small-press books.

Located at 134 Maine St, Brunswick, ME 04011, Gulf of Maine Books is open Monday through Saturday from 9:30 to 5:30.

Phone: 207-729-5083.

Email address: **gulfofmainebooks@gmail.com**.

kahtoola®

Since 1999, Kahtoola has been creating reliable gear that makes the outdoors more accessible and rewarding. Based in Flagstaff, AZ, and deeply inspired by the wonders of the Colorado Plateau, Kahtoola values the importance of public lands and advocates for their protection and preservation, not only for future generations of people but also for the wildlife that lives on them.

In September 2019, Kahtoola helped local nonprofit Grand Canyon Trust receive $50,000 in grant funding from the Conservation Alliance. The funding will aid collaborative efforts lead by Native American tribes in the fight to make permanent a standing 20-year ban on uranium mining, as well as combat dam proposals, mega resort development, and the many threats facing Grand Canyon.

Learn more at kahtoola.com and find them **@Kahtoola** on Facebook, Twitter, LinkedIn, and Instagram.

patagonia®

Patagonia is an outdoor apparel company based in Ventura, California. Since 1973, activism has been at the heart of the company's work by supporting efforts to defend our air, land and water around the globe. Through a self-imposed Earth tax, 1% for the Planet, Patagonia has funded thousands of environmental nonprofits and can count contributions of more than $100 million in grants and in-kind donations to date to local organizations.

Learn more at patagonia.com and find them **@Patagonia** on Facebook, Twitter, LinkedIn, and Instagram.

Made in the USA
Columbia, SC
04 June 2020